# Welcome to the Woke Trials:
# How #Identity Killed Progressive Politics

## Julie Burchill

# Welcome to the Woke Trials:
# How #Identity Killed Progressive Politics

**Julie Burchill**

**Academica Press**
**Washington~London**

Library of Congress Cataloging-in-Publication Data

Names: Burchill, Julie (author)
Title: Welcome to the woke trials : how identity killed progressive politics |
Burchill, Julie
Description: Washington : Academica Press, 2021. | Includes references.
Identifiers: LCCN 2021949414 | ISBN 9781680532333 (hardcover) |
9781680532340 (paperback) | 9781680532357 (e-book)

# DEDICATION

FOR JIM OWEN
And for the Terven Tribes across the world and our male allies -
especially Harry 'Fair Cop' Miller - **Venceremos!**

# CONTENTS

# INTRODUCTION

When we consider the phrase 'Flaming June' we might think of the famous portrait by Frederic Leighton showing a sleeping woman in an orange dress which Samuel Cortauld once called 'the most wonderful painting in existence.' But the June we lived through in 2020 was not a month of sensual slumber and molten gold sunsets. It was a conflagration of sensibilities as one cultural artefact after another went up in flames lest it offend some petulant cry-bully. The summer of 2020 - and the days ever since, right up till now as I write this in the autumn of 2021 - will be remembered for the vanity of the bonfires.

You'd think that everything that happened last year would have made this book a piece of gluten-free cake to dash off at top speed. But I found it something of an embarrassment (literally, for the perpetrators and capitulators) of riches. This was both the easiest and the most difficult thing I've ever written because by the summer of 2021, not each new day but each new hour brought some new snippet of Woke insanity. So each morning I would read back the previous day's work, only to find that half a dozen new acts of idiocy had taken place while I slept. I'd go to bed reeling from the fact that rambling was racist and wake up to the glad tidings that cyclists wanted to be included in the ever-lengthening queue of those who may be eligible for Hate Crime status.

As the insanity picked up velocity, I was increasingly reminded of the tsunami of sound that comes at the end of the Beatles song A Day In The Life, that cacophonous orchestral crescendo which John Lennon instructed George Martin should be 'a tremendous build-up, from nothing up to something absolutely like the end of the world.' Imagine it now as you read this.

First they came for our fond memories of television, which had seemed such an innocent babysitter at the time: Fawlty Towers (mentioning the war), The Dukes Of Hazzard (Confederate flag), Brum (the mischievous car who 'may reflect language and attitude of the 90s') and Songs Of Praise (Cat Lewis, a producer of the programme and self-professed 'campaigner for a better world' Tweeted of Rule Britannia 'Do those Brits who believe it's OK to sing an 18th Century song about never being enslaved, written when the U.K was enslaving and killing millions of innocents, also believe it's appropriate for neo-Nazis to shout 'We will never be forced into a gas chamber''?) Then they came for cartoons; on the Disney streaming service, Dumbo, Peter Pan, Lady And The Tramp and The Jungle Book are preceded by the dire warning 'This programme includes negative depictions and/or mistreatment of people or cultures - 'these stereotypes were wrong then and are wrong now.'

Then they came for the music; in the winter of 2020 the BBC announced that the audience for sweary Christmas favourite Fairytale Of New York would be segregated; older listeners could hear the original on Radio 2, while over on Radio 1 the word 'faggot' would be removed lest it offend tender young ears. There's the whole weirdness of Woke right there; old people want the unabridged version while youngsters want the censored one. It's meant to be the other way around — if rock and roll was invented these days, old people would be out there dancing to it and young people tut-tutting about how offensive it was.

They came for the museums (the Natural History Museum's Charles Darwin collection because he had voyaged to the Galapagos Islands in the course of 'colonialist scientific expeditions') and they came for the old houses as the National Trust appeared to have mistaken itself for the National Front when it published a list of nearly 100 properties under its management which it claimed had links to slavery and colonialism. They came for full stops, which intimidate young people when used in social media communication as they are interpreted as a sign of anger and insincerity according to linguistic experts. They came for the female genitalia: a college in Michigan decided to cancel its production of The Vagina Monologues because it was discriminatory, given that 'not all women have vaginas.' They even came for the rainbows, when someone called Kirsty Conway complained in the summer of 2020:

> 'Not long after lockdown was imposed, I was pleasantly surprised to see a rainbow flag on my drive home from work. However, as I saw more rainbow flags I quickly realised that these were not intended as support for the LGBTQ+

community, but rather as support for the NHS. I felt saddened, and disappointed. I am proud to work for the NHS, and of course public support for the NHS, and all other essential workers, can only be considered a good thing. However, I couldn't help feeling that taking the rainbow flag, which has been a symbol of LGBTQ+ pride and protest for more than 40 years, and repurposing it to represent support for the NHS, was at best thoughtless, failing to consider what this symbol means to our community, and at worst an act of erasure, sending a message that LGBTQ+ rights are not considered important.'

Racism was the big one, suddenly detected everywhere, a parallel deadly virus. Master bedrooms were racist. Chessmen were racist. Brunch was racist, according to the actor Alan Cummings, reeking of 'white privilege.' Sherlock Holmes was racist, the countryside was racist, fried chicken was racist, the anti-racist film In The Heat Of The Night was racist. As the One Little Indian record label became One Little Independent, the whole lazy lip-service aspect of virtue-signalling was summed up gloriously by the NME headline ONE LITTLE INDIAN CHANGE NAME TO HELP FIGHT RACISM. Yep, that seems sensible - never saying the world 'Indian' again will surely defeat one of the greatest evils on earth.

Hawaiian shirts, camping, gardening, biking, hiking, jogging, mathematics, trees, botany, libraries, roads, lawns, soap, craft beers, peanut butter, dieting, wine, spelling, Thomas The Tank Engine, robots, interior design, surfing, hockey, the Smurfs - ALL RACIST! I'll leave it there but it's a fair bet that by the time you get to the first proper chapter of this book, something else that made you think or laugh will have been cancelled or castigated for fear of attracting the wrath of a group of people who appear to have a deep distrust of thinking and laughing. Monstrous regiments of Violet Elizabeth Botts have joined the Stasi and started up a series of deranged sideshows detracting from the very real ills of a society with a risible level of social mobility all across the colour chart - white working-class boys do worse in education than any other group, don't forget.

The star turn of these witch trials is J.K. Rowling, who has nothing to do with racism but who has attracted the considerable ire of the small, well-financed, extremely loud trans-lobby who have never seen a drama that wasn't about them, even if it was the killing of a black man in Minneapolis. After a period of attempting to placate the geek chorus, Rowling was recently re-born as a fearless and funny feminist who responded to the proposed book-burning of her Harry Potter bestsellers with 'Whenever somebody burns a Potter book the royalties vanish from my bank account. And if the book's signed, one of my teeth falls out.' That the Harry Potter actors who turned on her are from privileged backgrounds while as an impoverished single mother she once worked in cafes (and went on to drop from billionaire to mere multi-millionaire status due to the sheer amount of money she gave away) made the situation even more grotesque. I don't think the fact that Rowling is self-made and they've been feather-bedded all their lives are completely unconnected with this wrangle; the more privileged people are, the less they understood how women without money are vulnerable to male incursion.

In the interests of harmony and time-saving, shall we just cut to the chase and ban everything - every book, film and TV show, reinstating each one in turn only when a worldwide referendum has established that no one in the world is offended by them? Because surely if some people are offended a statue of a man who led the armies which defeated Hitler, then they can be offended by anything; I fully expect Flat Earthers to start pulling down statues of explorers soon. Think about it - Swan Lake has the good white swan and the bad black swan, David Bowie had sex with underage girls, Manet used prostitutes, John Lennon used the N-word and Dickens was mean to his wife.

Selected fragments of pre-Woke culture may be allowed to survive - but only if it has been *re-booted* to take all the nasty bits out, and can now slip down like that unctuous stuff in cans they give to old people who can't eat any more. (No teeth, please - we're skittish!) And of course the same old boring boundaries of who you can provoke and who you can't will still stand; Paris Jackson, alleged daughter of Michael, portrayed a *re-imagined* lesbian Jesus, but don't hold your breath for Maxine Peake as a re-imagined lesbian Mohammed any time soon. Wuthering Golan Heights with Heathcliff as a Palestinian and Cathy as the daughter of a Zionist settler? Will some chancing publisher think 'Hmm, I bet I could shift a few more copies of Great Expectations if Pip was a

BLM activist, Estella was a non-binary and Miss Havisham had dementia…'?

Far from being daring, as the clowns who commission these things seem to believe they are, re-imaginings are the misshapen spawn of a scared-stiff culture in which history must be policed and statues must wear red letters lest some snivelling snowflake has a tantrum. In these stupefyingly censorious times, those who yearn to burn books but are frightened of fire can always destroy them another way - by *re-framing* them so blandly that no one will want ever to read them. There will be a huge void where truthful, exciting entertainment used to be. But I'm sure that Generation Bedwetter can easily replace it with ukulele solos and social distanced dancing flash mobs. Let's give a try - everything must go! Because it's not like burning books ever leads to anything bad, is it?

My own book - this book - was burned metaphorically, but to be fair I never saw a conflagration I didn't want to run towards. Due to my own drunken stupidity on social media I had my first contract cancelled in the winter of 2020; a not altogether bad thing, as Hatchette had already asked me to remove the word 'Woke' from the gloriously playful and appropriate title. Sure enough, in May of 2021, The Bookseller published an *open letter* from a selection of closed minds working in the publishing industry - with the ineffably creepy title 'The Paradox of Tolerance' - stating that 'transphobia is still perfectly acceptable in the British book industry' and demanding 'quiet statements of acceptance from companies and organisations within our industry' before rushing en masse to their bedrooms and slamming the door.

It transpired that Hachette, my erstwhile publisher, had launched a partnership with something called 'All About Trans' in 2020, donating £10,000 to Stonewall U.K - the very organisation that had 'urged' the employers of lesbian barrister Allison Bailey to sack her after she criticised it for 'appalling levels of intimidation, fear and coercion' during one of their regular crusades to erase women who don't believe that penises can be female. If I'd known that, **I'd** have cancelled **them!**

It's funny that I got into my bit of bother on Twitter while defending a friend; I've never admired loyalty as a character trait, and the events of the last few years - starting with Brexit - have made me feel even more cavalier about friendship. I'd far rather be loathed for who I am than loved for what I'm not; the best definition of friendship is seeing someone clearly and liking them anyway. Losing a friend is not the end of the world and there are always more along; as the late Peter Ustinov memorably quipped 'I do not believe that friends are necessarily the people you like best, they are merely the people who got there first.' Losing free speech, however, **is** the end of a world - the world of freedom and fearlessness which is the only world I want to be part of, a world which won't return once banished. You can always make new friends - but you can't make new principles. And I would rather be a pariah in the tiny minds of the Woke - even though they increasingly hold both the floor and the purse strings - than be sundered from the greater part of humanity that still has the guts to say the Woke emperor has no clothes and is waving his 'girl-dick' in our faces out of sheer ill-tempered triumphalism.

The chief of MI6 puts his pronouns on his Twitter now. But the Woke aren't getting it all their way as I write this in the fall of 2021, on a serious note, the magnificently named Higher Education (Freedom of Speech) Bill, announced in the Queen's Speech, and the frankly thrilling idea of an Academic Freedom Champion - an office tasked with proactively applying the law and ensuring that universities promote academic freedom - will make campuses safe for freedom (as opposed to being safe **from** freedom) once more.

On the fun front, Caitlyn Jenner - the high priestess of lady-penis-possessors - spoke out against men competing in women's sport, no matter how much mascara they wear: 'I oppose biological boys who are trans competing…it just isn't fair. We have to protect girls' sports in our schools.' It was hilarious to see the Troon legions - who had previously elevated Jenner to some sort of spiritual Mount Olympus, drooling over their pronouncements on life, the universe and everything - suddenly turn on the twentieth century's greatest Olympian for talking about what they absolutely knew about - sport.

The day may soon come when the Woke wake up and realise that they **are** the new Establishment and their belief system is just another way of corralling and controlling the masses who, if not constantly belittled, might themselves wake up and find that, even without the privilege, they certainly have the numbers. As I write this the green shoots of seditious sense are struggling to break through the permafrost of pig-headed prejudice. It's been a long hard winter on Planet Plague, when the West was almost devoured by self-flagellating delirium. But I have a feeling that setting sunlight upon the silly and the sinister alike will rob the pandemics - both of them - of their power.

Julie Burchill, October 2021

# CHAPTER ONE

# FIRST WITCH AT THE WOKE TRIALS: MY BEAUTIFUL FRIENDSHIP, RUDE AWOKENING AND SEVEN-YEAR SHUNNING

It was all going so well.

Women, homosexuals and ethnic minorities - in the West - seemed to be moving inevitably towards parity with the people who had always presumed to know better, from the last century seamlessly into the present one. A female British Prime Minister in 1979, a black American President in 2009, more gays than you could shake a rainbow-striped stick at on prime time TV - all of them pulling down the barriers one block at a time. Right-wing bigots defending the old order looked increasingly ludicrous and desperate.

And then Woke came along and it all went wrong. As progressive thinking somehow lapped and ate itself, a looking-glass world came into being where it was fine for alleged Left-wingers to demonise Jews who supported their ancient homeland, feminists who didn't believe that the poorest women in every society should be reduced to hiring themselves by the hour out as sexual spittoons and lesbians not interested in having sex with men in dresses.

Woke-taunters (amongst whom I proudly include myself) have largely swallowed the line which the special snowflakes themselves like to propagate; that they are rebels with many causes, each one more daring and progressive than the last. But having been of a rebellious bent all my life, this never sat well with me. Because the more you examine what the Woke want, the more they emerge as reactionaries rather than rebels - leading to the surreal situation, as we enter the third decade of the twentieth century, wherein censorship, misogyny, racism and homophobia now comes principally from the Left. How in the world did we get here?

The word 'Woke' - meaning anything other than the opposite of being asleep - was probably first used in the 2008 Erykah Badu song 'Master Teacher' with its repeated, somewhat wearisome insistence 'I stay woke' after which it became a watchword among sections of the black American community. After the 2014 shooting of Michael Brown in Ferguson, Missouri, by police, Woke became entwined with the Black Lives Matter movement; instead of just being a word that signaled awareness of injustice it signaled a refusal to put up with this state of affairs. It must be said that even when used by such an obviously underprivileged people as black Americans, there is something creepy about the word; compared to the 'I have a dream' of the black civil rights movement it sounds curiously smug and inactive, indicating that one is somehow inherently better than other people without actually having to do anything to prove it. But it wasn't till the smuggest, most inactive people on earth - privately-educated and over-protected students - got their hands on it that the true folly of Woke was revealed in all its gory glory.

Youngsters who might previously have marched against actual war and oppression were suddenly Woke by the clammy kiss of identity politics, probably the most deranged force to hit public discourse since the Flat Earth Society. No longer up to analysing society from a no-nonsense economic Marxist standpoint - Karl Marx was just another Dead White Male, after all, and a Jew with it - and though officially places of intellectual challenge, universities were soon refurbished as pity-party play-pens where feelings trumped facts every time, as they do for infants. When the veteran feminist Julie Bindel - feared and loathed by the Woke for her insistence that men cannot be magicked into women if they wake up one morning preferring pink to blue - was de-platformed at a college in Texas the reason given was that 'This is the students home and their safe space - and that comes before anything else.'

Though the Woke think of themselves as the most enlightened group in any society, both their beliefs and the way they express them hark back to a darker time. Over-indulged by parents who foolishly told them they were special, they are terrified by the adult world of healthy competition and thus rage against capitalism; cutting their wisdom teeth in the echo-chamber of social media, their pursuit of those who refuse to parrot their claims (men can be women, prostitution is work like any other, Jews don't have a right to one principally Jewish state but Muslims have a right to more than fifty lands labouring under sharia law) at times resembles every witch hunt from Salem to Hollywood. A recent survey by The Policy Exchange think-tank claimed that fewer than half of British university students support freedom of speech.

It's not just the style but the content of their arguments which make the Woke reactionary rather than revolutionary, taking in activists who claim that lesbianism is *transphobic* and that sportswomen should accept second place to competitors who were born male, fauxminists who believe that a permanent underclass of prostituted women is acceptable and that wearing a hijab is subversive, American *antifas* and Corbynite clowns who repeat ancient anti-Semitic tropes about the Jews - and Woke princes who seem to believe in the divine right of kings never to be criticised. Their analysis of class oppression is conspicuous in its absence, fitting for a group to whom only the personally experienced is political; thus an unemployed middle-aged manual worker in the American Rust Belt has more *privilege* than Meghan Markle, Duchess of Sussex, due to being a white male. There was a pleasing exchange on social media along these lines; a Woker wrote with typical smug superiority of poor unemployed Americans in the rust belt that it was amusing to see so many 'dumb whites' screwing up their 'White Privilege' and a young socialist answered 'I know, right? And there **are** so many of them! It even starts to look like society might be organised on the lines of, IDK, **class oppression** or something, and not to do with White Privilege at all…'

Wokeness is the roar of the entitled mediocre, desperate to hold centre-stage and terrified by any challenge to their flimsy sense of self - a temper-tantrum with a socially concerned alibi. The Woke are self-centred to the point where they care so much about *micro-aggressions* towards themselves that they don't seem care about atrocities which happens to others in 'faraway countries of which we know nothing' to quote Chamberlain on Czechoslovakia. Hence being called 'Darlin' by a bus-driver = Evil: female genital mutilation = It's Their Culture.

The old saying 'Youth is wasted on the young' has never been so true as it is of the Woke. As well as being averse to rigorous thinking, they are the first generation to want **less** of everything - less sex, less booze, less travel as opposed to the easy-going sexagenarians now pushing up the senior STD and cirrhosis rates. And definitely less laughs; this appears to be the first generation bred without a sense of humour. It's grimly predictable that Lou Reed's 'Walk On The Wild Side' has been denounced by Canadian students as 'transphobic' - being both sexy and funny, it must be bad.

The Woke would be less objectionable if they lived up to their own pristine standards but they fall woefully short. In an inversion of Carl Jung's great saying YOU ARE WHAT YOU DO - NOT WHAT YOU SAY YOU'LL DO, once you have identified yourself as Woke you can get away with anything. Thus the Sussexes feel free to lecture others on climate change while taking private jets and Justin Trudeau seems as compulsively drawn to blacking up as his mother was to screwing pop stars; after the third example of him doing so was revealed this year, he admitted that he had actually lost count of the number of times he'd done it. Nevertheless, he was defended by minority spokesmen and liberal commentators. It's what the social commentator Daniel Norris dubbed the 'Wokescreen' at work; from behind this magical canopy, privileged cliques can rob women of their hard-won private spaces or enjoy the brutish thrill of Jew-baiting - and because they've ticked the box which says Brotherhood Of Man, it doesn't make them bad people! Those people over there are the bad ones – like Jacob Rees-Mogg's 12-year-old son, so let's all scream at him.

But perhaps what I hate most about the Woke is the way they have done the dirt on feminism. The irony of *The Handmaid's Tale* is that it is set under a Right-wing American regime with Canada, just across the border, as a safe sanctuary from feminism. But look at the state of Trudeau's Canada; public funding removed from women's shelters which insist on protecting women-only spaces, crimes no longer recorded by sex, rapists sent to female prisons and endless harassment of feminist activists, all in the name of Wokeness. *The Handmaid's Tale* is always used as a warning against the growth of right-wing ideology, but look at the female

American protestors marching against Trump or Swedish female politicians visiting Iran, all of them voluntarily hijab-ing up; Woke handmaids playing dress-up to suck-up to the most oppressively patriarchal of religions while brave Muslim women all across the Middle East are tortured for taking their shrouds off.

This is Sharia Syndrome - and like the new Fresh'n'Funky anti-Semitism, it stems solely from the Woke.

The one consolation amongst all this nasty nonsense is that Woke may well have peaked. When I started this book at the start of 2020 I was looking at an alien landscape full of melting clocks and angry unicorns in which even such comforting cultural artefacts such as knitting, of all things, had been contaminated by Wokeness. In 2020 the journalist Gavin Haynes made a remarkable BBC radio programme which, once one had ceased believing that the original broadcast date had been April the 1st, made one goggle-eyed with the sheer molten mentalism of it:

> 'Nathan Taylor, an Instagram knitting star, unwittingly triggered a race row after attempting to reach out to people of colour using the hashtag Diversknitty. Nathan watched in horror as a wave of accusations of white supremacy and Nazism flowed into his inbox. This brush with the toxicity of a Purity Spiral was so severe that Nathan was hospitalised by his husband following a suicide threat.'

A Purity Spiral is extreme cyberspace bullying in the name of righteousness; what Haynes calls 'vicious cycles of accusation and judgement which see communities engaging in moral feeding frenzies. As a result, individuals are targeted and savaged by mobs who deem them problematic.' It's positively surreal to reflect that a way of thinking which started as a legitimate response to police brutality has mutated over the space of a few years to bickering about the race-bias power-balance between plain and purl.

And then Woke came for the Wombles. In early 2020, a trailer was featured on social media, with an Instagram post showing two creatures of indeterminate sex and different colours embracing under the words WE'RE ALL EQUAL and above the quote: 'Diversity is beautiful. In humans, in animals, in nature. The best way for us to protect the planet is together' - Alderney.

Talk about rewriting history!

To quote Wikipedia:

> 'Wombles generally have a low opinion of other animal species, though they are never unkind to them. They have a poor opinion of humans.'

Why get the Wombles involved in Woke? They were surely Woke enough the way they were, forever bustling about recycling any bit of rubbish they could get their paws on. Though no one actually used the word 'racist 'of them, demanding 'diversity' of them definitely implied that the scavenging sods weren't being 'inclusive 'in who they hung out with on Wimbledon Common. You could hardly blame Marcus Robertson, the son of their creator Elisabeth Beresford, for defending their honour in the *Mail on Sunday* after being led to believe that his mother's creations were in some way racist and unfit for furry purpose in our multi-cultural times:

> 'Wombles have grey fur and orangey-brown faces. They're not white. They're not black. Wombles are Wombles. I don't believe in black or white Wombles and neither did my mother, because Wombles are Wombles. We believe in the diversity of humans, but Wombles are not ethnic humans. I feel like I've failed Mum in allowing it to get like this. Now I need to retrieve the soul of the Wombles. I want to be able to walk past her ashes at a church in Alderney and say 'We've sorted it, Mum.''

As if the situation could be rendered more comic, lawyers for the Wombles new owner opined loftily:

> 'Mr Robertson's views are not shared by Wombles Copyright Holdings Limited or the Wombles. WCHL and the Wombles believe in an inclusive and diverse world, where everybody should be treated equally.'

Of course it doesn't matter a fig what colour some fictional beasts are. But, once again, it's the ceaseless drip-scold of being told what we should think or say in any given situation which has the actual effect of making people far less tolerant and far more reactionary than I believe they would otherwise be because endless attempts to set us on the right path as if we were wayward children invariably make us want to do the opposite. The poem which describes my adopted home county of Sussex now stands for all of us who have a healthy amount of self-respect and scepticism in relation to Wokeness:

> 'Some folks as comes to Sussex,
> They reckon as they knows
> A darn sight better what to do
> Then silly folks like me and you
> Could possibly suppose
> But them as comes to Sussex,
> For Sussex will be Sussex,
> And Sussex won't be druv.'

When we feel dismayed at the Woke way the world appears to be going, we must always remember that they're not just sinister, like other witch-hunters; they're also singularly silly, and this being so it's highly likely that they will bury themselves with their own foolishness and hypocrisy. For instance, how can you believe in the evils of cultural appropriation - even down to getting angry about non-Hispanics wearing sombreros - yet believe that a man can become a woman because of a 'feeling' he has? Misogyny has always been the poor relation of racism and it may well take people *feeling* that they are ethnically different from how they actually are which will derail this danse macabre. In the November of 2019 the University and College Union announced: 'We have a long history of enabling members to self-identify, whether that is being black, disabled, LGBT or women.' A year earlier a white theatre director claiming to be 'African born again' won public funding intended to help ethnic minorities develop careers in the theatre. No wonder Trevor Phillips, former chairman of the Commission for Racial Equality - target of his own Woke Trial in the spring of 2020 - said that allowing people to self-identify their race meant that ethnic minorities 'lost out.'

Like Political Correctness before it, Wokeness started out as an admirable aim and ended up as a despicable smugness, inhabited by people who need never tackle their own shortcomings while there is a demonised Other - chav, gammon, Brexiteer - to unload upon. It would be interesting to know how many hardcore Wokeists suffer from bi-polar syndrome as a great many of them appear to experience the term known as 'splitting' - a polarised way of viewing the world in, which in order for one's own side to be totally good, the other side must be totally evil. Not unique to the Left, this mentality invariably leads to show trials driven by anything from not being the right kind of Communist (as in 1930s Russia) to being even a tiny bit sympathetic to Communists (as in 1950s America). The result is invariably grim; a reign of fear and a desiccation of culture.

The trans-activists hashtagging #BeKind while threatening TERFs with rape and murder do not appear to see the contradiction in their behaviour - and this is the very real danger of virtue-signaling. It's not, as defenders claim, just a wordy way of being decent; it actually becomes a cover either for doing nothing at all to contribute anything good to society (at best) or a cover for behaving very badly indeed. I loathe virtue-signaling - the semaphore of the Woke - not because I despise virtue (my history of philanthropy and volunteering would indicate otherwise) but because those who yell loudest about the importance of being good are so lacking in any practical demonstration of it.

*

COVID-19 came to us quietly in the year 2020, driving humankind from the streets and ushering a strange sort of super-spring in which Mother Nature, the bossy old bitch, sent us all to our rooms and filled our cities with her mute outliers; mountain goats graced the streets of Wales, wild boar brought home the bacon in Barcelona and coyotes left their mark on the heart of San Francisco.

I wrote this book during lockdown, when we were all reassessing what was really important to us and what could go out for the noble bin men when we emerged blinking in the sunlight of the other side. I wondered for a couple of weeks whether I should write it at all - #allinthistogether and all that jazz. Luckily, the ceaseless whining and ill-will from Wokers at a time when everyday people proved to be humdrum heroes and the Conservative government was acting like Robin Hood gave me renewed purpose.

For instance, I heard a right-on half-wit on the radio complaining that in dangerous days like these, *we should have more diversity in the cabinet if they are to be credible* 'because when everyone looks the same, it doesn't give people confidence in the government.' This would be the cabinet in which the four main offices of state are occupied by a woman of Gujarati-East African extraction, a man of Punjabi-East African extraction, a man of Eastern European Jewish extraction - and a bouncing, bumptious blond man whose great-grandfather was the Turkish politician Ali Kemal who served under the Grand Vizier of the Ottoman Empire. Did the radio half-wit perhaps believe that diversity was being ill-served by there being too few Anglo-Saxons in the Cabinet? Of course not; she was merely appalled by *the wrong type of diversity*, one which had come about through effort and merit rather than quotas and patronage.

Why, even during the greatest threat to the human race in living memory, were the Woke still such nit-picking naysayers?

Just as the plague was peaking, a group of jolly Devon nurses wore white headbands and stripes of black face paint to perform the ceremonial Māori haka dance whilst chanting 'You'll never beat us' at images of the coronavirus. A few moments of harmless, morale-raising fun from a group of people doing more than any other to save their fellow citizens from a terrifying disease and ceaselessly putting their own lives on the line in order to do so? Wash your mouth out with antibacterial sanitiser! Twitter predictably got its ever-wetted knickers in a twist where it accused the nurses of 'mocking Māori culture' and a Maori *expert* (interestingly, not *spokesperson*) named Tania Ka'ai denounced it as 'blatant cultural abuse verging on racist':

> 'Haka are not about being simply angry at the world. They are a fierce display of a tribe's pride, strength and unity. This is an example of the dominant Western culture trivialising an aspect of Māori culture and abusing our language which has struggled to survive since the signing of Te Tiriti o Waitangi in 1840.'

The hospital responded:

> 'We want to offer a wholehearted apology to those we offended with a video we posted on Twitter at the weekend. The video was intended as a show of our commitment as nurses to continue to work hard and care for people as we fight coronavirus. We've really enjoyed seeing the video messages from nursing colleagues up and down the country and we are really sorry that our choice of delivery caused offence. Upsetting anyone was the last thing we wanted to do.'

Wokers are like those dogs you see in pubs sometimes, who aren't really angry, but utter one bark every ten minutes just keep their equipment running. Are their lives so profoundly dull and their personalities so intrinsically uninteresting that they need to ceaselessly create problems in order to feel alive? Whatever the reason, they're totally in denial, and whereas generally people are in denial about Bad Things - as a coping mechanism - the Woke are the only group who are permanently in denial about Good Things, such as the **real** diversity of the Government. They're cowardly people as a rule (I'd love to know how many Woke got their worthless hides out there during the lockdown and actually **helped** anyone) and they loathe the working-class; it must drive them nuts that we're finally moving towards a **real** socialism, as opposed to the performative brag that's their bag.

Like all those snobbish socialist eugenicists of the olden days (the fiery pro-Brexit socialist firefighter and trades unionist Paul Embery once quipped to a heckling member of the Fabian Society 'What you gonna do - sterilise me?') Wokers swear they're speaking on behalf on The People but are secretly filled with fear and loathing at the thought of actual people, who have a tendency to do illogical things such as vote for the political candidate who didn't call them Deplorables. With the possible exception of the murderous rhetoric they employ against rebellious women who won't toe the line over the claim that penises are not necessarily male, it's when they're lashing out at the working classes that we see the Woke in all their inherent nastiness.

Sensitivity is portrayed as a positive character trait but interestingly the flip side is often cruelty and callousness, as heightened sensitivity indicates a person who has never made the effort to master their feelings and thus become a self-controlled adult. They are those people referred to historically as those who 'can dish it out but can't take it.' In 2015 I named a new *type* in an essay in the Spectator:

> 'This is the age of the Cry-Bully, a hideous hybrid of victim and victor, weeper and walloper. They are everywhere, these duplicit Pushmi-Pullyus of the personal and the political, from Celebrity Big Brother to the frontline of Islamism. I don't care for monarchy, but the old saw the Windsors they are said to live by -Never explain, never complain - is a sound one. The Cry-

Bully always explains to the point of demanding that one agrees with them and always complains to the point of insisting that one is persecuting them. They really are the very worst sort of modern moaner.'

I've never heard of a pro-Brexit Woker and I had a feeling that as soon as my side scented victory the C-word would not be long in coming from our self-anointed superiors And sure enough in that week's *Sunday Times* report from the Glastonbury Festival, there it was: "The chavs have won,' whined one cut-glass raver. 'I'm already looking into dual citizenship." Elsewhere in the paper a Brighton Remoaner commented 'If you give a vote to every man and his dog, you have to be prepared for the answer you get.' WELCOME TO CHAV BRITAIN was a friend of a friend's Facebook status the morning of the result. Sorrowful snowflakes quickly began demanding that London be allowed to secede from the rest of this churlish isle, with perhaps a stylish little shuttle-service to keep them connected to Scotland. Though the prospect of getting shot of 99 per cent of man-buns and clean-eaters in one fell swoop was thrilling, what did these Little Londoners plan to do with the whopping 40 per cent of Londoners who voted Leave? Presumably they'd be allowed to live there to service the Remainers, grieving the loss of their Eastern European slaves.

The pathetic petulance which emanated from the Remainers in the wake of our glorious victory stemmed from the fact that many of those who prided themselves on being progressive were, actually, differently-styled parts of the Establishment all along. They also saw themselves as supreme humanitarians who genuflected before the altar of the European Union due to their generous-spirited membership of the brotherhood of man rather than their stingy desire to hire cheap household labour. Similarly, the ugly utterances of the most savagely splenetic of the Remnants - everyone from the novelist Ian McEwan (yearned for yet another referendum once older Brexit voters were' freshly in their graves') to the broadcaster Terry Christian (hoped that a 'good virulent strain of flu' would hit people who 'voted to destroy our lives') - were revealed as the genocidal fantasies they always were when the senior citizens they blamed for Brexit began to fall in their thousands in the face of the pandemic. (It's amusing to note that McEwan is in his 70s and Christian a mere stripling of 60, despite their demonising of the old; perhaps they possess what I once coined a Magic Mirror, which are owned by a sizeable section of unappetizing geezers who look into them only to see a young Adonis gazing back.) The strange hatred of the Woke for the masses in the time of plague was summed up sorrowfully by a friend who posted on Facebook: 'Just heard my wonderfully eccentric step uncle died of Covid-19 today - make no mistake, it is a vile way to go. Last week I saw a Bristol musician's comment on a friend's FB post':

> "Bring on Covid-19, I'm just about ready for a cull.' He was referring to the working classes; it made my blood boil then as it still does now. I hope I never meet this revolting creature; peak Woke wankerdom.'

A letter to the Guardian, which like much of that newspaper reads like rib-tickling Tory satire of Wokedom, gloated 'My daughter, Maude, wisely said last week that we, humans, are the virus and Covid-19 is the solution.' I'd keep an eye on Maude if I were her mum, as this sounds quite like something a littler Hitler might say.

It may be a subconscious nagging knowledge of how little they actually contribute to life which makes the Woke shout so loud to hide it. Whatever the causes, their insecurity and fear of lively debate shuts down societies in both serious ways - censorship - and frivolous ones - they seek to steal our sunshine and make us all as boring as they are, licking self-inflicted wounds in the safe space of a sealed-off echo chamber. Sometimes I think it's my fierce love of freedom which makes me hate Wokeness; sometimes I think it's my fierce love of fun. It's probably both, but whatever it is, I won't be druv. If you too feel this way, and you've got nothing nice to say, why not sit right down by me and read this book?

*

One afternoon early in 2013, I was innocently wasting time on Facebook when it came to my notice that a friend, the writer Suzanne Moore, was being threatened with violence on social media by militant trans-activists due to a line in an essay in the *New Statesman* entitled 'Seeing Red: The Power of Female Anger':

'Women are angry with ourselves for not being happier, not being loved properly and not having the ideal body shape – that of a Brazilian transsexual.'

Though I am impervious to haters myself I'm never one to shy away from a scrap where my mates are concerned. And I had *previous* with Suzanne; I felt a deeper bond with her than I did with other friends because of our shared status as rare working-class women in the media. My mum had asked me how *the typing* was going when I was a teenager determined to become a famous writer; hers had been heard to say 'Suzanne's depressed - she's reading.' I'm emphasizing this not just to show off (though of course I am very proud of myself for becoming a famous writer despite not having had rich parents, books in the house or a university education) but because I maintain that Wokeness is, at heart, merely the latest attempt by the privileged to corral and control the scary proletarian hordes; a repressive movement rather than a progressive one, despite the narrative of social justice the Woke peddle. I believe that the mutual class origin I shared with Suzanne was responsible for much of the furore which would subsequently ensue.

But to be honest, righteousness was only part of the reason I cleaved to her. We had a pleasurable friendship in which my role as Bad - possibly Mad - Cop to hers as Good Cop was based in fact but exaggerated to a hilarious degree. For instance, when I tired of my second husband in the 1990s and was casting around for a suitable stand-in to take the edge off of his sexual jealousy and thus hopefully make him more amenable during the divorce settlement, my eye fell on Comrade Moore, who shared my somewhat vulgar, Betty-Boopish brand of sex appeal; rinky-dink voice, staggeringly high heels and cleavage before noon. After weeks of appearing appalled - 'Julie - NO! Not even YOU could want THAT!' - she eventually cooperated and, as with everything we've been though, we had a good laugh about it.

It was an earlier bit of mischief, though, which eerily previewed the tsunami of sass I would serve in Suzanne's *defence* ('No matter what troubles I face in future, I'm going to tell myself 'This could be worse - Julie Burchill could be leaping to your defence'' - the late Deborah Orr) against the monstrous regiment of Arthurs-turned-Marthas-on-Mondays-and-Sundays. Our opponent on this outing was Germaine Greer, now a fellow TERF (Trans Exclusive Radical Feminist - we're sort of the Round Earthers of the gender politics world) which demonstrates how pleasingly the transsexual debate - like Brexit - has smashed old biases and created new alliances. For some reason (or maybe none - she has a long history of being bitchy to other broads, sort of an 'I'm the only feminist in the global village' stuff) the Professor had subjected Suzanne to a random-generated word-soup insult-emetic way back in 1995, lashing out at her alleged 'bird's nest hair' 'fuck-me shoes,' 'three fat inches of cleavage' and 'so much lipstick it must rot the brain.' Suzanne was the very model of a dignified bluestocking - 'If Germaine attacked me for my writing, it would be far more worthy than to attack me for my shoes' - but where's the fun in that? I was determined to put myself between my two warring sisters - but only so I could have a ringside seat, and hopefully make the conflagration carry on for far long after it would have died a natural death had not a trouble-maker like me got involved.

I tried to see both sides. Perhaps Dr Moore **had** been cheeky to start with, writing that Professor Greer had undergone a hysterectomy when young; if it's rude to insult someone's shoes, it's probably even worse to have a go at their ovaries. But how were we to know that what this antagonistic Amazon had wanted most of all all along was a **liddle baybee** to dote on? We're not mind-readers! Quoth the Prof:

> 'It's pretty painful when you have spent a goodly part of your life struggling to have children, to have this young woman - who is lucky enough to have two children of her own - suddenly announce that I had myself hysterectomised at 25 because I didn't want kids. How could she be so stupid? I think that level of incomprehension is inexcusable in someone who calls herself a feminist.'

Replied the Doc:

> 'Germaine's womb is the centre of her universe, but it isn't for me. Obviously I was upset by what she said, but nonetheless I have a lot of admiration for her. She's absolutely right in saying that women need to be angry and she's absolutely the person to write passionately and polemically on it. But people want a catfight.'

Well, I certainly did, so when ABC - the Australian BBC came calling - I was delighted. Dr Moore was in her element: 'Julie, you can't say that!' she squealed repeatedly as I laid into Prof Greer's ovaries and even, for some reason, that she had seen fit to give names to all her chickens. 'It's not Suzanne's fault that Professor Greer's been mugged by gravity,' I finished in a caring manner. 'Or that she's barren.'

Appetite whetted by this warm-up, I went on to have a few one-on-one scraps with Greer of my own over the years. She was always nice as pie in person, albeit never missing a chance to show the upstarts who was boss bitch: 'I hope you don't mind me flirting with your husband so flagrantly on TV,' she twinkled once as we waited to appear on Woman's Hour.

I looked blank on purpose. 'Which one? There's been so many!'

She wasn't expecting that. 'Tony!'

'O, that one! Yes, I left him when the still looked half decent so obviously I'm not going to get jealous now he looks like a sick rhesus monkey. Fill your boots!'

We smiled civilly at each other before going into the studio and attempting to turn each other into twelve tins of cat food. But this looked like a 'Ladies Excuse Me' dance compared to my scrap with Camille Paglia. She: 'I am read around the world from Japan to South America...you are completely unknown outside England.' Me: 'It's great to see an academic cube like yourself get with it. I'm very glad you're big in Japan.' She: 'You think yourself madly clever but you seem trapped in juvenility.' Me: 'Fuck off you crazy old dyke.'

I'm reminiscing here to show that feminists have always disagreed - often to the point of slander - but because we understand that well-behaved women never change history, we've never tried to get each other censored, blacklisted or cancelled. We're sure enough of our own arguments to be confident they won't crumble to dust the moment they're challenged. Whereas in 2015, a petition at Cardiff University sought to ban Greer's talk on women in political and social life because her of her 'misogynistic views towards trans women.' Here was the best example yet of the lunacy that informs trans-activism, if indeed you can dignify the process of fondling your cock in the ladies lavatories and yelling death threats at actual women *activism*.

The talk went ahead anyway, with uniformed police officers standing guard outside the lecture theatre and security men guarding the doors inside. It was perhaps the last gasp of common sense on the part of this country's police force where the TERF Wars were concerned; by the end of the decade we would see them revealed as a bunch of misogynist mitherers, apparently under the delusion that it is the responsibility of the forces of law and order not to protect free speech from violent attack but rather to hover over social media all day like a bunch of flat-footed Kardashians busying themselves with the heinous crime of *misgendering* while the streets of the nation's capitals runs red with the blood of young people. I can imagine these PC PCs poring over the morning Twitter-feed as they sip skinny lattes and catch up on who's hurt whose feelings while minding their pronouns ('Cis TERF bitch disrespected my brave and stunning kween - they's going down!') before skipping off to bravely confront law-abiding free-thinkers over the latest 'non-crime hate incident.'

Anyway, during the lecture Professor Greer made in clear in the bluntest of terms that she did not accept that post-operative men were women:

> 'I don't believe a woman is a man without a cock - you can beat me over the head with a baseball bat, it still won't make me change my mind. Being a woman is a bit tricky; if you didn't find your pants full of blood when you were 13 there's something important about being a woman you don't know. It's not all cake and jam.'

A flyer distributed by protesters featured a quote of hers from the Guardian: 'Nowadays we are all likely to meet people who think they are women, have women's names, and feminine clothes and lots of eyeshadow, who seem to us to be some kind of ghastly parody, though it isn't polite to say so.' Splendid splenetic stuff - and what a triumph of the squabbling sisterhood to see none other than Dr Moore standing in solidarity with her erstwhile sparring partner on Twitter: 'Germaine Greer was a right cow to me many years ago So what? She is Germaine Greer and she should say what she likes. Banning her is ridic.'

But to return in our TERFY Tardis to 2013. On seeing that my amiga was being monstered on Twitter I posted a few bitchy comments in support of her on Facebook and a commissioning editor from the Observer joined the conversation to ask me if I would make them into a column. I refused as I was on my way out; they offered me double the money so I did it, went on my merry way and thought nothing more of it until Sunday, when I went out and bought the paper. My column **did** read well - full of the rampant vulgarity I am notorious for, my feelings about which is summed up so well for me in that quote by the architect Clough Williams-Ellis 'I would rather be vulgar than boring - especially to myself.' I know I'm not everyone's cup of Kool-Aid, but I write to please myself and get paid in that order and I usually succeed. I certainly did not disappoint myself in the chortle department with that now notorious column of January 12th 2013:

> 'The writer Suzanne Moore and I go back a long way. I first met her when she was a young single mother living in a council flat; she took me out to interview me about my novel Ambition for dear dead City Limits magazine. I have observed her rise to the forefront of this country's great polemicists with a whole lot of pride. With this in mind, I was incredulous to read that my friend was being monstered on Twitter, to the extent that she had quit it, for supposedly picking on a minority – transsexuals. Though I imagine it to be something akin to being savaged by a dead sheep, as Denis Healey had it of Geoffrey Howe, I nevertheless felt indignant that a woman of such style and substance should be driven from her chosen mode of time-wasting by a bunch of dicks in chick's clothing. To my mind – have given cool-headed consideration to the matter – a gaggle of transsexuals telling Suzanne Moore how to write is quite like the Black & White Minstrels telling Usain Bolt how to run.'

With this in mind, I was incredulous to read that my friend was being monstered on Twitter, to the extent that she had quit it, for supposedly picking on a minority – transsexuals. Though I imagine it to be something akin to being savaged by a dead sheep, as Denis Healey had it of Geoffrey Howe, I nevertheless felt indignant that a woman of such style and substance should be driven from her chosen mode of time-wasting by a bunch of dicks in chick's clothing. To my mind – have given cool-headed consideration to the matter – a gaggle of transsexuals telling

Suzanne Moore how to write is quite like the Black & White Minstrels telling Usain Bolt how to run.

My only experience of the trans lobby thus far was hearing about the vile way they had persecuted another of my friends, the veteran women's rights and anti-domestic violence activist Julie Bindel, picketing events where she was speaking about such minor issues as the rape of children and the trafficking of women just because she refuses to accept that their relationship with their phantom limb is the most pressing problem that women (real or imagined) are facing. Ignore the real enemy – they're strong and will need real effort and organization to fight. How much easier to lash out at those who are conveniently close to hand!

But they'd rather argue over semantics. To be fair, after having one's nuts taken off by endless decades in academia, it's all most of them are fit to do. Educated beyond all common sense and honesty, it was a hoot to see the screaming-mimis accuse Suzanne of white feminist privilege; it may have been this which made her finally respond in the subsequent salty language she employed to answer her Twitter critics: 'People can just fuck off really. Cut their dicks off and be more feminist than me. Good for them.'

Suzanne, the other Julie B and I are part of the tiny minority of women of working-class origin to make it in what used to be called Fleet Street and I think this partly contributes to the stand-off with the trannies. (I know that's a wrong word, but as their lot describe born women as 'Cis ' –sounds like syph, cyst, cistern; all nasty stuff – they're lucky I'm not calling them shemales. Or shims.) We know that everything we have, we got for ourselves. We have no family money, no safety net. And we are damned if we are going to be accused of being privileged by a bunch of bed-wetters in bad wigs.

It's been noted before that cyberspace, though supposedly all new and shiny, is plagued by the age old dreariness of men telling women not to talk, and threatening them will all kinds of nastiness if they persist in saying what they feel.

The trans lobby were now saying that it wasn't so much the initial piece as Suzanne's refusal to apologise when told to that 'made' them drive her from Twitter. Presumably she was meant to do this in the name of solidarity and the 'struggle' – though I find it very hard to imagine this mob struggling with anything apart from the English language and the concept of free speech.

To have your cock cut off and then plead special privileges as women – above natural-born women, who don't know the meaning of suffering, apparently – is a bit like the old definition of chutzpah: the boy who killed his parents and then asked the jury for clemency on the grounds he was an orphan. Shims, shemales, whatever you're calling yourselves these days – don't threaten or bully we lowly natural-born women, I warn you. We may not have as many lovely big swinging PHDs as you, but we've experienced a lifetime of PMT and sexual harassment, and many of us are now staring HRT and the menopause straight in the face – and still not flinching. Trust me - you really won't like us when we're angry.

This was fairly standard stuff for me - I've been going for people's ankles since I was a 17-year-old cutting pop stars down to size on the New Musical Express - and I knew there was often comeback. I'd had loads of death threats in the post (which now, with the demise of letter-writing, take on the illuminated glow of courtly love) as well as figuring in the fantasies of an ocean-going loony who'd started out writing to me from Scotland, promising to do all sorts of gory stuff, and then increased his angry ardour with each southward city he stopped in on the course of his perverted peregrination to me. I was a Guardian columnist at the time and one day - perhaps because my pen-pal had taken to drawing angry-looking genitalia on the envelopes - one of the do-gooders on the staff went and opened the billet doux and was quite horrified by what they read.

'Ooo, go on - what is it?' I urged down the phone. I was quite getting into these mucky-minded missives by now.

'Julie, YOU DON'T WANT TO KNOW!'

'O, I do - I really do!' I insisted.

'No - it's HORRIBLE - I'm sending it straight to your local police!'

Within 24 hours there was a fresh-faced PC on my doorstep; a mixed blessing as these were the good old days when I'd throw three-day cocaine-fuelled pool parties at my pink palace in Hove and invariably the place would end up looking like someone had burst a huge bag of sugar over all flat surfaces. I unlocked my porch door and did my best impersonation of a good person with a bad cold as I nodded earnestly between sniffles at their concerns and sympathy, not expressing disagreement until they proffered the notion of a panic button.

'No way! They're for old people that fall over! And besides - I gestured smugly at our immediate surroundings' - 'I have **a porch door**.' With this I smiled beatifically and made to close the door on the issue. The PC stuck their foot betwixt it and the jamb and for a good five minutes the words 'Panic button' and 'Porch door' were batted back and forth like a Wimbledon of words. Eventually they retired exhausted and I bounced off to lick my mirrors in celebration. (The nutter eventually turned up at the Guardian offices - believing I'd work in an office with **that** bunch was truly proof of his tenuous grasp on reality - where he made to push past the security man, was bounced straight back out onto the pavement and never heard of again.)

But I wasn't just accustomed to being a magnet for the attention of dyspeptic elder feminists or off-message madmen. I was also a repeat offender when it came to the libel laws, inspiring extortionately expensive wars of words. For instance, in 1994, reviewing the film Frankenstein, I described the character of 'The Creature' in as being 'a lot like Steven Berkoff, only marginally better-looking.' A small fortune was spent on legal eagles by both sides before, as sensibly summed up by the barrister Paul Magrath:

> 'Miss Burchill made a cheap joke at Mr Berkoff's expense; she might thereby have demeaned herself, but his Lordship did not believe she had defamed Mr Berkoff. His claim was as frivolous as Miss Burchill's article and the court's time ought not to be taken up with either of them.'

I'm recounting my history of public conflict partly because I find myself endlessly fascinating but just as much to demonstrate that I was used to having pushback, and relished it. Nevertheless, nothing had prepared me for the sheer babyishness of the trans-lobby; how fitting (if creepy) that a large number of them *identify* as little girls. It's not just me who found them singularly unwilling to test their arguments rigorously; in 2019 I met a respected documentary maker who specialised in talking to both sides of an armed conflict – he'd made a film on both sides of a sectarian frontline in the Syrian civil war, and had made a number of award-winning films about the Arab-Israeli conflict. These warring sides were quite content that he was also filming with their enemies; when he told a senior press officer for the IDF that he was going to be filming with leaders in Hamas and Islamic Jihad, the press officer smiled and simply said 'That'll be interesting!'

He continued:

> 'With trans-activists, however, it was different. When I began making a film that questioned the huge rise in young people transitioning in the U.K, not a single advocate of trans-children would take part, saying there was 'Nothing to debate' and that they didn't want to take part in a film that would be 'one-sided' - not realising that by not taking part they were making such an outcome more and not less likely.'

Or as the gay writer Philip Hensher put it in March 2016:

> 'The phrase 'enter into debate' is being used in interesting new ways. The transsexual activist Paris Lees, who has always refused to appear if my admired friend Julie Bindel was to speak, claimed on Newsnight that Julie 'refused to enter into debate.' (Newsnight issued a retraction of Ms Lees's claim) May I suggest a new meaning for 'enter into debate,' viz, 'Agree with me unconditionally on a subject I don't understand'?'

A favoured phrase of the trans-lobby is 'Words are **literally** violence.' This is, of course, the logic of the lunatic asylum; words are the opposite of violence and can often delay or negate violence altogether. From Mrs Burchill informing the child me that sticks and stones might break my bones but names would never hurt me to Mr Churchill advising that jaw-to-jaw is better than war, we have history to show us that words are literally the opposite of violence and that people only resort to the latter when one or both sides give up arguing logically. Looking back, we may see that perhaps the most remarkable achievement of the trans-lobby was to make surrealism seem like nagging.

The Observer skirmish was my first taste of what would become known as Cancel Culture - where the battle is won not by the side with the best arguments but by the side that screams the loudest. You can't blame a dog for barking, but you can certainly blame a bystander if, when that dog bites you on the ankle, rather than helping you that bystander sinks his teeth into your hand for good measure. I wasn't shocked at the shrillness from the female-impersonator camp but you could have knocked me down with a feather boa when the Observer chickened out. The oldest Sunday newspaper in the world acted like a skittish adolescent having a panic attack at a high school debating society when challenged to put into actual practice. What a long way - all downhill - they'd come since the heady days of 1989 when Charter 88 (the pressure group which advocated a written constitution) was launched in the Observer with a letter signed by a whopping five thousand of the Great and the Good (hormonal excitement must have been high in Hampstead on that historic day):

> 'We have had less freedom than we believed. That which we have enjoyed has been too dependent on the benevolence of our rulers. Our freedoms have remained their possession, rationed out to us as subjects rather than being our own inalienable possession as citizens. To make real the freedoms we once took for granted means for the first time to take them for ourselves. The time has come to demand political, civil and human rights in the United Kingdom. We call, therefore, for a new constitutional settlement which will:
>
> 1) Enshrine, by means of a Bill of Rights, such civil liberties as the right to peaceful assembly, to freedom of association, to freedom from discrimination, to freedom from detention without trial, to trial by jury, to privacy and to freedom of expression.'

Imagine my sophomoric surprise when instead of publishing and being bravely damned, this bastion of free speech backtracked under fire with all the slipperiness of a snake performing in a figure-skating contest by Monday morning. My column was published, and then pulled from the website. The Lib-Dem MP Lynne Featherstone - then Minister for International Development, now cooling her heels in the Lords after having to return £22,000 worth of Parliamentary stationery (perchance she identified as WH Smith) and losing her seat to Labour - accused me of 'inciting hatred' and said that no only should the editor sack me but also be sacked himself. I must say that I came to agree with the second part of this demand, when after apologising to fuming fuss-budgets everywhere and ringing me up to tell me that this wouldn't change anything, he never employed me again.

Reading it back now, it's certainly cheeky and provocative - but the *worst* lines had already been on my Facebook conversation and they were what led the Observer to ask me to write the column in the first place, which makes them hypocrites as well as cowards. As Suzanne said 'You don't commission someone like Julie Burchill to launch an Exocet missile and then say 'Oh dear, we only really wanted a sparkler.'' The Observer's action was a sinister and silly capitulation to a pressure group whose demands have become ever more unreasonable ever since. As Douglas Murray describes in his book The Madness Of Crowds, I was then sent into the professional wilderness.

Nothing's changed in those eight years; it's truly pathetic how those who consider themselves to be rebel voices serving it to the Establishment have most eagerly put their own blinkers and gags on. In the spring of 2020 the artist Stella Perrett published a cartoon in the Morning Star depicting an alligator telling newts in a pond: 'Don't worry your pretty little heads, I'm transitioning as a newt.' The Communist daily, after the by-now mandatory fit of the screaming ab-dabs from very cross-dressers, pulled the drawing from its online editions and issued an 'unreserved' apology for any offence caused. As Perrett says on her website: 'Between 2015 and 2020 I have been a regular political cartoonist for the U.K's only Socialist daily newspaper, the Morning Star, until I was 'no-platformed' by them for a feminist cartoon called 'Endgame,' which they published, and then changed their mind about, knowing it was a comment on the potential changes to the GRA and the erosion of women's rights in the 2010 Equality Act.'

Also in the spring of 2020, Dr Moore was in the word-soup all over again. (At the moment the roll-call of sexual grandstanding stands at LQBTQIA but the never-ending growth of this particular initialism is a gift to we popcorn-throwers as the ponderous types who go along with this sort of guff struggle to keep up to date and pronounce every last letter even at the risk of using up their whole allotted time when accepting their Stonewall award.) In a March column outrageously headlined WOMEN

HAVE THE RIGHT TO ORGANISE - WE WILL NOT BE SILENCED
Suzanne outraged public decency thus:

> 'Last Saturday, Selina Todd, a professor of modern history at
> the University of Oxford, was due to give a polite two-minute
> speech of thanks at an event at Exeter College commemorating
> 50 years since Ruskin College's inaugural National Women's
> Liberation Conference. The day before Todd was due to speak
> she was disinvited on the grounds that she had addressed a
> meeting of the group Woman's Place U.K, which was formed
> in 2017 after proposed changes to the Gender Recognition Act.
> The group campaigns for women to have separate spaces and
> distinct services on the basis of our biological sex. Todd, an
> esteemed professor of working-class history, has, as a result,
> been accused on social media of being transphobic. Woman's
> Place U.K was recently defined as a 'trans-exclusionist hate
> group' in a pledge put together by the Labour Campaign for
> Trans Rights which the Labour leadership candidates Lisa
> Nandy and Rebecca Long-Bailey signed up to.'

And shamelessly raking up the past and daring to refer to her own
personal experience:

> 'I know from personal experience the consequences of being
> deemed transphobic by an invisible committee on social media.
> It has meant death and rape threats for me and my children, and
> police involvement. I also know that the most vicious stuff takes
> place online and not in real life. Still, I can't stand by. As
> Roman Polanski was being rewarded for his latest film at the
> César awards, Todd was being silenced. This latest silencing of
> women is a warning. You either protect women's rights as sex-
> based or you don't protect them at all. You can tell me to 'Die
> in a ditch, Terf' all you like, as many have for years, but I self-
> identify as a woman who won't go down quietly. There are
> more of us than you think.'

The trans-lobby often reminds me of the two masks which
represent modern theatre, paired together to show the two extremes of the
human psyche. As Thalia, muse of comedy (which symbolises how foolish
humans can be) they often pose gurning on social media, clad in little more
than a garter belt and a rictus grin, lying to each other than they are
*stunning and brave* - an echo chamber in a hall of mirrors. And as
Melpomene, muse of tragedy (which signifies dark emotions such as fear)
they break out like a syphilitic rash all over social media, gathering

Twittermobs to help them take down the latest woman who has dared to say boo to a goose (or rather, gander.) In a remarkable demonstration of the latter - even considering how high the ballet barre was - a *trans-woman* called *Jess* dramatically resigned from the Guardian[1] in protest over Dr Moore's uppity words - before, of course, returning to an editorial meeting in order to flounced out all over again, but this time tearfully and with an audience. In a politics as purely performative as *trans* nothing which is not done in public can really count as being done. As the amusingly appropriately-named Huffington Post put it:

> 'A deepening row about The Guardian's coverage of trans rights issues saw a trans woman dramatically announce her resignation in front of colleagues on Tuesday. It is the third resignation from the paper's U.K office in months over the issue. The worker confirmed to HuffPost U.K she had handed in her notice a few weeks earlier, but chose to speak out in the busy news meeting on Tuesday over what she called 'the straw that broke the camel's back.''

The camel in question, though, was not remarkable for retaining water but for shedding lots of it in copious unicorn tears. Before Their tantrum, *Jess* had Tweeted:

> 'I'm literally fucking crying reading this utter garbage fire, how is this allowed to be published??? "m an EMPLOYEE @guardian and I'M SCARED TO GO INTO WORK TOMORROW" I've already had transphobic Editorial views to me…Whats next after this threat?'

Though appearing to be a particularly snide Private Eye parody of the sub-literate sub-editors who work for the famously ham-fisted Guardian, this was in fact an actual thing.

But who would the famously freedom-loving staff of the newspaper choose to back? Dr Moore, winner of the previous year's Orwell Prize 'awarded to the best commentary or reporting which comes closest to achieving writer George Orwell's ambition to 'make political writing into an art'' with what the judges hailed as her 'stubborn and brave commentary' - or a person whose greatest writing achievement was a series of obfuscating Tweets? Not just bleating about being scared to go into work and face Dr Moore's deadly arsenal of cleavage, beehive and fuck-me shoes, it transpired, but also being in an open relationship with the truth last year when Them claimed to have been attacked by a pair of knife-wielding transphobes and asked for *donations* before deleting said Tweets when it emerged that this had only happened in Their deranged dreams.

Did you guess right? Yes, a whopping 338 Guardian/Observers employees - more than a fifth of its workforce - signed a letter lamenting the decision to publish Suzanne's column, deploring it as part of their newspapers 'pattern of publishing transphobic content.' Naturally I wanted to step in one more time but for some reason was not encouraged; indeed, another so-called friend of the Doc's saw fit to snark back to Round One: 'Julie has poured oil on troubled waters, then set fire to the oil, killing several sea birds.'

Abandoned by her craven comrades on the Left, who could blame the good Dr for hotfooting it to Amsterdam and getting off her box on drugs while at home it was publications of the *Right* which supported her right to free speech? Censorship now comes overwhelmingly (and over-wroughtly) from the Left; still, it was wicked fun to see the Spectator call her 'the great Suzanne Moore' and to read the great Brendan O'Neill in Spiked:

> 'Suzanne Moore once said she wanted to vomit on me. So I'm guessing she's not a fan. Alas, defending freedom of speech, standing up for the essential liberty of intellectual and moral dissent, often means defending people who despise you. Even people who want to puke on you. And so I must defend Ms Moore from the army of censorious misogynists keen to shut her down because – let's be frank – she thinks that if you have a dick you are a man, not a woman.'

In a true End Of Days move, Miss Moore then popped up in the pages of the Spectator herself, doing that old more-in-sorrow-than-in-anger act which has proved such a reliable straight-man to my own flagrant wickednesss:

> 'After all the online abuse, I thought someone might ring me and see if I was OK, but they didn't. The emails then came pouring in from people who wished they could say what I had said. I wished people would stop calling me brave. Columnists are meant to be made of titanium; I felt more like papier-mâché.

> But the orthodoxy which demands that Mary Beard must refer to an ancient statue with a little penis as 'assigned male at birth' is powerful. I like freaks. I like fluidity. I just don't like one set of rules being replaced by another. I was hurt that so many of my 'colleagues' denounced me, but I suppose everyone needs a hobby.'

Never mind, she'll bounce back; like me, she is the opposite of a snowflake - a snowplough, perhaps, pushing all the slushy and ill-sorted modern mewling which passes as radical politics before her. And as the title of her essay collection admits, my dear Dr Moore was always 'looking for trouble' - and in this most interesting of times to be a feminist she has certainly found it. We all have.

---

# Notes

[1] https://www.huffingtonpost.co.uk/entry/dfgdfgdfgfd_uk_5e5e7444c5b6732f50e8d509

# CHAPTER TWO

## FAUXMINISM AND
## THE RISE OF THE WOKE BROS

Suzanne and I haven't always agreed throughout the three decades we've been friends. There was the time I left my job at the Mail On Sunday to chase fresh opportunities and when I subsequently found myself unemployed, it wasn't the most snuggly feeling in the world to find my dear Doctor Moore tucked up tidy in my former cushy billet at the MOS - my dear, the money! There was the time she had her teeth fixed and acquired a second home, the double-whammy of which struck me as so irretrievably bourgeoise that I fell into the habit of berating her furiously about both in public when intoxicated, to which she would bafflingly reply 'O, just go and buy a tractor, Julie!' It was funny how our positions had reversed over the years - with her once the council flat-dwelling Marxist firebrand and I the founder of D.O.T (Daughters Of Thatcher, a pure theoretical club for women of lowly origins who had made it in the media and whose membership comprised the two of us - except she didn't know about it) but in any relationship which is not dead or dying there will inevitably be change.

Whatever political journey Suzanne and I have taken over the years we have always had one constant; feminism; for us it has been the immutable centre in the maelstrom of modern mores and manifestos. We would no more say we were not feminists than expect a black person to say that they didn't believe in equal race rights - it really would be that weird and Stockholm Syndrome. We know that without the women before us who fought for, were tortured for and died for our rights, we'd be scrubbing someone's front step if we were lucky or serving as sexual spittoons for some disgusting man if we weren't. Feminism isn't a hat we wear - especially not a pink *pussy* hat - but a part of us, like the colour of our eyes. And you poke us in those eyes at your peril, sonny.

I'd always prefer to be hurt and set free by the truth than happy and trapped in a lie, because the first you can recover from and start something new but the latter will use up all your juice and leave you broken at the side of the road. Many feminists traditionally bought into the lie that the Left is more of a friend to women than the Right partly because it just feels so big and lonely to be out there on your own and partly because girls are socialised to see male approval as a necessity only slightly less vital for survival than food and defecation. This has led Left-wing women to put up with a long history of Left-wing crusades against women's rights, starting with socialists who were against the suffragettes because they claimed that women tended to vote more conservatively. Emmeline Pankhurst tried to join the fledgling Independent Labour Party but was initially refused membership by the Manchester branch on account of her sex, though she was later 'allowed' to join nationally; her daughter Christabel later wrote of her mother's enthusiasm for the ILP: 'In this movement she hoped there might be the means of righting every political and social wrong.'

Fortunately, she wised up; in 1914 the suffragettes put their campaign on hold to support our war effort and in 1915 the National Union of Women's Suffrage Societies threw out pacifist members. Emmeline and Christabel became prominent in the White Feather movement which from the entry of Britain into the First World War in 1914 saw bold bands of females - many of them teenagers - roaming English cities and handing white feathers (now an addlepated signal that a moulting angel is near, but then a symbol of cowardice) to men of fighting age wearing civilian dress. Interestingly, far from being approved pets of the ruling class, these sneering sauce-pots sent waves of pearl-clutching moral panic throughout the soppier parts of the Establishment, as social commentators of the time condemned these brazen flappers who actually had the nerve to judge strange men and find them lacking - as men have always done to women, of course. Physical violence to women always being the resort of the inadequate man, it's not surprising that many of these men who weren't brave enough to fight other men had no problem at all with striking women who drew attention to their craven cowardice. They were the type of men of whom John Stuart Mill memorably wrote:

> 'A man who has nothing which he is willing to fight for, nothing which he cares more about than he does about his personal safety, is a miserable creature who has no chance of being free, unless made and kept so by the exertions of better men than himself.'

In recent years, the smarter sort of feminist has become wary of the Woke Bros; men who talk a good feminist game in order to put women at their ease before behaving just like unreconstructed creeps. In liberal Hollywood, a creature like Harvey Weinstein could hide in plain sight because he donated to feminist causes, supported Clinton and gave an intern job to Obama's teenage daughter. It's likely that the suffragettes were the first feminists to deduce that wimpy men were as likely to be the enemy as more obviously macho men, while not even having the useful qualities of traditional masculinity, and by 1926 Mrs Pankhurst was standing as a Conservative candidate, her political journey from hostile Left to welcoming Right complete.

Feminism went quiet for quite a few decades - there was so much happening, from Hitler to the birth of rock and roll, that we understandably took our eye off the ball for quite some time. But suddenly in the year 1970 - in the shape of a gang of shoddily-groomed and sexually frank younger sisters of the suffragettes - 'Women's Lib '('Burn your bra!') was born in a hail of flour bombs and flash bulbs when the Miss World contest was enlivened by protests from females sick of being promised jam tomorrow if they were free with envelope-stuffing and blowjobs today. Ever since I was a 12-year-old militant feminist teenybopper dividing my time between getting stuck in to my shoplifted copy of The Female Eunuch and being propositioned in the street while wearing my school uniform by grown men, I had a hunch that the attitude which 1960s 'revolutionaries' displayed towards women was nothing short of vile; the historian Dominic Sandbrook[1] called out Richard Neville's *classic* counter-cultural manifesto Play Power as 'infantile and grotesquely misogynistic' largely due to the bit where Neville boasts about a 'hurricane fuck' with a 'moderately attractive' 14-year-old girl he picks up outside a local comprehensive school. Men who fear women often have paedophile tendencies and in the nasty counter-culture crew we saw skin-crawling examples of this, especially in the case of the late John Peel.[2] Like many an ugly Englishman, the public school munter sought his fortune in America after the Beatles made it easy for British men to pick up women. 'All they wanted me to do was abuse them, sexually, which, of course, I was only too happy to do,' Peel once told the Guardian. Girls, apparently, 'used to queue up outside - oral sex they were particularly keen on. I remember one of my regular customers, as it were, turned out to be thirteen, though she looked older.' The alleged Sexual Revolution of the Sixties was not a bid to advance women's rights, but rather to turn back the clock and push the brave new young working woman back to being barefoot and pregnant. Even the approved appearance of hippie women - long skirts, long locks - spoke of an earlier era, before girls raised their skirts and bobbed their hair and went out to earn a living. Thus the Women's Liberation movement of the 1970s was as much a reaction to the 'revolutionary sexism' of the 1960s as it was to millions of years of reactionary patriarchy.

It was fitting, therefore, that the final year of the best decade for feminism since the suffragettes won us the vote saw the election of Margaret Thatcher. Let impotent socialists sneer that she 'never did anything for women' - the real test of a worthwhile life, in my opinion, is whether it inspires or not. Mrs Thatcher didn't need to mouth dreary platitudes about feminism; she just rolled up her sleeves, hoisted her handbag and piled into various useless males wherever she found them, from her own party to Brussels. In the early 1980s a friend's small daughter mocked a boy at her kindergarten when he said he would grow up to rule the country thus: 'You can't - you have to be a lady to be Queen. Like Mrs Thatcher.'

Though I found Mrs Thatcher fascinating, I never voted for her; I'd been brought up in a Communist household with such a hardcore Labour father that for much of my infancy I believed 'Capitalist' literally to be a swear word. I wish I had though; she was a rebel and just my kind, far more than the stale, pale, male Labour leaders I so mindlessly kept wasting my vote on because the patriarchy in the shape of my own dear pa had told me it was the proper thing to do. Despite the lazy liberal slurs determined to find a neurotic repression at the root of all that bossiness, Mrs T was never an old–fashioned girl; voting for her was a bit like buying a Vera Lynn record, getting it home and finding the Sex Pistols inside.

There's a lovely photograph of the punk singer Poly Styrene, the novelist Jackie Collins and the campaigner Mary Whitehouse attending the 'Women of the Year Lunch'[3] shortly after Mrs Thatcher's victory, all smiling at each other as they pose for photographs. It says something good about the late 20th century that such different women were happy to be seen together; I wonder, because of the narrow-mindedness of identity politics, whether this could happen now? Regrettably, I rather think that instead we'd have some bloke referring to himself as 'They' centre-stage - and the women shooed off to the sidelines.

That's certainly what happened in the Labour Party. What had they been doing while Mrs Thatcher was leading little girls to believe that you couldn't rule a country unless you were female, pray? They were electing a selection of variously dinosaur dudes as leader - duds as disparate as James Callaghan and Michael Foot - while ignoring the female talent in their ranks. Perhaps due to the influence of the trades unions - the monolithic smorgasbord of beer and sandwiches at a union-friendly Number 10 left no place for a small white wine and a finger buffet for the little ladies - they hadn't perked up their ideas about a fair deal for the fairer sex since Mrs Pankhurst was refused membership for running like a girl. When Maureen Colquhoun,[4] the Labour MP for Northampton North, left her husband for a woman in 1975, it caused an uproar, with her local party huffing: 'She was elected as a wife and mother…this business has blackened her image irredeemably' before attempting to deselect her, citing her 'obsession with trivialities such as women's rights.' She survived and held on till Mrs Thatcher's landslide when she lost her seat to a Tory; a tough woman lost out to an even tougher one, whose party had apparently far less fear of tough women.

The most efficient and exciting politician of her generation - Barbara Castle, the evil genius behind the Equal Pay Act of 1970 which was, incredibly, opposed by many Labour MPs - was repeated overlooked in favour of mediocre males but even so was still considered uppity by men from her fellow Labour MP Gerald Kaufman ('the Norma Desmond of politics, always ready for her close-up') to the trades unions whose bully-boy tactics she attempted to tame with her 'In Place Of Strife' policy.

Sadly, even the Red Queen internalised the misogyny of her party and just a year before her death in 2002 opined 'One of the biggest dangers women face today are men-haters. I love men. If there's a great deal of love you can get a great many things done. You don't have to be a man-hater to be a successful woman. In fact, all it can do is impede your progress.' Was she thinking perhaps of the way the suffragettes won the Vote, perhaps? Because obviously they didn't do anything unpleasant like smashing windows, setting postboxes on fire, slashing nude paintings and yelling 'VOTES FOR WOMEN AND CHASTITY FOR MEN!' No, it's common knowledge that Emmeline and Christabel put on their prettiest frocks, popped out for a pampering pedicure and gave Lloyd George and his cabinet a whole lot of neck rubs and savoury snacks. Because, like Barbara, they knew that a) the way to a man's heart is through his stomach and b) if there's a great deal of love you can get many things done. Those Pankhursts, they knew the importance of Pussy Power!

Finally in 1997 Labour found themselves landed with an electable leader in the shape of Tony Blair, a modern metrosexual man who was half Thatcherite and half entertainer. He came equipped with high-flying wife Cherie, who nevertheless goggled up at him in public like a teenager who'd won a meet-and-greet with her fave member of a boyband. He also had the dubious distinction of fronting his very own cheerleading squad: the Blair Babes, as the 101 female Labour MPs were known to nobody but tabloid editors, after the Principal Boy posed on the steps of Westminster flanked by a whopping 96 of them. It's interesting that the refuseniks numbered amongst them Kate Hoey, Clare Short and Glenda Jackson - all of them natural leading ladies rather than part of anybody's chorus line.

When Gordon Brown finally wrested power from his erstwhile chum Blair (a power struggle I am unable to contemplate without thinking of the naked wrestling scene from Women In Love) a tenor of manly hysteria took hold of the Labour Party and Brown's brooding macho style (Heathcliff to Blair's Cathy) made the People's Party a bleak place for women. For a man so steeped in politics, it was strange how tone-deaf he could be; when in 2010 he tangled with Gillian Duffy, the 65-year-old ex-

Labour voter who heckled him over immigration on the Rochdale hustings, the real disgust in his voice as he spat the words 'that bigoted woman'[5] was as ugly as it was ill-judged - and held a world of contempt which one had the unpleasant suspicion would not have sounded half as derisive had the subject been a bigoted man. Looking back, this was the tiny Japanese knotweed seed which would pull down the mighty Red Wall a decade later and deliver Labour's heartland to the Tories.

After three years of glowering and growling, Brown finally loosened his grasp on the barely palpitating throat of the Labour Party in the spring of 2010, the capable Harriet Harman taking over as wet nurse for the summer season until the helpless bundle was delivered to Ed Miliband. For the five years he kept perilous hold of the bouncing bundle of fun, Miliband resembled nothing so much as daffy young husband from a 1970s sit-com, forever getting into easily avoided scrapes while slipping on banana skins and bacon sandwiches. When he finally dropped it, Nurse Harman was there to step up for the May to September shift once more, reprising her role as Chief Fluffer to the People's Party.

With almost three decades on the front bench, twice acting deputy leader and the first Labour woman to feature at Prime Minister's Questions, Harman is the definitive Nearly Woman — as are all capable Labour women, trapped in a party which having signed up to the brotherhood of man seems quite happy to ride roughshod over their sisters. That the Tories were not so inclined became obvious with their election of Theresa May as both party leader and PM in the summer of 2016 - just a year after Labour chose a man to lead them who appeared as much a fan of misogyny as any other weirdy beardy from friendly neighbourhood mosque to local Real Ale Society.

Jeremy Corbyn may have named Mary Wollstonecraft as his hero, but talk is cheap. Not only have the Conservatives had two female leaders while Labour have achieved the grand total of a dick-swinging zero, but as the Labour MP Jess Phillips[6] said to me 'People on the Left are champions of sex equality until they see that some of their power is being taken away from them - whereas the Tories willingly gave it over.' It was unfortunate that the woman of colour who Jeremy Corbyn promoted highest in his Shadow Cabinet was an ex-girlfriend and even sleazier when a comrade recalled how he showed off his dusky prize to the rest of Chess Club - sorry, his fellow soldiers in the socialist struggle - way back in the street-fighting, free-loving 1970s. According to a helpful nark in Rosa Prince's book Comrade Corbyn: 'One Sunday autumn morning...we were out leafleting. And for some reason he called four or five of us and said: 'Oh, we've got to go back to my flat and pick up some leaflets.' It seemed a bit odd – 'Why the hell didn't you bring them with you, Jeremy?' So we all bowl along to his bedsit, follow Jeremy into the room; there on the mattress on the floor in the one room is Diane with the duvet up to her neck, saying: 'What the fuck is going on?''

See the smouldering smirk of Steptoe which oversaw the Labour announcement in the summer of 2017 that ONLY LABOUR CAN BE TRUSTED TO UNLOCK THE TALENT OF BLACK, ASIAN AND MINORITY ETHNIC PEOPLE you'd be forgiven for thinking that there was more 'Mandingo[7]' than Mandela about the whole mucky business, having as it does a whiff of fetishising The Other. Ethnic minorities are more than capable of helping themselves without having the Great White Leader help himself to their booty, as the Conservative MP James Cleverly pointed out with his pleasing meme of his equally attractive colleague Priti Patel: Priti Patel, Secretary of State, Conservative politician, candidate in Witham. Waiting for Corbyn to unlock her potential.

Sensible Labour supporters breathed a sigh of relief when Corbyn was replaced by Sir Keir Starmer in the spring of 2020. But as a lifelong Labour voter who was one of the millions who had found themselves in the surreal position of voting for an old Etonian Tory in the last general election as only he could be trusted to respect the wishes of the British working-class when they overwhelmingly voted for Brexit, I wasn't that impressed. A soft (en)titled Southern Remainer was hardly the heavy lifter we needed to rebuild the decimated Red Wall.

And as a woman, I could hardly have been more underwhelmed. We were lucky to have dodged the 'favourite' Rebecca Long-Baily[8] who was not only anti-abortion but, somewhat repulsively, boasted that she calls her young son 'The King' because 'We serve him - we are his servants' - handmaid, heal thyself! But Sir Keir (or 'Dame Drear' as the waspish social commentator Carl Stanley dubbed him) was hardly the feminist's friend. As the young activist and abuse survivor Lucy Nevitt wrote shortly before the Dame took delivery of the poor old flogged horse which was once the noble Labour Party:[9]

> 'In her role as Home Secretary, Priti Patel has already crafted the attack lines the Labour Party will face if Sir Keir Starmer becomes its next leader. After having been appointed head of the Crown Prosecution Service (CPS) in November 2008, Sir Keir's half decade in the position oversaw cases as large and polarising as the Rochdale grooming gang scandal, mass sexual abuse scandals involving entertainment figures such as Jimmy Savile, and the John Worboys case. Patel noted Sir Keir has a complete 'lack of interest in prosecuting horrendous crimes against women' - a statement hard to argue with when presented with his record.'

Each lost Labour voter - and there are millions of us, as the fall of the Red Wall in the general election of 2019 proved - has a particular moment when they realised that the party formed to represent the oppressed against the oppressor had become the oppressor itself. Many Jewish supporters realised it when in the spring of 2019 Labour had the dubious honour of joining the BNP in becoming only the second political party to be investigated for racism by the Equality and Human Rights Commission when it transpired that they had been backing anti-Semites against Jews within their own ranks.

I am not a Jew - despite my teenage attempts to pass as one - and in recent years it has come to my notice that once one is past adolescence, pretending to be (or 'identifying as') something one is not is probably not the most honest thing to do. But I am undeniably a woman and for me my party jumped the shark when each of the female Labour candidates for leadership were asked their positions on the Gender Recognition Act and each and every one of them - identifying as a cis rather than a sister - said that they were fine with male-bodied rapists being put into female prisons so long as they went by the name of Karen just to remind them not to rape anybody else.

In this age of safe spaces for all, the spaces where women are most vulnerable - toilets, jails, women's refuges - were suddenly flung open to any rapacious trucker who had happened to hear Shania Twain's greatest hit while he soaped his scrotum in the shower that morning and decided that man, he felt like a woman. When A Woman's Place[10] U.K - a long-standing socialist feminist group - pointed out that sex is a protected characteristic under the 2010 Equality Act they were reviled as a 'trans-exclusionist hate group' and told that their supporters would be expelled from the Labour Party. Labour leadership and deputy leadership candidates as apparently disparate Lisa Nandy, Rebecca Long-Bailey, Emily Thornberry, Angela Rayner and Rosena Allin-Khan queued up to witch-hunt fellow women at the behest of blokes in blouses; one of them, the triumphantly silly Dawn Butler (who had the dubious honour of replacing Diane Abbott as the token over-promoted and under-performing flack-catching black woman in the Shadow Cabinet and whose laughably inaccurate title was Minister for Women and Equalities) had proved herself the Shackleton of anti-scientific stupidity when she claimed in 2019 that perhaps 90% of all giraffes were gay. Ah, so that explains their outrageous garb and languid glances!

> 'If you can teach gayness, then who speaks giraffe? 90 per cent of giraffes are gay. So who the hell speaks giraffe, what does that sound like? You can't teach it, and it's not a disease either. Being who you are and your true, authentic self is not a disease.'

This was the week when Labour jumped not the shark but the giraffe. Somewhat embarrassingly, even considering the climate of perpetual foot-in-mouth-ism which ruled the roost inside Jeremy Corbyn's Labour Party, it took her comrade Lachlan Stuart - Corbyn's senior adviser on domestic policy - to put her 'straight' when he took to Twitter to point out that though male giraffes can often be seen 'necking' with younger males, they actually have something a good bit beastlier than the love which dare not speak its name on their minds, to wit bullying:

> 'It is a ludicrous, offensive, homophobic claim...akin to describing Deliverance as a 'gay romance' because the effete city boys are put in their place by the locals by getting beaten and then raped.'

Ouch! - as a young male giraffe might have said. But the eminently unqualified Ms Butler could not stop herself from returning to this knotty subject any more than a dominant male giraffe could stop himself from lusting after his uppity young herd-mate and the following year she could be heard claiming on Good Morning Britain while defending Labour's crazed position on the GRA that 'A child is born without sex.'

Congratulations - it's an It!

The party which had in its infancy rejected Mrs Pankhurst as a member on grounds of her sex was right back where it started from, but this time it was old enough to know better. And this time it wasn't defensive working-class men scared of losing the one bit of superior status they had who were demonising uppity women. This time it was men mired in privilege - the Woke Bros. Mind you, they did turn out to be non-discriminating destroyers to a degree; it's pretty fair to say that Wokeness was the main weapon which wrecked the erstwhile party of the people, losing it the vote of the working class and rendering it little more than a toy of the bourgeois, in turn a playpen and something to chuck out of the pram. It was these well-bred buffoons of whom the glorious ex-glamour model and working-class Labour MP Gloria de Piero was thinking of when she said 'If any other institution was as posh as the Labour Party, we in the Labour Party would be the first to point it out.'

Why do Woke Bros who like to think of themselves as revolutionaries have such a blind spot when it comes to feminism - indeed, why increasingly these days are their attitudes to women far more reactionary than those of men in the Right? There's a reason why men who would rather remove their own testicles with pinking shears than be considered racist don't seem to have a similar problem with being sexist. The answer, as with so much of apparently unconnected life, comes down to our old friend Sex; that is, Good Sex, in which men get to ejaculate inside of various parts of biddable women rather than Bad Sex, which insubordinate women claim they're discriminated against because of and why they might be inspired to withdraw Good Sex from men if they become too conscious of this unfairness.

A privileged man can work towards ending racism without much fear of losing his privilege - it's going to take the average underprivileged BAME citizen quite a few generations to be knocking at the same doors, career-wise, so he has the luxury of virtue-signalling without ever actually having to give anything up. It's notable that when oppressed racial groups start to make progress under their own steam - such as the Jews - and start to outstrip dim and privileged indigenous men in the professions, they cease to be protected pets of the Left and will be accused of employing all sorts of dark arts as an explanation for them out-performing Whitey. But if feminism takes hold, men of all belief systems are affected; the bourgeoise liberal man - the Woke Bros of today - will take a hit from women no longer being complicit in their own oppression as much as his Conservative cousin will.

The one place you cannot virtue signal is in an intimate relationship; if no man is a hero to his valet, how much less is he to his wife. I would imagine that a good number of the women killed by male 'partners' or exes each year - two a week - die not because 'My wife doesn't understand me' but because she understood her killer all too well; he couldn't stand to see himself reflected in all his inadequacy in eyes which did not reflect him back at twice the size. I've known educated and enlightened men who were wife-beaters; in fact I've never met an uneducated wife-beater. Political principles do not signify in the secret sewers of misogyny; a woman I know was once knocked unconscious by her boyfriend with a huge coffee table book about the plight of the Palestinians while another humanitarian once confessed to me that he had to stop reading about the sexual torture of Chilean women under the Pinochet regime as it invariably aroused him. It's fair to say that men of all classes, creeds and political colours frequently stand united over the broken body of the universal woman, their squabbles briefly forgotten. Isn't the Brotherhood of Man a wonderful thing!

To stop us from seeing this, Woke Men have promoted the idea of white privilege being more oppressive than male privilege, which separates the sillier sort of bourgeois broad from her sisters of other colours, her whiteness to be weaponised against her to the point where she will pay for women of colour to reduce her to tears at special show-trial dinner parties. (It's telling that Woke Bros do not pay black men to hector them over a game of darts.) A woman convinced that she is inherently privileged above certain groups of men will be a confused creature, guilt-ridden, malleable and a lot less likely to seize upon feminism as the answer to her problems, thus rendering her a far more useful doormat in the domestic arena.

Covid 19 threw this into sharp relief when during lockdown not only domestic violence soared (any excuse) but domestic labour became women's work once more. A young woman called Grace, sharing a London house with friends of assorted sexes, told Grazia magazine:

> 'When the pandemic struck we lost our weekly cleaner and, it seemed, any iota of civilisation. By April the women in the house had to down tools as we were so sick of cleaning up after the men. And they have the cheek to call themselves feminists!'

The operative word here is 'call' - it's the easiest thing in the world for a man to call himself a feminist and it means absolutely zero. Only actions matter; the best male feminist I ever met was my blue-collar nightshift-working father who was frankly mystified by 'Women's Lib' but performed around three-quarters of all cooking and childcare in the home of my youth simply because he was full of energy and my mum believed that she was Mariah Carey. (Who was not yet born, making her delusion even more unfathomable.)

Generally, once men have said they're feminists, they feel free to behave in whatever scummy manner they see fit towards women. The reason I loathe virtue-signalling so much is not because I'm against people bigging themselves up (I'm a colossal show-off so that would be self-loathing) but because boasting only makes sense when it's about something you do well. People who do nothing worth talking about will invariably boast about the way they are; their virtue-signalling is not a prelude to virtue but rather a substitute for it. In fact it can encourage them to behave even worse than they would otherwise; one thinks of those men working for charities who will happily head into a disaster-zone and make whores of the poverty-stricken female population. Heads of international capitalist corporations, though more wicked in theory, don't do this as much, aware as they are that no Wokescreen stands between them and public revulsion. On a personal level, when I think of the people I know who've been keenest on calling me 'bad' or even a 'psychopath' (me, with my decades of volunteer work and ceaseless philanthropy) while themselves identifying as 'good' they've often been people who've exhibited the most self-centred behaviour.

Wokeness is King Midas in reverse, tarnishing any noble cause it touches, but on no body of struggle has it left as many filthy fingermarks in inappropriate places as on feminism. With smoke and mirrors and sleight of hand worthy of a wicked misogynist magician, it has midwifed a monstrous creature, a fauxminism which is centred solely around the stations of the hallowed penis. Under the strictly impartial guidance of the Woke Bros, Woke Handmaids found a very feminine fulfilment in giving lip service to male supremacists whether they were Islamists pushing the most patriarchal religion in the world, cross-dressers demanding that vaginas should give equal-opportunity access to every last Arthur-turned-Martha on the planet or the men who run the billion-dollar sex industry. The cuddling up to Islamofascism and the bartering of women to trans-colonisation I will tackle in forthcoming chapters. But I will tackle the very real war against women - from the portrayal of sexual violence for the pleasure of punters and the profit of pornographers to actual femicide - right here, right now.

Lesbians have always been the mavericks of feminism; free of the desire to live with men, they have no reason to cater to them. When you're not sleeping with the enemy, you can see him clearly; up close, pleasure has a habit of closing one's eyes. Under the reign of Woke fauxminism lesbians would be attacked as never before by alleged 'progressives' basically for not being like the lesbians these men had grown up masturbating over in the online pornography which had shaped their idea of what sex should be. Woe betide the woman who stands between a man and his all-important wank fantasies; for daring to contradict the world view of inadequate onanists with their actual lived experience, lesbians are now routinely told that they are fun-spoilers at best and fascists at worst. One of the very toughest veterans of the sex war, the unrepentant lesbian That Julie Bindel, summed it up beautifully in the Spectator in 2020 in a piece ominously called Feminism For Men Is Bad News For Women:

> 'In my 40 years as a feminist activist campaigning to end male violence, I have never felt so engulfed in a culture of woman hating…something has gone terribly wrong over the past decade. Some young women, particularly privileged, university

students, appear to have become convinced that everything that is bad for them is in fact good. The sexual harassment we fought hard to expose and legislate against? According to trans activist and self-identified feminist Paris Lees there is little more liberating and pleasurable than being 'catcalled, sexually objectified and treated like a piece of meat by men.' Why are so many young women celebrating this culture of misogyny and insisting that porn can be liberating? Partly because of the pressure coming from so-called progressive men. I am contacted almost every day by women of all ages, telling me they are sick and tired of men deciding what women's liberation is. No amount of stripping, choking, wolf-whistling or porn will help us. But it does help the men who are desperate to keep hold of their power.'

Why are old-fashioned feminists so, like, 'uptight' about sex, the Woke wonder? Why can't they stop doing draggy stuff like helping women exit prostitution and be 'sex positive' instead? The feminist outreach work which has been a practical and compassionate way of opening up a better life for the generally wretched women condemned to it ever since Mrs Pankhurst took her gloves off was now declared 'whorephobia' and those who concerned themselves with it SWERFS - Sex Worker Exclusionary Radical Feminists. If they have to be lesbians - which is 'transphobic' as it excludes 'girl-dick' - why can't they call themselves 'gender-queer' and dye their hair blue so they look like the Manga Pixie Dream Girls of the Woke Bros clammy fantasies? In fact, what's the point in lesbians at all if men aren't allowed to watch? What sort of lesbian completely ignores her calling as toss-fodder and instead insists on dedicating herself to making life better for other women?

The infant's denial that anything might be more important than their immediate demands and the child's delight in interfering with its own faeces combines in the the Woke Bros and their Handmaids to create a perfect storm of stupidity where actual feminism - as opposed to to prancing about in 'pussy hats' and showing off their unremarkable udders on 'Slut Walks' - is concerned. The Woke are by their nature young and still crave popularity to a pathetic extent, especially the young middle-class women involved; thus the type of feminism they perform for male approval often appears to have been influenced more by the sex industry than by the suffragettes. One thinks of the photos of white female allies at the 2020 race riots holding up placards saying I ONLY SUCK BLACK DICK and I LOVE BLACK DICK SO YOU WILL HEAR ME SPEAK (I have to admit I couldn't help but adore the brazen illogicality of this one) or of another snap, this time of the social commentator Owen Jones pointing at his young female friend wearing a T-shirt bearing the promise WILL SUCK DICK FOR SOCIALISM. It's notable that Owen, a proud homosexual, felt no need to wear this garment, though he'd probably sucked far more dicks than his friend - he is a Serious Writer, after all, and what do women have to contribute to any struggle except a set of holes? It's an easy mistake to make, if one has spent too long interfering with oneself over snaps of the Black Panthers, whose leader Stokely Carmichael who once stated[11] that the only position for women in the struggle was 'prone' - though I'm sure he might have bent the rules to embrace the public toe-sucking which took place on the streets of the U.S.A in the grovelling Woke wake of the Black Lives Matter riots.

Magic Socialist Grandpa Bernie Sanders poor old ticker must have been working overtime in 2020 - maybe it's why he had to drop out of the presidential race - when he saw all the #hotgirlsforbernie. (The ugly girl supporters of Bernie were no doubt employed to make the coffee and stay well out of view.) It makes me laugh now to look back and remember all the times I was told that Mrs Thatcher was no friend to feminism; compared to the Woke Handmaids of today, she was practically Valerie Solanas.

For the Handmaids a naked selfie paints a thousand well-meaning words. Or maybe they're just so inarticulate that they have to let their T&A do the talking. At the start of lockdown model Bella Hadid posted a nude snap urging people to stay at home to save 'literally the entire world.' The model and 'naked philanthropist' Kaylen Ward raised more than half a million pounds selling nude images of herself to 'relieve' the victims of wildfires - in the process relieving a whole lot of other people who were victims of nothing worse than their own libidos. Emily Ratajkowski's Instagram feed must be the only 'feminist magazine' (her words) to cause mass masturbation - but why on earth shouldn't she get her kit off? As Ursula Andress said when asked why she stripped for Playboy 'Because I'm beautiful.' There's a certain admirable sort of spiteful feminist triumphalism in showing sad-sack men exactly what they can't have. It becomes somewhat less straightforward when the weasel word 'empowering' is dragged in; be clear that when you get your tits out for public consumption the only thing you're empowering are erections. Don't mistake giving someone a stiffy for terrorising the patriarchy, as some of the sillier Millennial minxes do.

There is a lost-girl quality in the nude feminists of Instagram; a topsy-turvy land where women show men their disapproval of man-made rules by delivering up exactly what men want from them. Women have spent decades protesting about wanting to be seen as more than bodies by men - and now the trend is to literally make tits of themselves in a bid to prove that they're independent women. I'm certainly not morally outraged by them - I wasn't averse to popping out of my corset top as a teenage punk when the snakebite was flowing - and I'm extremely suspicious of the concept of 'modesty' as a desirable thing for women. But there's something so infantile about such actions, adding to the image of the Woke as laxly-parented giant toddlers forever yelling for attention.

However, the relative youth of the fauxminists is no excuse for their truly impressive ignorance once they've calmed down and put their clothes back on. Though it's understandable that youngsters will always be inclined to 'cheek' the generation that went before - feminists are spirited by nature and as we saw in the previous chapter, I couldn't get enough of dissing Professor Greer when I was young - the line in the sandpit surely has to be drawn when their insurrection becomes sheer silliness. And of course when you get the feeling they're dissing us old broads to give the Woke Bros a cheap thrill from the sight of a bluestocking catfight, then one really does feel emboldened to pull their pigtails and bark 'Get back, Shorty!'

Perhaps one of the reasons why activists like Bindel aren't keen to spend their valuable time remaking our hard-won liberation creed for the approval of the planet's dedicated self-abusers and their porn-producing puppet-masters might be because feminism is needed in the world as much as it ever was; in March 2020 a whopping survey by the UN Development Programme called on governments to introduce legislation to address the engrained prejudice against women in every country on the planet. 'We all know we live in a male-dominated world, but with this report we are able to put some numbers behind these biases,' said Pedro Conceição, director of the UNDP's human development report office. 'And the numbers, I consider them shocking.'

The survey found that almost 90% of people are biased against women, with 91% of men and 86% of women holding at least one bias against women in relation to politics, economics, education or reproductive rights; almost a third of men and women found it acceptable for a man to beat his wife. Of the seventy-five countries studied, there were only six in which the majority of people held no bias towards women - Andorra, Australia, the Netherlands, New Zealand, Norway and Sweden. But even these weren't free from sex-based bigotry; Sweden was one of several countries – including South Africa, India. and Brazil – in which the percentage of people who held at least one sexist belief had increased over the nine years the data covered.

The logical outcome of finding one group of people less valuable than another is to value their lives less and accordingly worldwide domestic violence causes more deaths of women aged 15-44 than cancer, malaria, traffic accidents and war combined. A quarter of women in the United Kingdom will experience violence from a partner at some point in their lives; two women a week are killed by a partner or ex-partner, accounting for half of all killings. (I've always hated the word 'partner' when used of a person one is intimate with, though I might use it if I ran a legal or medical practice with another person or if I regularly played a racquet sport with them. In the context of being murdered by one it sounds especially bleak, as this most passionless and practical of words is subsumed in the most primitive of rages.) There are three times as many animal shelters in the U.S.A as there are refuges for battered women. There are many more sex-based murders than racial murders but we see no popular uprisings insisting that Female Lives Matter; instead we have the ineffably sorrowfully-named Counting Dead Women, the 'Femicide Census'[12] created by Karen Ingala Smith and Clarissa O'Callaghan in 2015, 'a unique source of comprehensive information about women who have been killed in the U.K and the men who have killed them' which might well be subtitled Female Lives Never Mattered, as we see the lost line of women of all ages and races killed by those who professed to love them and whose deaths were regarded merely as the collateral of being female rather than something to righteously riot about. If a racial or religious minority faced the same scale of ceaseless attacks that females do, we'd call it terrorism, persecution or genocide. When it happens to females, we seem to see it as the luck of the draw.

You'd think that the caring, empathic Woke would have something to say about such a relentless massacre, but I don't recall one of those very many marches ever focusing on femicide. They're far fonder of taking the part of transsexuals, which the police and the judiciary appear to agree with, considering the reluctance to prosecute rapists and the contemptuous sentence handed out to domestic offenders. It's extremely illogical how attacking a man dressed as a woman is a Hate Crime, but attacking an actual woman is not; many trannies are built like brick shit-houses (albeit ones which have bad wigs perched atop them) and therefore more than capable of fighting back.

Other hatreds come and go - but it's always open season on women. The threat of femicide is always there in the background, like white noise - the mood music which accompanies the danse macabre of misogyny - and authorities seem intensely relaxed about statistics which would provoke a frenzy of breast-beating if it involved any other group. When in 2002 statistics came out showing that murder rates in British cities were the highest in a century, the Home Office made the usual concerned noises about tackling violence - but an amazingly creepy look-on-the-bright-side addendum was then made by a chirpy spokesperson. Things weren't really as bad as they looked - because 61% of the killings of women were 'domestic.'[13] That's all right, then! Imagine the Home Office telling us not to worry because a third of all murders were of ethnic minorities or of gay men. Yet they can say that the large proportion of women killed by partners or exes makes the murder rate not so shocking. Why? What world are these people living in? Don't they have daughters, sisters, mothers who cohabit with men? To add insult to fatal injury, shortly afterwards selected police chiefs and lawyers from the crown prosecution service suggested to the Home Office that certain alleged criminals should be allowed to avoid prosecution and jail by apologising to their victims and signing a 'going straight' contract.

And which crimes will earn their alleged perpetrators a Get Out Of Jail Free card? Shoplifting, burglary - and domestic violence. Not men accused of racial or homophobic violence, you'll note - just men who beat up women. After two decades of government and police propaganda about how there must be 'zero tolerance' of domestic violence,[14] people who influenced policy were seriously suggesting that it becomes once more a crime akin to shoplifting, one that an apology can wipe out. Not a hate crime at all; a love crime, perhaps - a crime passionnel! Don't men who commit racial and homophobic assaults and murders feel passionate about what they're doing? Of course they do. So why is it that only the assault and murder of women is excused by some cretin feeling strongly about something, however unreasonably?

Whenever the rights of women clash with the rights of others, those in power seem extraordinarily keen on letting the side who aren't women win - and their attitudes seem creepily in accord with those of the Woke Bros. For example, the British police force - PC Plod has been born again as PC PC - seem far more interested in bothering people for online 'misgendering' than they do investigating threats by blokes in brassieres to rape TERFS. We hear a lot about systemic police racism, but one of the most repulsive elements of the grooming gang phenomenon - which saw thousands of girls as young as 11 raped, tortured and trafficked by men of mostly Pakistani origin - was the way the police actually bent over backwards not to go after the men involved simply because they were not white and thus their exposure might inflame racist feeling. (That this lack of action in itself would inflame racism far more than simply treating them as regular pimps and paedophiles when it eventually came out - one rule for them, another rule for us - apparently did not occur to the half-wits who formulated this under-the-carpet credo.)

This was the first sighting of PC/PC Snap, when the police took on a Woke agenda - here, the elevation of racial harmony above all else, even the welfare of thousands of tortured children. Islam alone of religions has been elevated amongst the Woke, promoted to a race (it's not) and understandable wariness of it mocked as a phobia (which instantly makes criticising it an irrational illness - but strangely there's no Christophobia, which can be mocked with impunity and sanity) with that magic wishful thinking they're so good at. Perhaps the reason that many Leftist men have so much time for Islamism are the suppressed feelings of resentment towards the march of feminism which they could never in a million years admit to but which became blatant with the dawn of Woke. After years of being yelled at by female comrades whenever they inquired about the likelihood of a hot beverage being imminent, imagine how excited Left-wing weeds were watching big bad men in balaclavas selling 'slave girls' in a sweltering marketplace.

What a shame they couldn't have changed places with the wretched girls of Rotherham - or Rochdale, or Keighley, or Newcastle, or Peterborough, or Aylesbury, or Oxford, or Bristol - where they would have been abandoned to their heart's content to the brutality of their Mohammaden masters. The Woke attitude to the white working class, which logically includes the female half of it - that they are uneducated, animalistic bigots who deserve everything they get - was apparently shared by the police, who to be fair have never claimed to be scourges of the patriarchy, with their notoriously insensitive attitudes to women. But you would think that social workers - who were woke before Woke was a thing - might have read a few books down the decades on how the sexual abuse of children is one of the sickest secrets of every society, and with their duty of care to the vulnerable might have rushed to the aid of these abject children. But they didn't; they became the final betrayers in the unholy trinity of abusers and police who dismissed these girls as 'white slags.'[15] Or to give them their full names, White Slags vs Diverse Members of a Vibrant Society who are to be shielded from hatred at all costs, even if that hatred was in this case fully justified.

Why do the police find it so difficult to believe women? Cynics used to say that any woman being raped should shout 'Fire!' if she wanted to attract police attention but 'Hate crime!' would be a better choice these days. While endlessly sensitive to racial slurs and quite kinkily eager to bend the knee to the Black Lives Matter Movement, every new initiative the law attempts to improve the pathetic rate of rape conviction, for example, just makes them sound more misogynistic. In 2019 it was announced that alleged rape victims would be compelled to hand over their mobile phones to the police; something which seemed like a silly gimmick at best and a sinister strong-arm tactic at worst; would our Woke constabulary consider taking the phones of people alleging racial abuse to see if they ever used the racial slang so popular among the young when having 'bantz' with their mates? Would they take the phones of transgender people alleging misgendering to see if they had ever referred to themselves privately as men? No, because these crimes must be handled with seriousness and sensitivity rather than the toxic blend of bullying and condescension with which too many policemen treat women in general and rape victims in particular.

The police force are by their nature masculine; policewomen are so forced to adapt to the locker-room culture that Britain's only female police chief rejoiced in the handle of Dick. This masculinity is of course desirable when it comes to chasing dangerous criminals but not so great when it comes to bullying law-abiding citizens for not being up to date with latest favoured mode of address required by female impersonators, the second of which appears to be a far more enthusiastic police pursuit in recent years. Add sex to the mix and the masculinity evoked may well be of a toxic rather than a chivalric kind. Of course not all of them are as vile as the police officer who was found to have masturbated over photographs of a woman who complained of being stalked, soon to be murdered. Sometimes they keep their cocks inside their trousers and suffer merely from the misogyny branch of Munchausen's-by-proxy like the mundane monsters who franchised out the murder of the Brighton teenager Shana Grice[16] to her ex-boyfriend in 2016 just months after she was fined with 'wasting police time' for repeatedly reporting his stalking to them.

Until I began researching this book, I was under the impression that policemen would be more more law-abiding than other men, and though they certainly commit less opportunistic burglaries their impulse control sadly does not extend to crimes of domestic violence, leading the the Centre For Women's Justice to submit a 'super-complaint' to HM Chief Inspector of Constabularies in 2020, detailing how victims of 'partners' who are policemen feel even more isolated than your average terrorised wife: 'They experience the powerlessness that most domestic abuse victims experience, but in addition their abuser is part of the system intended to protect them.' Police officers and staff were reported for alleged domestic abuse almost 700 times in the three years up to April 2018, according to Freedom of Information responses - more than four times a week on average. Just 3.9% ended in a conviction, compared with 6.2% among the general population; less than a quarter of reports resulted in professional discipline. Greater Manchester Police, one of the country's biggest forces, secured just one conviction out of 79 reports over the three year period.

It's a fascinating aspect of Wokedom that men who might be normally found on the wrong side of a police horse often turn out to be brothers in arms with the boys in blue when it comes to treating women as second-class citizens. They both appear to believe that women are not really oppressed - but that if it transpires that they are, they should stay that way, as it makes life so much more easier and more enjoyable for men. Recently women who believe that men should be severely punished for their some of their exhaustingly comprehensive crimes against women have been awarded a brand new slur, but a classier one this time, befitting for a female sociologist; a 'carceral feminist,' if you please, is the term for a woman who believes that violence against her sisters is best addressed by a lovely long prison sentence which will not only keep the man in question from damaging more females but also hopefully introduce him to the experience of having someone stronger set about him, preferably with a rough and ready bout of *prison-sex* in mind.

This was what the splendid American judge Rosemarie Aquilna seemed to be hinting at when in 2018 she sentenced Larry Nassar, a doctor who had molested young gymnasts in his care:

> 'The constitution does not allow for cruel and unusual punishment. If it did … I would allow some or many people to do to him what he did to others.'

This was a bold defence of getting back what you'd chosen to deal out, which was a long time coming in a country where 994 out of alleged 1,000 rapists walk free. Who could possibly object except rapists themselves?

The answer would be, those who oppose 'carceral feminism' and appear to believe that there's no point in seeking justice for women until we can achieve wholesale utopia. Raped, beaten, domestically murdered? Don't worry your pretty little head - you just sit tight until the Woke Bros have masterminded the world socialist uprising from their mum's basement between restorative bouts of masturbating over Ethical Porn and don't get mad, or attempt to get even - it will all come out in the downfall-of-capitalism wash. Women must always be the caretakers, the caregivers; traditionally we were socialised by the Right into doing it for our loved ones at the expense of our own ambition and dignity. But Wokeness goes one up on this; Wokeness wants women to abnegate our own autonomy on behalf of those who are not just not our loved ones, but on behalf of strangers who would happily damage us. Meet the new boss - same as the old boss, with Woke bells on.

What's wrong with this picture? Well, no Woke Bros ever told a black man to turn the other cheek, swallow his pride and wait for the social justice which revolution would eventually bring. No one tells the beaten-up homosexual or the misgendered trans not to seek justice. But once more, women must suck it up (literally, according to the sexy socialist T-shirts cited) and wait for other, more important issues to be addressed. And then just when you thought Wokedom couldn't be anymore toxic to female health, the crazy days of misrule which followed the cabin-fever of Covid-19 came up with a cracker when, in the wake of the police killing of George Floyd, the cry went up from Woke local councillors in a swathe of American cities 'Defund the police.' In New York City, Washington D.C, Baltimore and beyond (all those serene little backwaters where folks leave their doors unlocked) there were demands for billions of dollars to be slashed from police budgets, with the money instead going to social workers, counsellors and the intriguingly-named 'violence interrupters[17]' - ex-criminals who are paid from public funds to intervene and prevent escalations of mostly gang-related crime. What a surprise when some of these urban martyrs were accused of assaulting women while on the job!

Already finding ourselves living in aftermath of a pandemic where we as free Western women are encouraged to cover our faces and not touch unrelated men, in the manner of some mullah-infested Middle Eastern hellhole, the last thing we need is a further dip into Medievalism where women are left to the tender mercies of their own 'communities'- that's how the witch trials started, how wife-beating was normalised for centuries and how incest flourished. The cosily-named 'Family Courts' which seek to avoid the 'adversarial' position of other courts were accused of being 'not a safe place for women who have been abused' by a letter signed by more than a hundred lawyers, and the same could be said of the religious courts, both Jewish and Muslim, which seek to keep the abuse of *their* women as a private matter rather than a public concern. If women think they have a hard time getting The Law to take their grievances seriously, wait till it's a clique of *community leaders* telling you to stay with your abuser and not bring shame on the all-important community you had the misfortune to be born into. For many women community is first and foremost the place where they are corralled, controlled and judged - home is where the heartache is. We already have the example of brave black women who have come forward to expose their sexual molestation by powerful black men and are then demonised as both traitors to their community and tools of white oppression; think of Clarence Thomas reacting to Anita Hill's accusations by calling them 'a high-tech lynching.'[18] We can easily imagine black women being guilt-tripped not to turn in this wife-beater or that paedophile boyfriend because America puts too many black men in jail.

Policeman kills black man and white men declare a state of anarchy - and the already precarious safety of women will be the savage currency squandered on this experiment in dismantling the level of civilisation we've fought so hard to reach which the Woke Bros seem so intent upon, for some strange reason of their own, which may have its shady roots in their own squalid, solitary, savage amusements, to be examined in the next chapter.

## Notes

[1] https://hotcopper.com.au/threads/richard-neville-the-paedophiles-the-poster-boy.28
94949/

[2] https://www.independent.co.uk/voices/john-peel-allegations-metoo-radio-1-jimmy-savile-a9097866.html

[3] https://www.womenoftheyear.co.uk

[4] https://www.theguardian.com/politics/2021/feb/08/maureen-colquhoun-obituary

[5] https://www.theguardian.com/politics/2010/apr/28/gordon-brown-bigoted-woman

[6] https://www.spectator.co.uk/article/lunch-with-the-future-leader-of-the-labour-party

[7] https:// www.spectator.co.uk / article / did-jeremy-corbyn-forget-to-unlock-diane-abbott-s-talent-

[8] https://www.thetimes.co.uk/article/rebecca-long-bailey-bows-to-her-boy-king-some-feminist-qfv6t3mhb

[9] https://medium.com/@lucynevitt/starmers-shambolic-cps-affabd38bb6d

[10] https://www.theguardian.com/society/2020/feb/20/womans-place-uk-is-not-a-trans-exclusionist-hate-group

[11] https://socialistworker.co.uk/art/50457/Stokely+Carmichael%C2%A0+What+we+gonna+start+saying+is+Black+Power

[12] https://kareningalasmith.com/the-femicide-census/

[13] https://www.bbc.co.uk/news/newsbeat-51572665

[14] https://www.bbc.co.uk/news/uk-scotland-41817068

[15] https:// www.independent.co.uk / voices / rotherham-grooming-gang-sexual-abuse-muslim-islamist-racism-white-girls-religious-extremism-terrorism-a8261831.html

[16] https://www.bbc.co.uk/news/uk-england-sussex-49155333

[17] https:// www.vox.com / 22622363 / police-violence-interrupters-cure-violence-research-study

[18] https://historynewsnetwork.org/article/170071

# CHAPTER THREE

# HOW PORNOGRAPHY BECAME A HUMAN RIGHT AND WHY FEMICIDE DOESN'T COUNT AS HATE CRIME

Back in cosy old Blighty, a page of the Sunday Times carried a pair of items whose proximity would have been funny if it hadn't been so grotesque. There's an old journalistic in-joke practice of avoiding libel charges by putting a pair of items on the same page wherein without linking them, insiders can feel smug that they know the link between a story about a prostitution ring being bust and a famous actor telling the world how much he loves his family; i.e the family man is well-known to we hacks as a frequenter of call girls. On May 31st 2020, one headline was CPS BACKED OFF ASSAULT CHARGE OVER FEAR OF 'ROUGH SEX'DEFENCE and below it

RAPE AND MURDER AMONG 2 MILLION UNSOLVED CASES CLOSED BY POLICE.

The Rough Sex defence was the most audaciously misogynistic attempt yet by the notoriously male-dominated law process to blame women not merely for their own rapes but for their own murders. Imagine if all these dead women had wanted to be killed - were *empowered* by it even, living the Fifty Shades Of Grey dream! What a lovely way to go, doing something you loved - which in this case would be your *partner* choking the last living daylights out of you, and giving the nuptial vow 'Till death us do part' a whole new meaning.

Imagine a victim of robbery being told 'the suspect could say you consented to giving away the Rolex.' (It does happen - I've given away three.) As the Labour MP Harriet Harman succinctly wrote to Max Hill, the director of public prosecutions when asking him to review the case 'If that's what is going to happen, there could be no prosecutions of sexual offences at all, because in every case the defendant could say 'She wanted it.'"[1]

Since 2010 the Rough Sex defence (sometimes called the Fifty Shades Of Grey defence, in honour of the books by E.L James which helpfully originated in 2011) has been used to help over sixty sub-human males justify the deaths of women they were having sex with, though as these women are conveniently dead it's impossible to be sure that even the sex, let alone the death, was consensual. No doubt the cheeky phrase 'a bit of slap and tickle' comes to the wholesome mind when we think of 'sex games' accompanied by the comforting soundtrack of Sid James and Barbara Windsor sniggering; on the contrary, the campaigning group We Can't Consent To This assembled evidence of 115 cases reaching back to 1997 involving women whose attackers claimed they consented to acts including 'waterboarding, wounding, electrocution, asphyxiation, beating, punching, kicking, and, in one case, a shotgun fired intimately.' (Just to make this last one every bit as grotesque as it is, I'll throw in the Merriam-Webster definition of 'intimate' here: 'marked by a warm friendship developing through long association.')

Many of those men convicted of over-enthusiastic intimacy had their sentences reduced from murder to manslaughter or were not jailed at all. Most of these women died by strangulation, like the British backpacker Grace Millane, murdered in Australia the night before her 22nd birthday. As an extra bequest from her killer to her loved ones, whenever her birthday now comes around, her broken parents will remember that she spent the last few hours of her life in terror, after which she was stuffed into a suitcase and dumped. Thus it is those who loved her who will serve life sentences, while her murderer continues his worthless life. In Grace's open, sunny face we see a life of limitless potential snuffed out by some scum who had chosen to use his miserable existence subsuming himself under so much pornography that everything else, including the continuance of another human life, faded into mere background noise compared to the importance of his own pitiful ejaculations. Because of this, I sometimes wonder if we can truthfully call sex offenders fully human; of course they are biologically, but when one's own sexual satisfaction has become the governing principle to the extent that other people are only meat-puppets which act as objects to facilitate it, surely they lose that intangible yet recognisable quality we call 'humanity' - the stranger who runs towards danger to help someone they have never met or who queues up in the rain to give a part of their body to some poor soul lacking a vital part.

The porn addict - as Grace Millane's killer was, and as most sex-killers are - does the opposite. They have 'de-humanity' - using someone they will never meet as a masturbation aid and offering up their own unwanted body part repeatedly to the poor soul who is the receptacle of their disembodied desire. Grace Millane's killer was not only inspired by pornography, but turned her dead body into his own customised wank-fodder by photographing her afterwards, recalling the words of Andrea Dworkin, a survivor of the skin trade, speaking many years before revenge porn and rape porn became the norm: 'You have the great joy of knowing that your nightmare is someone else's freedom and someone else's fun.'

I've had a lovely life, but sometimes when I read about the worldwide lot of women, I can't help but think of a particularly vicious parody of Shakespeare's Seven Ages Of Man. First she is an aborted female foetus, then a cyber-bullied schoolgirl, then a raped and trafficked victim of a grooming gang, then a judged predatory Lolita responsible for her own molestation by some dirty old man. And that's just before she's old enough to vote. In young adult life, at the height of her beauty, she will be groped, grabbed and molested in the street as she goes about her daily business. Seeking refuge from this, she may put herself under the protection of one man through marriage or co-habitation. If he doesn't kill her, she will lose her beauty and become the despised battle-axe butt of a million mother-in-law jokes until she will be an unwanted old woman dying for a drink of water on an NHS hospital ward. Considering that life under the patriarchy can be such a slog, it's a feat of evil genius and the throat-choking cherry on the cake that the Fifty Shades Of Grey franchise managed to beautify male bullying of women and sell it back to them in their millions as exciting erotica.

Not just grown women but blameless babes in arms were swept along in a merchandising maelstrom, clothed in rompers and changed on mats proclaiming NINE MONTHS AGO MY MUM READ FIFTY SHADES OF GREY. Under the headline MORE 50 SHADES BABY NEWS the blogger Mom 365 gushed somewhat revoltingly in 2012:

> 'Earlier this summer, we brought you news of a professor who was predicting a 50 Shades Of Grey-inspired baby boom in 2013. Now, it looks like that prediction may be coming true, as more and more moms-to-be are citing the steamy BDSM series as inspiration for their latest creations. We know that plenty of you new moms are enjoying the books, too - but do you think it could lead to a new arrival?'

If you're a universal feminist like me (that is, one whose immediate reaction to brown-skinned women being maltreated by brown-skinned men is not the really rather racist Woke reflex 'But it's their culture!' which effectively asserts that only white women should be allowed to lead decent lives) you might imagine how this would look to a child bride in some Medieval hellhole, forced to give birth at thirteen and totally broken by the experience. That women in the West could be so carefree with their freedoms that it took a book about a woman being controlled by a man to persuade them to procreate; well, if only we could do an en masse Freaky Freedom Friday thing, and the Western women who fantasise about Christian Grey could truly live trammelled by a tinpot tyrant while the Third World girls pursued their educations. But if you have a malicious sense of humour like mine, your anger on behalf of underprivileged females might be leavened by the mischievous observation that, babies being a particular passion killer, many a new mother who starts out finding such mucky-minded merch quite the hoot may well, a few months in, be swearing at EL James under her breath as she wrests her wriggling spawn from its kinky rompers and deposits its deposits on the similarly taunting changing mat. Hubby, by this point, may well be locked in his study 'working' - working on downloading yet more rough sex pornography, no doubt. Ah, sweet circle of life! It's also worth noting, for another cheap laugh, that while it's generally men who end up in A&E claiming that they accidentally sat on a Magimix, 2012 - the year after the first Fifty Shades book was published - saw attendance at emergency rooms rising 50% from 2010 by women with injuries related the over-enthusiastic use of alleged sex *toys* during BDSM sessions. They're actually 'sex aids' and, yes, that was a judgmental tone; 'sex toys' brings a creepy air of infantilism to this most adult pastimes. It's pitiful that two people — presumably equipped with the usual supply of hands, mouths and sex organs — need to set about each other with bits of garish, cut-price plastic to reach the realms of ecstasy.

But how every last seat-sniffing pervert must have savoured the success of Fifty Shades - SEE, THEY REALLY DO WANT IT ROUGH AFTER ALL! However, let she who is without guilt cast the first cat o'nine tails lash. I've always been keen to 'finger' myself first when I criticise the behaviour of others - partly because I'm extremely honest, partly because I'm an attention-whore - so it behoves me to 'fess up' to my own youthful adventures in S&M. I was just 17 when I knocked on the door of one of London's most notorious sadists and suggested that he show me what it was all about; my interest in being thrashed lasted well into my thirties, after which my highly developed sense of the ridiculous finally out-ran my kinkiness and I couldn't so much as look at a pair of nipple clamps without howling with laughter. S&M, like love-bites and Maoism, can look lovely on the young and pretty - but there's few things funnier than a fat middle-aged fetishist of either sex. In my youth I was also responsible for writing the ultimate sexy-greedy (O.K - pornographic if you really want to point the finger) Eighties blockbuster Ambition, in the course of which the heroine undergoes a number of ordeals (classily based on the Seven Labours Of Hercules) including having SOLD tattooed on her forehead and being suspended by her nipples from the ceiling of a lesbian fetish club. (Is that even possible, let alone desirable?) Originally published in 1989, it was reissued in 2013 to ride E.L James' tsunami of lubriciousness and indeed I boasted proudly on the cover blurb that it 'Makes Fifty Shades Of Grey look like Anne Of Green Gables.' Regrettably, I bet more people got themselves off over Anne of Green Gables than my heroine Susan Street on her second outing, as sales were underwhelming. Truth to tell, I was probably a little envious of E.L James - I'd only made a lousy few hundred thousand from my shameful scribblings whereas she was sitting on a murky mountain of millions. But equally truthfully, there are some things which feel a whole lot better than making money - and, for me, knowing that you haven't added fuel to the endless fire of they-love-it-really woman-bashing is one of them.

It was a relief all round when the Conservative government announced in the summer of 2020 that the Rough Sex defence would be outlawed in new domestic violence legislation. But that this was needed at all said much about the contemporary attitude to sexual violence and how, curiously, the situation appeared to have regressed at a time when respect and protection of other oppressed groups had become the new religion. In 2019 a BBC survey found that more than a third of British women between 18 and 40 had experienced unwanted slapping, choking or spitting during consensual sex; the Centre for Women's Justice responded that the figures showed 'the growing pressure on young women to consent to violent, dangerous and demeaning acts…this is likely to be due to the widespread availability, normalisation and use of extreme pornography.' Which will probably not come as news to that most paradoxical fan-club of pornography, the Woke Bros.

Leftists of the past had varying attitudes to sex; I remember being pleasantly surprised on reading as a teenager that Chairman Mao in his early days ('before he went mad' to quote Ken Livingstone on Hitler) offered promotions to soldiers who married prostitutes. While in the Soviet Union the emphasis was more on *re-education* - that interesting word wherein the wagging finger and the kicking boot become interchangeable - which in true noble Soviet tradition led to the gulags. What no Leftist men have done before Woke is to actually cheerlead for the sex industry, and in the course of doing so ignore both the sad reasons why the vast majority of women go into it and the sensible reasons why the vast majority of women want to get out of it. It's like all that time the Woke Bros were carrying a copy of Das Kapital around throughout their formative self-fondling years they had a copy of The Happy Hooker stuffed inside it, and somehow one stuck in their minds more than the other. Rebecca West famously said 'People call me a feminist whenever I express sentiments that differentiate me from a doormat or a prostitute.' With Woke Bros, it sometimes seems that the only feminists worthy of the word are those who identify as doormats and prostitutes - our old friend WILL SUCK DICK FOR SOCIALISM. Could this be because they are the first generation to be raised with access to free online pornography, and because a woman who performs in pornography is to some extent a hybrid of both prostitute and doormat? Let's have a look!

It's so funny to think about the time before FOP (free online pornography - amusingly, one definition of fop in Merriam-Webster is 'fool, dupe') when feminists routinely got incensed about girls in newspapers wearing nothing but a suntan, a smile and a strategically placed scarf. The Labour MP Clare Short was forever losing her rag over Page 3 girls; in 1987 she tried unsuccessfully to introduce a Commons bill outlawing topless models in newspapers and in 2004 the Sun fought back after she called their pin-ups 'degrading pornography,' childishly using a montage of Ms Short's face superimposed on a topless model. This might now be seen as a primitive form of *revenge porn* all the more remarkable for having been overseen by the feminist editor Rebekah Brooks, yet to be unmasked as the fun-loving criminal who would rock a publishing empire.

I'll come clean and admit that I wrote an equally childish piece for the Sun against the ban; LET'S SEE BOOBS NOT BURQUAS might have been the headline. It's the usual excuse of the journalist to say that we don't write our own headlines but I've got a sneaky feeling that this gem was pulled fully intact from the actual piece. One of the few things I dislike about ageing is that increasingly I see both sides of an increasing number of arguments. I do think Clare Short was picking a petty fight. But on the other hand, the Sun's attitude was pathetic, especially when they urged Page 3 girls to call her 'fat' 'ugly' and 'jealous.' You could almost see the porn-addled words passing from the fish-bait lips of Sun hacks to the pretty shell-like ears of these girls, like a creepy man using a life-size naked sex doll as a ventriloquist's dummy. Jealous - really? A woman of humble origins, now one of the most recognisable politicians in the country, jealous of females doing a job that would see them on the scrap-heap at 30?

One item of faith of a porn-addled brain is the secret but strongly-held belief that any woman who could do so would choose to become a performer in pornography; porn-addled men (PAMs) believe that not only female politicians would, but that nuns would, kindergarten teachers would and probably even believe that not only female politicians would, kindergarten teachers would and nuns definitely would. (The exception would probably be the Queen and the PAM's mum. And daughter. And sister. But definitely his sexy sister-in-law, the dirty bitch.) Maybe they're onto something; one day, with revenge porn and rape porn and trafficking porn, it's entirely likely that more women will have been featured in pornography than not, though this will largely be without their consent, let alone be the glorious fulfilment of a burning ambition to be tossed off over by strange men. To fiddle with the old Andy Warhol saw; 'In the future, every woman will serve as masturbation material for 15 minutes.' What innocent hinterlands the Page 3 Girls now recall - sex as a smiley, sunny, saucy romp, where clothes just fall off and a good time is had by all. When she finally put her gear back on for good in 2015, she seemed as archaic as an antimacassar. But it was free online pornography, not feminism, which saw her off.

A 2008 report into youth exposure to online pornography (carried out in the U.S.A; can't you just see the Brit Woke Bros sneering that those nasty American men are different from their own spotless selves?) found that of 5000 undergraduates, 93% of boys and 62% off girls had seen internet porn before the age of 18 - the average age of first exposure to it is 11. They are effectively being groomed by proxy to mistake masturbation for sex; their groomer is not an inadequate individual, but the massive worldwide pornography machine - annual revenue around $90 billion a year compared to pre-plague Hollywood's $10 billion. Child pornography accounting for $3 billion, one avid viewer of which was the ex-Labour politician and born-again Woker Eric Joyce, *partner* of the ultra-Woke writer India Knight. With hindsight, his endless Twittering about the right of men to use female toilets (which are full of little girls) seems sinister rather than merely silly - the Tweets end abruptly when he admitted to viewing Category A pornography, including the rape of a baby. If they hadn't been on different continents, he could have shared a cell with the white, Woke American BLM organiser Christopher DeVries who was charged with six counts of possessing sixty images of child pornography in July 2020. Having said before the protests, which he arranged to take place on Father's Day, 'I feel like this is one of the best things I can do as a father...I don't want to live in a community where people are afraid of their local police' some people weren't at all surprised that a practicing paedophile was keen on abolishing the forces of law.

Dr Gail Dines (once described as the world's leading anti-pornography campaigner - now there's a job description that makes me jealous in a way that glamour model doesn't, like being some sort of maverick feminist pirate taking on the combined might of the world's putrid pimps) views pornography as a public-health crisis, hooking the male youth of all nations as the pornographers reel in those future PAMs too young to have credit cards by offering them swathes of free porn, which acts as a lure to paid sites. 'The first taste is always free' our teachers used to warn us about drug dealers; with porn, the first time - and the second, and the hundredth - a putative PAM sees a woman first taste sperm is always free. But one sunny day they'll find themselves paying for their pleasures when the stuff that comes for free can't make them come anymore; they'll save up their pennies and buy their favourites, like we used to do with hit singles way back in the twentieth century. Except that the thing they buy is a very sad song indeed.

Gail Dines has compared pornography to smoking, though I would point out with typical frivolousness that enjoying the first makes a man look about as ludicrous as it's possible for a man to look while enjoying the latter makes him look dead cool. It's also comparable to online gambling - but the suicides are among the performers, not the punters. It is the proud boast of many a modern man that he has never paid for porn, but he doesn't need to; women pay for it with their physical and mental health every day. And with their lives. Whereas the average life expectancy in the U.S.A is 78 years, the average life expectancy of a porn star is 37 years. Not shelf life - actual life. It's the only profession wherein the workers have a life expectancy less than half the national average, and though punters would probably like to believe that these women are dropping like flies through sheer pleasure overload, it's actually explained by overdoses and murder and - mostly - suicides. It's interesting to consider that the suicide of one man after his appearance on The Jeremy Kyle Show caused the popular programme to be axed forever whereas the ongoing suicide epidemic in porn is simply treated as collateral. Why, you'd almost believe that these women were worthless in the eyes of the society that nevertheless demands their use as a human right! Salman Rushdie went so far as to claim that the willingness of a society to accept pornography was a measure of how civilised it is.

I like men enough to believe that most of them would be perplexed rather than pleased about the fact that pornography kills its females performers. What's so bad about getting paid for having sex - not just paid, but getting paid double what most male pornography performers are, as the Woke Bros like to point out? Now that's feminism for you! Partly the higher fee would be a recognition that while for men the physical nature of sex is active, for women it involves being a receptacle - being used, in a physical sense. This can be a lot of fun when you fancy a man, but as a daily routine, with strangers, you can see why it might wear a woman down somewhat. And as I write, 'rosebudding' is the new trick in town, during which a rectal prolapse takes place and the walls of the rectum fall out of the anus. There's something seriously mentally wrong with any human being who believes that this is a reasonable way for another human being to have to make a living.

Another reason why pornographic actresses kill themselves so much might be the fact that a 2010 analysis of the fifty best-selling pornography videos found that 88% of the scenes included physical aggression, with the target of the violence being a woman. Every time a new atrocity comes to public notice - waterboarding, for example - it is quickly incorporated into porn with a predictability that makes one think that there might just be more to it than adults watching other adults enjoying themselves. And men who only watch *ethical* porn or porn where the actresses are well-nourished Americans rather than dead-eyed trafficked Europeans are never going to know whether those women were sexually abused as children, as a huge number of women who work in the sex industry are. It's ironic than in an age so concerned with mental health Woke Bros appear to give zero fucks about the mentally scarred women they continue to masturbate over.

In 2018, Peter Madsen raped, tortured, dismembered and killed the promising journalist Kim Wall, a journalist, for sexual pleasure, after searching the internet for *snuff* - and what volumes that short careless word speaks about the lightness with which we regard the killing of women in the course of men's perverted kicks. Of course the argument about the link between pornography and femicide has supporters on both sides. The PAM - Porn Addled Man, remember - can quite rightly argue that femicide was established long before the first pornography and that women often have least rights in countries where even a naked chin cannot be glimpsed. However in data released by Google in 2015, six of the top eight porn-searching countries are Muslim states; Pakistan, Egypt, Iran, Morocco, Saudi Arabia and Turkey. Pakistan, incidentally, also has the honour in leading the way on porn searches for animals like pigs, donkeys, dogs, cats and snakes. Interestingly, Google Trends shows that several Muslim countries are also amongst the global leaders in homosexual pornographic searches though their religion strictly forbids homosexual acts - more hypocrisy, which PAMs have a-plenty. The fact that there's loads of gay pornography is one argument against the claim that pornography exists solely to objectify and humiliate women - youth and beauty are equally prized and one man - usually the 'twink' - will oft be apparently 'forced' to do something he doesn't at first seem inclined to do.

Once again, I need to 'finger' myself about my own pornography use here - and doesn't the word 'use' say it all? Isn't it the worst Woke crime to 'use' fellow humans? Apparently if you splatter, it don't matter! Anyway, mine is very rare, partly because once I learned how young the performers die, it put me right off; you'd need to have a whole other level of cognitive dissonance going on to get off on it after that, like an animal-lover seeing inside an abattoir and still eating meat. And partly because I'm very 'quick' - during my starter marriage, as a horny teenager, I used to ring up those primitive Sex Chat Lines (this was the 1970s and such things were still highly recherché, especially in Essex) and I'd be 'done' before the nice lady had even finished reading out the menu - talk about a cheap date. Having such a hair-trigger sexual response, I suppose I feel a thoroughly conceited contempt that some people need it to 'get them going.'

It's also a status thing - put plainly, I don't want to be a wanker; it's telling that this word still retains the power to offend. If I was doing it loads, I'd see it as indicating sexual failure on my part; all my life since I was 17, if I wanted to do a sex-thing, I'd do it. Between the ages of 18 and

55, I was a ferociously monogamous sex fiend through three marriages (with six months Sapphic time off for good behaviour) and when I wasn't doing it, I was anticipating it, recovering from it or imagining downright rotten variations on it. I was once walking along the seafront with my husband when a tall, dark and handsome Alsatian passed by; my husband looked hard at me and said 'Please tell me you didn't just say 'Phwooar!''

I'll come clean and admit that I started abusing myself at an early age; once, I did it so hard that I fell out of bed. When I read that my teenage heroine Patti Smith did it so much as a kid that she regularly lost consciousness, I was so full of admiration that I redoubled my efforts; I never rendered myself unconscious, but I had fun trying. However, I did not once think: 'Oooh, one day I'll grow up and masturbate even more!' That would have been like dreaming that one day I'd grow up and go to school even more. I was practising for sex, the ultimate Big Scary Ride which I was, due to height and circumstance, currently barred from. Just like it's O.K to have an imaginary friend when you're young but it gets a bit weird when you're over the age of consent, that's how I feel about middle-aged masturbators who escape from the expectations of real women into an imaginary harem, pulling themselves off over ladies of all races and hues and believing this makes them in some sad way Men Of The World.

In the world of wonder which the one-handed Woke Bros rule, no women wants to be a buzzkill. Until one day, she wakes up - and she wants exactly that, because as well as being the right thing to do, it's also the cool thing to do, because being cool is about owning yourself and kneeling to no one. Because the Woke Bro BS about all sex being good sex - even that in which a woman ends up with her rectum hanging out of her anus - is just as oppressive and twice as damaging as the old saw that no sex is good sex. They're both traps set up solely to control women. And as rulers always do, the Bros practice divide-and-rule; by persuading women that pornography is everything from a bit of fun to a human right, men have succeeded in dividing women not into madonnas and whores, as traditional had it, but into killjoys and whores. The old agony aunt advice to 'Take an interest in your boyfriend's hobbies' was suspect enough when it led girls to pretend pleasure in darts and draught beer - now they must reach visible realms of ecstasy watching their fellow females being defecated on. Progress!

Pornography is like cocaine - everyone wants to believe that regardless of the misery and broken lives which litter the production of everybody else's kicks, the source they alone opt for is magically free of exploitation, torture and death. But if you're any sort of person, giving up is the only moral option; like all alleged addictions, it's nowhere near as difficult as our infantilised society leads you to believe. I gave up cocaine overnight after thirty years and pornography after five; a slight tussle and then you're in the clear, out of your rat-run, the sky opening out above you. For me the moment of truth was the terrible comprehension of the average age of a porn performer's death; for others it may be a broken relationship. And don't kid yourself that free stuff isn't part of the problem, because you're 'not giving money to pornographers' - demand creates the supply and the suffering, and getting it for free simply makes you stingy as well as weak.

I remember once reading a piece about two exited female porn performers who had to check their impulses to 'perform' sex when they made love - their testimony to the hard work it took to get over this was singularly moving. It's a level of consciousness that no PAM will ever achieve, until he finds the guts to step away from his drug of choice. But there's always an excuse. Woke Bros who are hooked on porn like to kid themselves that they can use it in a way their less enlightened brethren can't; that they are pro-sex activists justifying it as their 'treat' after a long day fighting oppression (on Twitter) and claiming that the sex industry's just a job like any other - unless it's their mum, sister or daughter, of course.

To a Woke Bros, it sometimes seems, **everything** is sexist except actual pornography, which gets a magic pass; I recall a PAM of my acquaintance once railing against the fashion business 'making money from exploiting women.' Really? Last time I looked, the average age a fashion model died at was way higher than 37. But let's not forget that the A in PAM does indeed stand for *addled*. How deep does porn-sickness go? Due to the furtive nature of the beast, it's hard to tell. If a PAM is watching some sorrowing female being gang-banged (apparently crying is at a premium in such entertainments, as protests and pleasure are so easy to fake but tears are not) and realises at the moment of 'release' that he is watching his niece, say, being violated, what does he do? Stop in his spunky tracks? Be glad it's not his sister and get off anyway? PAMs are by their nature just so morally compromised, it's hard to believe anything they say; 'How do you know when an addict is lying?' 'When their lips move.' Still, that's his business - until his private perversions might possibly spill over (pertinent choice of words) into the public realm. A study by Dolf Zillman in 1982 indicated that prolonged exposure to pornography desensitises people towards sexual violence; after being shown some choice items, test subjects were asked to judge an appropriate punishment for a rapist. Chillingly, the test subjects recommended punishments that were significantly more lenient than those recommended by those who had not watched pornography. Because when she says no she means 'Yes, yes, yes!' And when she cries, they're tears of joy. And when she dies at the age of 37, it's probably from pure pleasure overload.

One in four men suffering from impotence is now under the age of forty - and pornography use is usually the cause. When we read about the impotence of young men - who should be at their peak performance - with young women - who are without doubt at the peak of their pulchritude and who then blame themselves - then we see how pernicious pornography is.

The answer is, apparently, to groom girls still under the age of consent to put the idea of pursuing their own pleasure to one side and perform like porn stars. As groomers so often do, though, once they've gotten themselves all worked up they rarely know when to stop. Even the professionally broad-minded were repulsed when the Beano of Woke, Teen Vogue, began to publish essays on how teenage girls could best enjoy anal sex - or rather, how best to perform the impression that they did for the benefit of pubescent PAMs keen for a new way to cut down to size the female classmates making them feel small academically.

Grandly describing itself as 'The young person's guide to conquering (and saving) the world, Teen Vogue covers the latest in celebrity news, politics, fashion, beauty, wellness and entertainment. No fluff here - just what you need to know now' that the porn-sick trans agenda had invaded the once-safe space of girls magazines (Teen Vogue already used such find-the-lady phrases as 'vagina-owners') was illustrated by the thoroughly inadequate reaction of one of its editors, Phillip Picardi, when called out over the Christmas 2019 bum-sex bonanza *A Guide to Anal Sex*: 'The backlash to this article is rooted in homophobia.' The young writer Peony Campbell in her 2019 response 'Anal Sex Is Awful' put him firmly in his place:

> 'It's not homophobic to say no. Of course it isn't. Men have prostates, so they have some kind of magical pleasure centers that are stimulated through this act. If the payoff is worth it to them — mazel tov. I'm not going to say all men who ask for anal sex are sadists, fecophiliacs, misogynists, or pornsick. But given the one-sided nature of the request it's only fair to ask Why are you even asking me for this?'

That Teen Vogue is the glossiest Woke grooming organ around today was made very clear when they ran a piece telling teenagers how to masturbate. What next - a class teaching dogs how to bark? The only possible people who could benefit from such a piece of prosaic pornography would surely be perverts of a paedophile bent.

Like all drugs, pornography starts out persuading users that it's opening up a big wonderful world to them - and only when it's too late to break free without enormous effort reveals that it has shrunk both the universe and the user/loser. The pornification of society, making the sexes double-dealing strangers to each other, forever comparing each other to others, is the exact opposite of why bold progressives started trying to educate people about sex in the first place. A young friend of mine has been told many times - always by Woke Bros - 'You should be in porn!' because of her genuine enthusiasm for sex. These half-wits believe they're paying her a compliment by comparing her natural inclination to a pay-per-view performance and are bemused when she doesn't choose to have sex with them again. Jarvis Cocker - no one's idea of a prude - summed it up with sexy simplicity when he told the Sunday Times in 2020: 'Fame is like pornography. Pornography takes an amazing thing - love between two people, expressed physically - and grosses it out.'

In these weird Woke times, we inhabit a topsy-turvy world in which chessmen can be considered racist but where portraying women as nothing more than a selection of ever-open holes - Whack-A-Mole with DNA - is a lovely way for for a Woke Bro to relax after a hard day daubing SLAG on statues of Queen Victoria. Porn is a cheeky abbreviation of a long and ugly word with a history rooted in female slaves bought and sold for the purpose of sexual use, but now re-born as a lovely little chum to all. You can buy baby rompers proudly proclaiming that that the powerless and incontinent wearer is a PORN STAR; Marks & Spencer were forced to change the name of their canned cocktail the Porn Star Martini after mothers complained that they did not need the extra bother of explaining to tots what a porn star was during a wholesome shopping spree. Oddly, the M&S defence was that 'porn star' was 'intended as a reference to a category of person rather than a sexual activity' - presumably purchase of the toothsome cocktail came with a guarantee of early suicide and a side order of incontinence. Typically of a Woke retailer (let's not forget the brave insertion of guacamole into a heteronormative BLT sandwich, thus rendering it an LGBT sandwich as the proud contribution to Pride week in 2019) Marks & Spencer's sensitivity seems to grind to a halt when it comes to the rights of females of all ages; selling padded bras for nine-year-olds so that they can understand precisely what they'll be valued for as women as well as full-body-covering hijabs for other nine-year-olds so they can understand that they'll be valued so long as they never feel the sunshine on their blameless limbs. As the Muslim commentator Maajid Nawaz, said, referencing The Handmaid's Tale 'Little girls are told it is 'immodest' to show their hair. And blessed be the fruit. Hijab is still imposed - only on women - by law in Iran and Saudi Arabia, and many other countries. This is gender apartheid. Marks and Spencer are free to sell confederate flag tee-shirts too, but I bet they never will.'

What's wrong with this dirty picture? How will they grow up, these little girls who after a brief period when society appeared to be striving towards a clear-eyed and relaxed approach to sex are coming to maturity in a Woke dystopia where a child must choose between sexy lingerie or a cover-all shroud by the age of ten? We are already seeing a rise in the age at which youngsters choose to lose their virginity, demonstrated by the 2018 publication of a fascinating study by University College London tracking 16,000 people born between 1989 and 1990 from the age of 14, it found that 44% of girls had lost their virginity by the end of their teens compared to 58% of their mothers. With boys the result was far more dramatic - 47% compared to a saucy 69% for their parents generation - while a whopping one in eight of both sexes were still clinging on to their purity by the time they reached twenty. Could it be a case of holding onto nurse for fear of finding something worse - anal incontinence, perchance? The verdict from the experts was very much one that pornography was probably to blame: 'Millennials have been brought up in a culture of hypersexuality which has bred a fear of intimacy' the psychotherapist Susanna Abse told the Sunday Times. 'The women are always up for it with beautiful hard bodies and the men have permanent erections. That is daunting to young people.'

You know when your mum tells you not to gorge on sweets or you won't be able to eat your dinner? That! It's a vicious circle jerk; young men watch pornography, become PAMs and therefore less attractive to/potent with young women, watch more pornography, become Incels (the crossover between Incels and Woke Bros is considerable) and the deal is sealed - the thighs stay closed. If we keep on like this, there's a good chance we may end up like Japan, where pornography has contributed greatly to the spectre of maybe a million young Japanese men — the 'hikikomori' — who have entirely forsaken adult life for the solitary pleasures of online gaming and pornography. They are an important component in what the Japanese government calls 'celibacy syndrome,' an imminent national catastrophe which has seen nearly half of their young women as well as more than a quarter of their young men 'not interested in, or despising, sexual contact.' Because of this the Japanese Family Planning Association predicts a whopping one third plunge in the country's population by 2060.

Is there any upside to this increasing state of (non) affairs? Well, as a radical feminist who has always found my habit of being cock-struck/sinking into the dick-sand one of my less attractive qualities, I'd be happily anticipating that a lot more lesbians will emerge. (We can already see this in the emerging number of celebrity female 'bisexuals' who don't want to scare off their male fans and then quietly come out as completely gay when their sex-bomb sell-by-date is past.) Not porn lesbians either, just killing time eating out until a delicious crumb of dick comes their way; proper lesbians who are physically perplexed by men and want nothing sexual to do with them. Never mind, PAMS, you can always go and masturbate over your imaginary friends, and why not get your mum to buy you a VR headset for your thirtieth birthday? Then you can watch 3D porn to your heart's content - and give Darwin's theory of evolution a thoroughly modern twist as no woman with one iota of sex appeal or self-respect will give you a second look, let alone a first fuck.

Is it the humiliating fact that they're getting less action than their dads did in their youth that makes Woke Bros so weirdly insistent that sex work is real work and that women who maintain that most prostituted women would rather being doing something else are 'whorephobic'? That's like calling abolitionists 'slavephobic' - and considering that the trafficking of female children, girls and women makes up a such a huge part of modern slavery, that's not a flippant statement. A 2016 study by the United Nations' International Labour Organization estimated that there are more than 4 million victims of sex trafficking globally, 99% of them female and 1 million of them children. Commercial sexual exploitation accounts for two thirds of the profits of forced labor; profits from forced sexual labor - rape, basically - are estimated at $99 billion worldwide.

How can men of the Left approve of this supremely savage spearhead of capitalism, red in tooth and claw? And if they're so enlightened, how can they support the existence of a sexual underclass which reinforces all the old dumb clichés about women's sexuality; that they are not built to enjoy sex and are little more than walking masturbation aids, things to be **done to**, things so sensually null and void that they have to be paid to indulge in fornication, and that they are property, bought and sold from one man to another?

This being the case, and these innocent females being such unconditional victims of a vile trade, what sort of monster once have written the following words?

> 'When the sex war is won, prostitutes should be shot as collaborators for their terrible betrayal of all women.'

## Reader, that monster was me

I've prided myself on complete candour in this book so far, but whereas before I was bumptiously pleased to serve myself up for examination (scenery-eaters such as myself only ever see the 'me' in 'mea culpa') I'm deeply ashamed by this. I'm afraid there can be no ambiguous interpretation of these shameful words I wrote in 1984.

What was I thinking of? Yes, I was young - 24 - but old enough to know right from wrong, even if I had been a teenage shoplifter. Yes, I was snorting speed like there was no tomorrow, but as I was still able to dress and feed myself without assistance, that's no excuse. In my defence I'd say I was still a Stalinist (o no, it's getting worse - back away from the shovel!) and trying to put some sort of lame-brain social class spin on it, with a bit of mystical Lawrentian tat shoehorned in:

> 'Making the lives of the working-class residents of the areas where they ply their poxy trade even more depressing...in many areas of London tenants keep baseball bats and buckets of water by their front doors in order to drive away both the monstrous, moronic regiments who fornicate in their gardens and the men who come banging on their doors looking for hookers...to bring something as humdrum and modern into this most mysterious, moral part of life, to make physical love a **job...**this makes prostitution an obscenity almost as much as the slimy condoms which litter children's playgrounds in the districts frequented by these Quislings of the quim...'

O, FFS!

It's no excuse but all I can say to support my claim of diminished responsibility due to temporary insanity is that I used to be against abortion and adultery too when I wrote that, for no other reason that I was as ignorant and extreme as youngsters generally are. (I was the Greta Thunberg of sex, but sexier.) A lot of gin has gone under the bridge since then, I've been divorced twice for adultery and have lost count of the abortions I've had and a few of my dearest friends over the past twenty years have been retired hookers. So I can look back over more than three decades and admit that I, on this issue, was literally a raving idiot. But that doesn't mean I don't think prostitution is **just work**, as the Woke Bros insist, and that pimps and johns are just regular guys doing nothing nasty by hiring women - real people, with real souls - as sexual spittoons by the hour.

One thing my ex-prossie mates have in common is not just a loathing of sex and men which makes them great fun, but also a loathing of 'amateurs' - sexually generous women who do it free of charge. The air is **blue** when they talk about this slag and that whore; if I told them not to be whorephobic, they'd throw their drink in my face - and then charge me for it. Pornography performers are not popular with my easily-offended escort chums either, though their antipathy seems a mixture of both outrage (having That Thing **filmed** - shameless!) and envy - they don't have to smell the breath and bear the weight of the male munters who get off on them and who are always kept at a masturbating arms length. You'd think that the burden of surplus male sexual desire had been taken off of the market by free internet porn but there will always be brave maverick men who wish to humiliate women themselves as opposed to simply watch other men humiliate them. What pornography has done is to make life far harder for those women in the frontline of sexual servitude in that men now expect prostitutes - not just *civilian* women - to act like porn stars. The repulsive *reviews* of punters on various online forums bear this out as women are rebuked most often for 'staying still' and 'looking sad' rather than pretending to enjoy being penetrated by strangers as porn performers do.

I am far from being a sexual moralist – ask my three husbands. I don't believe that taking money for sex makes one a scarlet woman – I have many friends who tried it a few times when they were young, flighty and curious, but whose sense of self-preservation meant that they didn't care for the way it felt and so quickly set about getting themselves proper jobs. But I do believe that prolonged and exclusive sex work is extraordinarily bad for the mental and physical health of those who do it. People like myself – who approve of the Nordic Model pioneered by Sweden in 1999 and since followed by Norway, Denmark and Canada, under which it is illegal to buy sexual services, but not to sell them, making punters, pimps, procurers and brothel-keepers rather than prostitutes the criminals – are often derided as killjoys. But there's precious little joy to kill in having sex with a slobbering drunk who could easily kill you if you don't live up to his porn-sick fantasies. I'd love those people who declare that it's a job like any other to have to deal with the fact that their own mother, sister or daughter did it for a living.

It's not just Woke Bros who are hypocrites. When the otherwise excellent feminist writer Caitlin Moran wrote that sex-workers were very similar to care-workers, I had to laugh. Tell your average robustly religious Polish or Filipina care-worker that she's on a par with a hooker and you're quite likely to get your caring, sharing face pushed in. And as Moran boasts of confronting men in the street who merely cat-call her teenage daughters, I feel unconvinced that in a few years she'd be proud to see them hired by the hour by the very same sad-sacks.

As well as exemplifying the anti-Semitism (truly 'The socialism of fools') which is an essential element of Wokeism, Jeremy Corbyn identified himself as the Grandaddy of Woke when he proudly announced his pronouns at the Pink News Awards in 2019 on International Pronoun Day in 2019. (As though that bearded moron could have been anything but a 'he/him.') He also took the Woke Bros line that sex work was just work like any other and in 2016 came under attack from some spirited Labour ladies as yet unpurged when in 2016 he backed decriminalisation of the sex industry with the impossibly limp plea 'Let's do things a bit differently and in a bit more civilised way.'

We already knew that men on the revolutionary wing of politics, from Sinn Fein to the SWP, often saw consent as a bourgeoise construct, so why would we be shocked that liberal men had a liberal interpretation of consent? #MeToo was a phrase coined in 2006 by the black American activist Tarana Burke, who was inspired to use it after finding herself without words when a 13-year-old girl confided in her that she had been sexually assaulted, later wishing she had just said 'Me too.' But it spread virally – like some mass cyberspace inoculation against isolation – in 2017 when the actress Alyssa Milano encouraged women who had suffered sexual abuse to Tweet it in the wake of the first revelations of Harvey Weinstein's decades of sexual bullying and blackmail.

Million of women responded. The first shock was how many men - decent dads and wholesome husbands - were actually sexual predators. The second was how many of them identified as humanitarian and hid in plain sight as feminist allies. In the spring of 2020 the gallery and club owner Alex Proud - a fifty-year-old married man with three children - was accused of creating a 'hyper-sexualised workplace' in which he freely harassed at least five young women, 'slapping, grabbing and spanking' them, as well as creepily nicknaming himself 'Daddy' and 'Papa,' once presenting an award engraved to 'Daddy's favourite daughter.' He had recently joined a 'round table' of entrepreneurs promoting the 'safety of female employees' working in nightlife and in 2019 wrote that a report on low rape conviction rates 'blew away many of my arrogant and sexist assumptions... If this is where #MeToo takes us, then bravo.' His confusion was almost touching as he blustered in his defence 'I have championed a progressive working environment where I have employed gay, lesbian and trans staff.' O, in that case, molest away, you wonderful man! It was the strangest thing - half-witted, even - how the most expensively-educated of Woke Bros really seemed to believe that paying lip service to feminism somehow *set off* a demand for oral sex from a female colleague. Like Green jet-setters having trees planted to offset their carbon footprint.

Men are often accused of dividing women into two types – the virgin/whore complex, as Freud had it. And maybe women, because we live with men, work with men and love men, have to divide men into two types, to preserve our sanity – the Monsters and The Good Guys. Except that, to his wife and daughters, and to the feminist organisations he donated to, and to Barack Obama whose teenage daughter worked as his intern, Harvey Weinstein was once a Good Guy. Having seen at first hand how the legions of Hollywood liberals protected and lionised the child rapist Roman Polanski, it's understandable that Weinstein couldn't really grasp what he was doing wrong.

From Hollywood to Holyrood, those Woke Bros just couldn't help themselves - they were lecherous legion. But one of the grisliest examples is Tez Ilyas, Jeremy Corbyn's favourite comedian (apart from Diane Abbott) judging by all the times they were photographed cuddling up in a fraternal fashion after Labour fundraisers. In 2019 Ilyas was chosen from a horde of slathering showbiz groupies for the mind-melting honour of taking over Corbyn's Instagram account during his live television debate with Boris Johnson; the social media equivalent of becoming The Groom Of the Stool - the most intimate of a monarch's courtiers, responsible for assisting in excretion.

Due to the rabid Islamophilia of the Western media, Ilyas rose quickly to prominence in the moribund pond of *stand-up* due mostly to his DNA; he is strikingly unfunny, even judged by the dire standards of the state-sponsored titter-merchants who mire the BBC. The BBC who, on their religious education website, added 'PBUH' (Peace Be Upon Him) after every mention of Mohammad and often added 'The Prophet' before his name. But he's only 'The Prophet Mohammad' if you believe in Islam, which the people who are forced to finance the BBC generally don't. If they insist on doing so, then for balance they should also call Jesus 'Our Lord and Saviour, Jesus Christ' - which they won't, of course, because that would interfere with their practically parasexual mania for sucking up solely to Islam in the religion department.

The same BBC for whom, predictably, Ilyas made a short film taking us through a day in the life of a fasting Muslim during Ramadan in 2015. From there on his career was a dizzy whirl of Eid Special Comedy Nights and galas celebrating fifty years of 'Asian' shows on the BBC until Radio 4, inevitably, commissioned three whole series of lectures dressed up as laugh-ins from him; the Tez Talks, in with Ilyas sought to enlighten we heathen 'kaffir' (literally at our own expense, remember) by 'defusing numerous misconceptions about Islam' to an audience playing the part of potential recruits to this delightful religion. Thus we were treated to the intricacies of his belief system alongside sneery speeches on the worthlessness of British society while explaining concepts such as jihad with 'unpatronising good humour.' The extent to which this creature was given a blank cheque to force his religion down our throats - while providing fewer laughs than the Christmas Day episode of EastEnders - completed the grisly castration of Radio 4 comedy.

Sadly, the Religion Of Peace wasn't the only thing Elias was interested in forcing down throats as after a decade of debatable fun the punchline was that this poor persecuted peaceful victim of systemic racism was in fact a serial sexual molester who specialised in forcing himself on insensible women. (He wasn't the only *funny man* more likely to bring forth tears than laughter, it transpired; as the funny and clever comedian Konstantin Kissin writer in June 2020: 'Shocking news from the world of comedy: despite the industry being populated exclusively by Woke male feminists, numerous female comedians are reporting sexual harassment and inappropriate behaviour. This surprising development has rocked the industry to its core as people suddenly question whether being good and going on about how good you are may not be the same thing.') Elias public apology, sodden with manly Twittering tears, was a sumptuous banquet of Woke Bros virtue-signalling.

Long story short - man got caught being rapey and would say anything to save his career. Just a thought, if Woke women were warning him not to be a sex-pest since 2017, as his tearful confession explained, it might have been an idea to have stopped? But of course he'd have been at the height of his state-sponsored virtue-signalling on our most respected radio channel then, telling we heathens how to behave decently, so how could anything he did be wrong? And how extraordinary that contact with all these 'incredible women' had still seen him go on to make jokes about grooming gangs as late as 2020? He certainly wasn't interested in listening to the young woman he called a *snowflake* on social media when she objected; as she herself said 'Thinking that joking about the systematic rape of thousands is off-limits for a sketch is very far from snowflake territory.'

Ilyas credits 'the dry humour of the people of his home town Blackburn' for inspiring his alleged humour; perhaps he was somewhat inspired by the grooming gangs of his calf country too when he serially 'used women for my own personal gratification.' And maybe, as with the gangs, he found it somewhat less 'just not OK' as they were white slags rather than Muslim women. Perhaps he even thought that he in his way and the grooming gangs in theirs weren't even being particularly bad Muslims; after all, Mohammad (PBUH) married a child. Of course men of all religions rape, but it's doubtful whether men of other religions pray before and after the act, as Yazidi women recall ISIS fighters doing. That's one fascinating aspect of the the ROP which Tez forgot to put in his Talks, I'll wager.

In the summer of 2020 the BBC turned on itself in a racism-routing fit of zealotry, removing episodes of such excellent comedy shows as Fawlty Towers and Little Britain. But, mystifyingly, Tez Ilyas' woefully unfunny work is still mired all over their iPlayer, as is that of the Sikh sex-pest Hardeep Singh Koli. Their most prolific sexual abuser was of course the whiter-than-white Jimmy Savile, in the course of protecting whom the BBC ignored extensive evidence of child abuse over decades, even airing a fawning memorial tribute to him on prime time TV, which incredibly included children. When it comes to sexual molesters, the BBC is indeed colour-blind.

One couldn't really write about Woke Bros and their fear of females/loathing of feminism without giving a big shout out to the corporation once called 'Auntie.' Even the nickname seems sinister now — and massively inappropriate. If the BBC is any relation at all, it's surely an uncle — a dirty uncle, probably not even a relation but a 'friend' of the family, who tells you that it's just your little secret between the two of you. In 2018, just weeks after the huge gap between the pay of men and women working for the corporation was exposed, rather than put their hand in their (our) pocket and pay women the same as men Auntie instead played a virtue-signalling blinder by appointing a 'Global Gender And identity' correspondent, Megha Mohan, who Tweeted excitably: 'Thrilled to start as the BBC's first global Gender and Identity Correspondent, reporting on issues concerning women, sexuality, race, etc.'

Love that 'etc'!

Sending up smoky Wokescreens galore, the BBC also announced that they would be addressing 'gender issues,' boasting - out of a whopping 21,239 number of staff - 786 gay men, 206 gay women and 365 bisexuals among the workforce. And last but never least, 417 employees who identify as transgender, who of course Auntie would be aching to 'support through a transition period' by giving paid time off to those undergoing a sex change. They didn't add at what point of the incredible journey male-to-female trans would be paid less

Might it not just be easier to pay both sexes the same and - as a gesture of goodwill towards the female workforce they had showed such discrimination against - not continue to hire men who molest women? But that would be too obvious; why do one virtuous thing when you can virtue-signal ten? They might better be renamed the WBBC - Woke Bros Broadcasting Corporation. As for 'Nation Shall Speak Peace Unto Nation' - 'Supporting Never The Racist, Always The Rapist' has a nice ring.

*

Was there a female angle to Covid-19? Yes, of course, just as there was a BAME angle and a senior citizen angle. Despite being repeatedly told by rich white men that we were 'all in this together' there were several different strands that made up the whole sorrowful story. Old people were more likely to die than young, fat people more than thin, dark people more than light...and men more than women. Regarding the last, there was a funny meme which showed a woman looking strong in a Rosie The Riveter pose, with words snarking how men died from coronavirus more than women, so that meant that women were better. Some Smart Alec had reTweeted it with the additional line 'Now try this with race...?'

And it **was** silly to try and score sisters-are-doing-it-for-themselves points from a deadly pandemic. Yes, more men were killed by it, as more men are killed in war, but being a woman in a danger zone brings unique peril. In wartime, rape, as victorious strangers pour into your conquered land; under lockdown, domestic violence, as defeated intimates decide to take their frustration out on you. The UN described the worldwide increase in domestic abuse as a 'shadow pandemic' alongside Covid-19, with domestic killings in this country alone up 160%, up from the usual *normal* two. The excellent Victims' Commissioner for England and Wales, Dame Vera Baird, said:

> 'Counting Dead Women has reached a total of 16 domestic abuse killings in the last three weeks. We usually say there are two a week - that looks to me like five a week. That's the size of this crisis. To save lives in this pandemic we are ordering some people to stay locked up for along time with people who will damage them.'

But no worries - Pornhub was at hand to save the day; a massive rise in masturbation took place during lockdown, as those of us with actual lives were forced to live the solitary existence of the dedicated onanist. And what better way to utilise all that lovely unexpected free time than by improving the shining hour than spunking over revenge porn?

As the Labour MP Dr Rosena Allin-Khan said, 'The most alarming thing is that people can be raped and their video can be posted online. That is absolutely shocking, there should be a national outcry.' Clutching their home-made pearl necklace, Pornhub tutted 'We have a steadfast commitment[2] to eradicating and fighting non-consensual content and under-age material. Any suggestion otherwise is categorically and factually inaccurate.' To show that posting real-life rape videos doesn't make you a bad person, Pornhub donated both money and masks towards fight against Covid-19, because nothing says 'Bad for business' than a world in which men are so scared of catching coronavirus that they won't get close enough to women to hurt them for the pleasure and profit of their brother man.

Indeed, Pornhub's Wokeness was a glory to behold: 'Pornhub stands in solidarity against racism and social injustice. If you are able, we encourage you to give to organizations like @bailproject @BlackVisionsMN @MNFreedomFund @splcenter @NAACP' The anti-pornography campaigners Click Off retorted sharply 'LIARS - The porn industry IS a social injustice. Women are categorised by race for men choose to masturbate over. This is a grotesque, using a real movement & struggle for your own ends. Enough.' While the activist outfit Fight the New Drug immediately asked the pertinent question 'If you're anti-racism, why do you host the following videos on your site? Black Slave Punished by White Master' – 'White Cops F*** Black Chick, Force Boyfriend to Watch' – 'Gang Banged by Blacks' – 'Skanky N****r gives a Blowjob' – 'Black Slave Girl Brutalized.'

Amusingly, despite the sex industry's best efforts to kid PAMs that knocking one out over a gang-banged black woman makes a white man Martin Luther King, the only angle of porn which causes Woke Bros any concern were concerned with was that **it might not be real** and thus an inferior *treat* to a PAM accustomed to craft beer and heritage tomatoes.

Woke Bros journalists who'd never written a word about dismantling Pornhub, on which revenge porn, child-trafficking and actual rape are routinely peddled as masturbation aids, were suddenly aghast at the idea that women might not be being genuinely mauled for their home entertainment but that these might be DEEP FAKES - Frankenporn! Because the Lord forbid porn shouldn't be composed of real women being used as sexual spittoons and loving it. We don't want fake porn; we want organic porn in which we can be sure that some desperate woman actually rented out her genitals by the hour. Yay, good guys! The name of the company which owns Pornhub speaks volumes - Mindgeek. We're not the enemy. We're not old-fashioned macho chauvinists. We're brains - we're geeks. Yes, we want to see women sliced and diced and hit on and shit on just like bad men from time immemorial do - but it's **not the same,** remember, cos we're the Good Guys. We're the Woke Bros and we know what's best for you, so open wide.

Or maybe when someone shows you who they are - especially when they're waving their angry little penis in your face - look past the Wokescreens and the one-handed virtue-signalling and believe them. Woke Bros are no brothers of ours and the only 'struggle' they're really interested in is seeing a terrified, attractive woman attempt to fight back against her attacker, all laid out for their cyber-delectation.

2020 was a tough year, but it was well-named, because we saw the men behind Woke - the perverts and paedophiles and pornographers and PAMs - in all their gory glory, like wanking Wizards of Oz, revealed at last from behind their Wokescreens. And to give them credit, Woke did women a great favour, though it certainly hadn't intended to. All those decades of being manhandled by the Left, presumably for our own good; to a smart woman, discarding socialism was the spiritual equivalent of finally taking off a pair of shoes two sizes too tight having walked a thousand miles in them, an enjoyable cherry on the top of the second childhood which comes with the menopause. You're meant to dread it but if you have assembled your character correctly, it sets you free from caring about what people in general and men in particular think of you and brings a whole new levels of insouciance and liberty; with no biological desire to build a home or family you are suddenly free to see men exactly as they are. Some of them are adorable - but many of them are mundane monsters, and many of those mundane monsters come clothed in the apparel of the enlightened. Late onset lesbianism is a sizeable social phenomenon of recent times and not for everyone - but even those of us in whom a lingering love of the male sex remains can certainly free our minds, no longer reliant on male approval. Of course lots of men won't like this - and lots of those men will be Woke. But that's their problem, isn't it? It's not like they can **replace** women with a pantomime version of them, uncomplaining parodies of femininity revelling in objectification....is it? (*Winks*)

One of the main aims of the feminist movement was to stop women defining themselves in relation to men; one of the sharpest and cutest minor milestones in this long hard slog was 'The Bechdel Test' which became a basic measure to see if women are fairly represented in a film. (It's also referred to as the Bechdel-Wallace test as Alison credited the idea for the test to her friend Liz Wallace; sisterhood in action.) To qualify, a film must have at least two female characters, they must both have names and they must talk to each other about something other than a man. This summed up so sweetly the tenderness and toughness of modern feminism; that we'd never, ever again fight other women over men - to be brief, sisters before misters. But women were about to take sides and fight over men in a way unforeseen and unimaginable outside of a very strange nightmare indeed.

We were about to fight over whether men could be women.

---

## Notes

[1] https://www.thetimes.co.uk/_FP_/closed_anonymous/article/cps-backed-off-assault-charge-over-fear-of-rough-sex-defence-nk6ghgcs8

[2] https://thetab.com/uk/2020/07/03/pornhub-petition-one-million-164546

# CHAPTER FOUR

## STUNNING KWEENS VS TERRIBLE TERFS - WOMANFACE GOES WOKE

As a child, I scorned the pantomime dames who afforded my inky-fingered cohort glee, being a shocking little snob from a proletarian background who was only interested in adults representing mystery and escape. The Dame seemed like a horrible warning of the way a working-class girl might end up if she relaxed too much into the role society had allotted her: 'Shut it, Widow Twankey!'[1] I would mutter as my sainted mother begged me one more time to stop gazing at the breathtaking view in the mirror and help out with the hoovering.

But then I saw Danny La Rue one night on prime time television. Mysterious as a mermaid (with whom he shared the quality of knowing that everyone was wondering about his genitalia while too in awe to ask) he surveyed all around him with an insouciant stare probably borrowed from Hedy Lamarr when they briefly bonded over a tall tale and a hip flask in the last carriage of the Orient Express. I recall gazing at him with absolute worship. The room grew silent; amazingly, my father, who distrusted effeminate men, did not get to his feet and tersely summon the dog for a walk, as he invariably did whenever male dancers appeared giggling and wiggling in our living room. The dog stopped wrestling with his Bonio, My mother sighed and for once we were united; I sighed too. What a vision of womanhood was this - yet so far above us as not even to inspire feelings of envy or inferiority. We watched it as we watched the Miss World competition, grateful that we belonged to the same species as these glorious creatures.

Like a beauty queen La Rue saw himself as a tribute to women; having nothing vulgar or comical about him, he insisted that he was not a drag artist but a female impersonator - and what a tribute to womanhood it was, that he saw us this way, and that his repertoire included Margot Fonteyn, Marlene Dietrich and Margaret Thatcher. Seeing the drag queens of today - Malestia Child, Anna Bortion, Cheryl Hole - Daniel Patrick Carroll would turn in his elegantly appointed urn at St Mary's Catholic Cemetery in West London.

A homosexual at a time when it could get you a jail sentence rather than a Lifetime Achievement Award, born in Cork but raised in Soho, the young La Rue was relocated to Devon during the Blitz and discovered a flair for amateur dramatics: 'There weren't enough girls so I got the pick of the roles...my Juliet was very convincing.' He served in the Royal Navy which must have been all sorts of fun for a young gay man before he went on to carve his long and luxurious career. He was a *trooper* according to showbiz myth - a good tipper, a carrier of suitcases for lone women and a chatterer to children before titans of Light Entertainment made this a sinister thing. Appointed OBE in 2002 - 'the proudest day of my life'[2] - they were wheeling him out on a chaise lounge to make innuendos when he could barely walk. Suffering in secret from several cancers, he died aged 81. 'I never want people to forget that I'm a bloke in a frock'[3] serves as a suitable epitaph regarding his working-class roots and tough good humour. La Rue wouldn't have fussed about pronouns; build like a brickie and a drinker of pints, he was a proud homosexual with no desire to hang around women's toilets - though they would probably have welcomed him with open arms and asked him to do their make-up if he'd wandered in.

I had been a child when I fixed Danny with the chaste look of love; I was a mucky-minded adolescent when I saw David Bowie put his arm around his guitarist Mick Ronson in the course of singing 'Starman.'[4] Hardly able to contain my delight, I looked sideways at my father, a cheery man who nevertheless seemed to watch Top Of The Pops solely for the purpose of angering himself. Here, at last, was the motherlode - and indeed, my mother, whimpering 'Ooo, Bill...what's he doing?' Father had spent the past few months enquiring rhetorically about the precise natal chromosomal origin - XY or XX - of everyone from David Cassidy to Eno as they strutted their stuff on my favourite TV pop show, and now he was in no mood to keep his counsel: 'Well, I'm not gonna ask if **that one's** a boy or a girl - because it's a **ruddy alien!**'

Flash forward four decades to Sam Smith announcing:

'I've decided I am changing my pronouns to THEY/THEM. After a lifetime of being at war with my gender I've decided to embrace myself for who I am, inside and out. I understand there will be many mistakes and misgendering but all I ask is you please, please try. Love you all. I'm scared shitless, but feeling super free right now. Be kind x'

This tale of two pop stars is perhaps the most beautiful snap-shot of how Woke ruins everything it gets its namby-pamby hands on. Before Woke: David Bowie, fearless, unapologetic, courting outrage and in the process probably changing more lives than the wheel. After Woke: Sam Smith boo-hooing and asking people to be kind. And incredibly, Smith was older than Bowie when they both added their most significant stitches to Rock's Rich Tapestry.

Why are the Woke gender-benders of today - the *non-binaries* - such a miserable lot? Though they drone on about being 'sex-positive' everything about them is negative - even in their chosen handle there's a 'no.' When I think back to my own adolescent adventures in sexual perversity – from Bowie to Patti Smith – I remember above all how mischievous we were. We took such delight in pretending to be gay/coming out as actual gay, even though – this is almost half a century ago – times weren't half so enlightened then. Why are today's gender-benders so carping and censorious? Is it a class thing, because they're indulged and entitled in a way we weren't? Is it a lack of talent thing, perhaps – that their sexual confusion is literally the most interesting thing about them and so they cling to it like a flasher with a crusty comfort blanket?

Woke Sex recalls that of Huxley's Brave New World, inflicted in anger and conformity rather than the glee and curiosity which impelled my generation. Like most aspects of Wokeness it is performative and porn-sick; what cheap thrill is there in the quiet marching of Martin Luther King and his disciples when you could be filmed kneeling to kiss the feet of quite understandably jeering young black men? And nowhere is this more evidence than in the rise of the monstrous regiment of extreme trans-activists gone gaga, hence the union of 'trans 'and 'goons.'

Believing that 'trans women are women' is the highest article of Woke cultism. Though it is 'cultural appropriation' for a white woman to wear her hair in cornrows, it is perfectly fine for a man - with a penis, as men tend to - to say he 'feels' like a woman. Any woman objecting to this gigantic slice of cultural appropriation will promptly be branded a bad feminist for refusing to embrace a hairy great plate of prong and two veg. She will, in short, be a TERF - a trans-exclusionary radical feminist, and a word as much as cis which is designed to isolate and demonise those adult human females who believe that incels in thongs are probably not the first people women want to share public toilets with.

When it comes to men in frocks, it seems they've utterly lost the ability to pull one on (or off) in a lighthearted and rebellious manner. What we have now is the mincing mainstreaming of drag on one hand - Womanface, which is nothing more than Woke Blackface - and the clod-hopping march of the Troons on the other. Silly Draggers and Sinister Troons are the garishly befrocked pincer action to erase and replace women, allowing only those females utterly compliant to the new orthodoxy to keep their place in public life; handmaidens whose lives should be spent servicing these Brave And Stunning Kweens.

That this small pressure group has risen so rapidly to own the narrative covering everything from Labour Party shortlists to endlessly deep corporate pockets is easily explained as just the latest ingenious way a misogynist establishment attempts to drive back the rights of women now that saying 'Women aren't as good as men' just won't cut it anymore. But dress selected men up **as** women, say they **are** women and hey presto! People with penises are able to grasp back everything that seemed in danger of being taken from them. Having failed to beat women from the outside, some mentally unhinged kamikaze squads would now attempt to do it from the inside.

Be clear, 'trans rights' is not a liberation struggle of some oppressed minority; it is a male supremacy movement, made up of wolves in ewes clothing, which rose up nursing its painful and unwanted collective erection alongside the incels, so up to their eyes in it that they can't see the forest for their wood. Their 'allies' are just as dumb, with Matt Healy of the pop group The 1975 opining loftily in spring 2020:

'Toilets are the new water fountains - it's not about the water fountain and it's not about the toilet.'[5] He's right - it's about the wanking. Because all black people in the segregated Southern states of the U.S.A wanted was to use the same toilets as other people; this lot want to masturbate in them.

That's because they are not 'trans' anything, implying as the word does some sort of journey from being one thing to another. A few creatures are capable of 'transitioning' ('across' 'beyond' 'through') like tadpoles into frogs and caterpillars into butterflies - but not human beings last time I looked. The lunacy that biology can be overcome by 'feelings' - that men can become women - is as frankly preposterous as putting a tiny saddle on a seahorse and expecting it to win the Grand National. As the American thinker Emily Zinos put it:

> 'The ontological impossibility of becoming the opposite sex is why there's such a frantic emphasis on passing gender identity laws: the only way to 'be' the opposite sex is through a legal definition. **Outside of words, gender identity simply doesn't exist.'**

They say that if you're going to tell a lie, make it a big one, and the modern Troon rarely even bothers to make the slightest concessions to looking like a woman, having grown arrogant in the assurance of \*allies\* that he is a Brave And Stunning Kween who just wakes up like that. On the contrary, they seem to take a delight in posting pictures on social media with three day's stubble boasting that no one can tell Stork from butter and that their 'girldicks' bring all the dishy straight guys to the yard. I will admit that I can rarely resist the temptation to post the pithy request GET THE PINTS IN, MATE! whenever I see such a creature, this phrase having become something of a rallying cry when my Mean Terf mates and I greet each other in cyberspace.

But even those who have The Operation - what we used to call a 'sex-change'[6] in my youth - while to be awarded A for effort are wasting their time. The 'neo-vaginas' - \*fauxginas\* - they spend so much time cooing over are nothing more than open wounds which must be propped ajar, often indefinitely, with dilators lest that awful old TERF Mother Nature tries to heal up what she registers as a life-threatening gash. Sex without lubrication is inadvisable, unless the proud possessor literally wants to be ripped a new one, which considering the competitiveness of some might appeal to many of them, possibly rendering them *twice the woman* than we insignificant born women. As wounds are wont to, the fauxgina will attract vast swathes of bacteria, causing alarming smells to emit from the downstairs department. And as if this wasn't mucky enough, many of these creatures boast of raiding the bins in the Ladies in search of soiled sanitary wear; not so much a Lady Garden as a Chamber of Horrors.

Still, once you've had your testicles lopped off, the skin of your penis turned inside out and your scrotum turned into a labia major, foraging for tampons must seem quite mild in comparison. Though their proud owners like to purr about how superior their souped-up pussies are, they're actually a bit of a bouillabaisse, and getting fishier all the time. In 2019 a Brazilian became the first lucky person to have a vagina made out of fish scales, after the fauxgina bestowed on them twenty years earlier collapsed. 'I'm absolutely thrilled with the result,' they rejoiced. 'For the first time in my life I feel complete and like a real woman.'

Of course, if people were paying for their own body modification, no one would mind if they went all the way with the marine life theme and became actual mermaids. Though one may consider the whole idea of attempting to change sex as ultimately futile, we don't tell those bright sparks who have their tongues split due to their longing to live their one and only life answering to the name of The Lizard King that they can't do what they like with their own bodies. It's when the state is called upon to indulge body dysmorphia that we need to ask ourselves questions about exactly why we favour some fantasies and not others. Before the law changed in 1999, transsexuals who could not afford £10,000 for the pleasure of turning their genitalia into Abattoir Pick'n'Mix would apply to their local health authority for assistance and failing that pay for themselves. In the first year after it was ruled by the Appeal Court that those who believed they were born into the wrong body were suffering from a legitimate illness, 49 people took advantage of the offer, with the usual bias of eighty per cent seeking male to female alteration. They were obviously satisfied customers because in the coming decade more than one thousand such ops took place, costing the National Health Service around some £10 million.

Of course this is a drop in the ocean. But is it really the place of a country's overwhelmed health service to cater to fantasies? Would a doctor tell an emaciated person suffering from anorexia nervosa that because she thinks she's overweight she really is overweight, and so offer her gastric band surgery in order to rid her of her imaginary fat? What about the 'transabled' community, who labour under a delusion recognised as Body Integrity Identity Disorder since 2013 and who in 2015 were the subject of a fascinating report by Canada's National Post?

'We define transability as the desire or the need for a person identified as able-bodied by other people to transform his or her body to obtain a physical impairment, explained' the Canadian academic Alexandre Baril.[7] 'The person could want to become deaf, blind, amputee, paraplegic. It's a really, really strong desire.'

I'll say. One dedicated fellow cut off his own arm with 'a very sharp power tool' so that he could go by the name 'One hand Jason'[8] and tell tall tales of a tragic accident. Yet another loss to the Brains Trust dropped heavy concrete slabs on to his legs in order to get them amputated; doctors worked hard to save them and he had to be satisfied with a pronounced limp while swearing to continue until his limbs are permanently sundered. One bright spark surveyed wanted his penis removed; you'd think the transgendered would embrace their comrade in kinkiness but many trans-activists have expressed hostility to the idea. Professor Baril,[9] himself trans and disabled, says: 'They tend to see transabled people as dishonest people who try to steal resources from the community, people who would be disrespectful by denying or fetishising or romanticising disability reality.' Not like those loonies who go ferreting through bins in search of bloody tampons are romanticising the reality of little girls dying in 'menstrual huts' all over the developing world. Of course body dysmorphia exists - but it should be treated as a mental illness, not indulged, any more than people who think they're Napoleon should be assisted in invading Russia.

The Frankenstein fauxgina being as unfit for purpose as it is, it's hardly surprising the vast majority of Troons wish to hold on (literally) to their penises, preferably in the Ladies lavatories. They are Autogynephiles ('The paraphilic tendency of a biological male to be sexually aroused by the thought of becoming a female, sometimes considered a form of gender identity disorder or transvestic fetishism') a long and unlovely word which sums up perfectly the repulsiveness of a group of hardcore PAMS (fuelled by the best-avoided *sissy porn* in which the connection between AGPs and paedophiles is there for all to see) who have somehow managed to make a sizeable part of society believe the supreme insult that a man need only say the magic words 'Think pink'[10] and he is automatically a woman.

Toilets are their frontline, proving how degraded and frivolous their alleged *struggle* is; many boast of urinating all over the seats in the Ladies with their dainty little *girldicks*. They really do use this word, hilariously, and without realising the revolting risibility of statements such as 'Straight men can just think of it as a clitoris which is really easy to find - surely an advantage?' As far as I can tell, a *girldick* is just a regular dick with delusions of grandeur, as in the case of the poor soul who looked like a Spinal Tap roadie posting a photo with the caption YES, MY GIRLDICK IS MASSIVE, STOP ASKING. They are male supremacists gone the sissified scenic route who don't want women to have nice things to themselves so they take them and spoil them; incels who have learned that tears get them their way more than threats, though threats are always available as back up. Their desire to tear down the fragile freedoms and modest celebrations which women have built up in the face of centuries of oppression and sorrow goes far beyond sexual perversion. Characteristically of male tyrants, they hate women to gather together, for fear of what rebellion they may be fermenting, and so they insert themselves into every situation possible. Like all bullies, they draw a dark nourishment from their hive mind, encouraging each other on in new ways to humiliate and erase women.

How do they hate us? Let me count the ways. First they take our prizes. In 2015 Caitlyn Jenner is awarded the Glamour Woman Of The Year Award; James Smith, widower of Moira Smith, the only female NYPD officer to die during the attacks on the World Trade Centre while facilitating the escape of workers, returns her posthumous award, writing in an open letter to the magazine's editor: 'I was shocked and saddened to learn that Glamour has just named Bruce Jenner 'Woman of the Year'… was there no woman in America, or the rest of the world, more deserving than this man?' By 2020 not just individual women's awards but even International Women's Day was taking the knee to the Troons, with the United Nations Tweeting a list of those being celebrated with special guest stars 'Womxn' 'Trans' and 'Genderqueer' while re-Tweeting the words of wisdom of one Aaron Philip, a black, disabled, transgender model:

> 'Trans women are women at the end of the day. Every woman is a woman. Women are multifaceted, intergenerational, international. They are limitless, formless ... women are the world.'

Are black people limitless and formless? Are disabled people? He makes us sound like ghosts, but without the individuality and personality of a cheeky Caspar or an audacious Slimer. As one feminist joked, no doubt wryly, wouldn't the day better be done with pesky women altogether and rebrand itself as the super-inclusive 'International Formless Void Day'?

It's not like the Troons don't already have many separate days on which to celebrate their brave and stunning selves:

> International Day Against Transphobia (May 17)
> International Pronouns Day (3rd Wednesday in October)
> International Transgender Day of Visibility (March 31)
> LGBT History Month (nowadays more T History Month) (February or October, depending on country, or why not both!)
> LGBT Pride Month (also now all about the T) (June)
> National Coming Out Day (Oct 11)
> Spirit Day (3rd Thursday in October, about LGBTQ+ kids)
> Stonewall Riots Anniversary (Marsha P. Johnson day) (June 28)
> Trans Parent Day (First Sunday in November)
> Transgender Awareness Week (Second week of November)
> Transgender Day of Remembrance (Nov 20)
> International Drag Day (July 16)
> International Men's Day (November 19)

And they still need to *muscle in* on us girls one special day - why, it's almost as if their craving for validation never ends. Almost like they need to have their fantasies endlessly refracted back to them, lest they wake up and smell the fish scales for a moment.

They take our sport. I'm personally opposed to exertion on philosophical grounds but for many young women sport is a vivifying way to navigate adolescence in a world where youthful female bodies can easily oppress their owners by attracting the non-stop male gaze. Imagine being a young girl finding out about all the ways a body can be without having to be starved, primped and laid out for public approval, relishing a camaraderie which is about competition that's nothing to do with male attention - and then some man a foot taller, two stone heavier and three times a lady in his own demented mind tramples all over every effort to excel you've ever strived for.

Any fool who believes that these people only want to be allowed to play nicely with women needs to check out the statements which mire Troon take-overs of sports from cycling and martial arts. Rachel McKinnon[11] is the pink-haired Canadian Woke Bro who went by the far more appropriate name of Rhys until the age of 29 and who in 2018 became the world champion of women's track cycling despite being biologically male. Pleasingly, his university thesis was subtitled 'Why You Don't Need to Know What You're Talking About' while a later book was called 'The Norms of Assertion: Truth, Lies and Warrant' in which he argues that 'in some special contexts, we can lie.' Would those be lies like answering the question 'Does my dick look big in these cycling shorts?' in such a way as to escape the wrath of this puce-locked man-mountain? A veritable hotchpotch of fear and loathing, McKinnon celebrated the death of the young feminist activist Magdalen Berns[12] by Tweeting that he was 'happy' when 'bad people' died and advised his followers 'Don't be the sort of person who people you've harmed are happy you're dying of brain cancer' and dismissed her complaining competitors as 'losers.' When in 2019 the Olympic swimmer Sharon Davies[13] Tweeted 'I believe there is a fundamental difference between the binary sex you are born with and the gender you may identify as. To protect women's sport those with a male sex advantage should not be able to compete in women's sport' McKinnon's reaction was to Tweet a photograph of Davies and accuse her of looking like a man. Pot, kettle, dirty great mug identifying as tiny tinkling teacup!

But McKinnon appears as threatening as a Tiny Tears compared to Fallon Fox[14] (born Boyd Burton) the ex-truck driver who became the first Troon MMA (Mixed Martial Arts) fighter, Tweeting that he enjoys 'smacking up TERFS…for the record, I knocked [two] women out…one's skull was fractured, the other not. And just so you know, I enjoyed it. It's bliss. Don't be mad.' Nevertheless this creature was inducted into the National Gay and Lesbian Sports Hall of Fame in 2014 and on its retirement in 2020 was named in Outsports magazine as 'the bravest athlete in history.' That'll teach women to seek mastery over their own bodies, and to dare to aspire to some branch of physical excellence beside inspiring Woke Bros to wank over them.

If sport seems a dangerous way that women may feel the power of their bodies, how much more threatening to inadequate men - befrocked or not - are political meetings where we gather, daring to dream of a world where we are not just bodies. One of the most grotesque developments of the recent years has been the sight of young men - Woke Bros to a man - yelling in the faces of women who have the audacity to organise, in Woke cities from Bristol in the U.K to Seattle in the U.S.A. A ghastly mixture of Little Lord Fauntelroys and Little Bo Peeps, their privately-educated voices yelling 'TRANS RIGHTS ARE HUMAN RIGHTS!' will bring a thrill of class-war contempt to anyone who has spent time on genuine picket lines which were more concerned with people keeping their jobs rather than the right to put on a pencil skirt and call oneself Penelope when one is clearly Pete.

Just because they're funny, though, doesn't mean they're not nasty. Looking at any massed ranks of Troons, one is struck by the sheer sex-starved unhingedness of them. Though one hates to resort to a sexist old slur, one can't help but wonder if (as so much about them is a parody of femininity anyway) they're Slaves To Their Hormones. Hormone therapy is a huge part of the transgender experience and it would be impossible for that all that estrogen, antiandrogen and progestogen (sound like characters from Waiting For Godot) to churn about in the male system without some sort of havoc being wrecked. Add to this the fact that these powerful drugs are available without prescription from online pharmacies and you've got the conditions for a perfect storm of saliva-soaked swearing whenever a hated TERF hoves into view.

These people will do anything to avoid a debate lest we 'let in daylight upon magical thinking' - the belief that one's ideas, thoughts, wishes, or actions can influence the course of events in the physical world, to misquote Bagehot on monarchy. Seeing the baying mobs of Woke Bros, Troons and transmaidens out at night attempting to stop some woman from speaking truth to penis, their faces covered, their voices full of impotent rage, is how this book got its title. It's like the Frankenstein film in reverse; here come the hordes of monsters with their pitchforks and flaming torches, bent on burning down biology itself. I daresay Frankenstein's monster considered himself the good guy as he blundered around crushing things - but ask yourself, would you really want him in the next toilet cubicle to you when you had your frillies down around your ankles?

One of the favourite Troon truisms is that 'words are literally violence;' something of a surprise to those of us brought up to believe that while sticks and stones may break our bones, words will never hurt us. The earliest citation of which is, interestingly, from an American periodical with a largely black audience, The Christian Recorder,[15] which added admirably in a 1862 edition 'True courage consists in doing what is right, despite the jeers and sneers of our companions.' How telling that black Americans more than a century ago had a more robust attitude to name-calling than the affluent white They of today!

One of the core achievements of the Enlightenment - the rise of reason - was the separation between word and deed. In olden dayes, people believed in magic; that thoughts and speech could affect the physical world. If we regress to equating word and deed, we throw away three hundred years of progress; without this understanding we would still be in the Middle Ages, and men would still be free to burn uppity women as witches. Woke: the only philosophy which sees Medievalism as Utopia.

Considering their stunning lack of wit (I **literally** cannot recall one trans-activist saying just one funny thing, though considering the way most of them look, maybe they prefer visual gags?) it makes sense that the Troons might feel better about themselves if we dropped language altogether and just grunted. This being the case it was dismayingly predictable that (as many men do in situations of domestic violence) some Troons would argue that physically attacking women was fine as they had been hurt by their words. The most notable of these was Tara Wolf who in 2018 went on trial for the assault of Maria MacLachlan the previous year when the outrageously feminist opinions of a group of feminists at Speaker's Corner proved too much for delicate Troon sensibilities. That Wolf was in their 20s and MacLachlan in her 60s led an especially cowardly air to the attack - basically, a hefty youth attacking a woman old enough to be their grandmother.

Showing the weaselly Wokeness which the law displays with wretched regularity, District Judge Kenneth Grant seemed more concerned with language than with literal violence, rebuking Ms MacLachlan 'The defendant wished to be referred to as a woman, so perhaps you could refer to her as 'she' for the purpose of the proceedings.'[16] To which Ms MacLachlan robustly replied: 'I'm used to thinking of this person who is a male as male.'

Maria told me:

> 'I didn't fear assault that day. To me, they looked like a bunch of silly but harmless kids. I wasn't impressed that they had followed a group of peaceful women to Speakers Corner to shout and try to drown out our voices but I recognised it was their right to do so and that I had the right to film them doing so. I was very shocked that a man of 25 would attack an older woman doing nothing more than filming and trying to talk to them. I am in no doubt that he attacked me because I was an older woman standing apart from the other women who'd gathered for the meeting - an easy target - while he had the support of his crowd of mates.
>
> In court, it was while I was having to watch a video recording of the attack on me and answer questions about it that the judge snapped, 'What's the problem?' He said the court had agreed as a matter of courtesy to respect Wolf's identity as a woman and suggested I might like to do the same and refer to him as 'she.' That I should be expected to afford a violent man the courtesy of indulging his fantasy blew my mind. I told the judge that I was used to thinking of Wolf as male because that's what he is. In his summing up the judge referred to my response as 'bad grace.' He came across as just another male bully trying to control and punish an uppity woman.'

The support for Wolf at the court was suitably thuggish: 'Two dozen individuals — mostly men with masks on, some in full combat gear — accompanied Wolf. Many were wearing the all black uniform of Antifa, replete with bandanas and sunglasses. Most were recognized by a member of our group as belonging to Class War, an anarchist organization that Wolf is also a member of. Three of Wolf's supporters brought fighting dogs, as well as a huge sound system blaring death metal. The machismo of it all was palpable,'[17] wrote Jen Izaakson in Feminist Current. As many men who assault women do, Wolf walked free from court with a derisory fine; indeed, the judge seemed crosser with Ms MacLachlan who he branded 'ungraceful' for failing to refer to Wolf as 'she' during the trial.[18]

Wolf emerged as something between the Little Orphan Annie and Michelle Obama, given the financial equivalent of a rap on the granny-bashing knuckles for her beating of a senior citizen. Her lawyer, tiny violin screeching, sought to exonerate Wolf due to her autism; very common in Troons, interestingly, which may explain their bafflement about how boyish girls and girlish boys could once happily exist without lopping off their genitals, not to mention getting a whole load of *action* from both sexes. They also suffer from something called Oppositional Defiant Disorder, which the Mayo Cinic defines thus:

> 'Even the best-behaved children can be difficult and challenging at times. But if your child or teenager has a frequent and persistent pattern of anger, irritability, arguing, defiance or vindictiveness toward you and other authority figures, he or she may have Oppositional Defiant Disorder (ODD).'

There's a funny and very telling finish to this serious case, vis a vis the fandom of the British police towards the Troon Army. Jen Izaakson concludes:

> 'Afterwards, we were ordered by police to stay inside the court due to the danger posed by the trans activists outside, almost all of whom were members of Class War. As we walked up the hill to a pub, a police van containing 10 police officers pulled up alongside the two lesbian feminists leading our group. The Class War activists had apparently gone to the pub, spotted these women walking up the hill, and called the police.
>
> Particularly ironic is the fact that Class War are loud critics of what they call "carceral feminism," a pejorative term used to

smear feminists who seek justice through the legal system. Class War criticize women who telephone the police about crimes, including male violence, yet the officers informed us that they had received a phone call from the "other group in court" alerting them of our arrival. Apparently, the Class War activists couldn't stomach our jubilation and camaraderie, or having to watch women relish a celebratory pint. What they could stomach, however, was throwing their anti-cop politics in the bin, phoning the police over a group consisting mainly of middle-aged lesbians. Some of them even came outside to smile at the police presence barring our crossing the road to the pub.'

Presumably quite dizzy from all that close contact with hunky men in uniform, later that evening Wolf posted a comment on Facebook saying that MacLachlan was 'a man' so therefore Wolf's violence was 'actually misandry.' Even later that night he changed his Facebook name to 'Tara The TERF Slayer' so one can easily imagine that quite a few sweet sherries were consumed that triumphant evening when a man in his twenties paid a tiny fine after being found guilty of attacking a woman in her sixties. [19]

How else do they hate us? They get us sacked from our jobs. With so little time and so many women to harass, it's understandable that a high proportion of trans-activists appear not to work but prefer to spend a good deal of their splendid lives scrounging on social media.

To skivers with a desperate need for attention, the simple truth that the best way to get attention is to work hard at something you're good at for a prolonged period of time could be scribblings in Sanskrit. Bitterly envious of female achievement (see above all Rowling, J.K) they don't believe that women should be allowed to have nice things like jobs, unless they are utterly compliant to the Troon agenda and thus have rendered themselves female eunuchs fit to serve in the hermaphrodite harem. Once more, my theory that Wokeness is reactionary, not rebellious, is demonstrated in the way the Troons care not a jot for hard-won workers rights but love to blab to the boss-class who can then promptly dump any employee who dares to have a non-approved view. It's a sign of the crazy times we live in that allegedly Left-wing people believe employers should be able to sack people for their private opinions.

Women's access to any work beyond the menial is relatively recent, their barring from higher education making sure that well-paid and high-status occupations were the preserve of men; astonishingly Oxford didn't admit women on the same terms as men till 1921, while Cambridge put it off till 1947. There was a belief that higher education would cause our uteruses to shrivel up - a lovely bit of male logical thinking in action. But the struggle wasn't over; as soon as we got our foot in the door, many men put their hands up our skirts. A 2017 survey by the BBC found that a full half of all British women have been sexually harassed at their place of work. As if we didn't have enough to put up with - giving the phrase 'the daily grind' a whole other sleazy meaning - with the rise of the Troons a new male threat to women's right to earn their own living emerged. Maya Forstater,[20] a tax expert at the Centre for Global Development, was not entitled to express her views on whether men can be women without losing her job in 2019. She told me:

> 'Like many people I came into this debate thinking that there must be a sensible way to find the answer on to how to support women's rights and transgender people's rights. I worked at a think tank. My colleagues were smart, analytical economists; serious about evidence and argument. I did not see it coming; that this was the one thing you could not talk about. I tweeted about the gender recognition act and I tweeted about Phillip/Pips Bunce - a man who works at Credit Suisse and who comes to work some days in a dress and a wig. He was given an award as a 'woman in business' by the Financial Times. I thought this was offensive. But some young women in the Washington DC office thought that it was offensive for me to talk about it. When they raised the issue, organisation crumbled. All of their commitment to robust debate and evidence fell away, they investigated me and eventually after five months they let me go.

> I am sure that none of the senior staff have any confusion about what a woman is. Like me they understand that sex is real and that the human rights of transgender people can be protected without rewriting reality. But the pressure to stay quiet is too great.

> I see this happening everywhere. People start off thinking that this is a simple matter of liberalism and inclusion, an extension of gay rights. Then if they read and think a bit more they realise that what is being asked is not just that adults can live their life as they chose, but that institutions deny the reality of sex and replace it with gender identity, and that children are told they

can be 'born in the wrong body.' A few people keep speaking up, and many have faced consequences; loss of friends, loss of work. Many are only able to speak up anonymously on Twitter, or in private, writing to their MP and talking to their friends. But those people in positions of influence that could have made the space to have a proper clear debate about how to balance human rights, have been silent or compliant. They have repeated the slogans 'trans rights are human rights' but refused to consider the implications of the idea that people can change sex just by saying so. They have kept their jobs by keeping quiet and looking the other way at the abuse of women. The silencing of anyone who could stand up to gender ideology has been brutal and effective.'

How else do they hate us? They take the safe spaces - how ironic that the Woke who talk so much about Safe Spaces are determined for those who really need them not to have them - which are so essential to those of us who have suffered male violence. In Canada the government has stopped funding rape crisis centres and women's domestic violence refuges if male-bodied female-identifiers are not allowed in. Because that's just what you want when you've been attacked by a man - a stranger with a penis in the next bed.

Though the Woke Bros in their struggle against *systemic* (the smashed avocado on toast of politics - once completely unheard of, now everywhere) racism lead the marches demanding the defunding of the police, they are very much brothers under the skin, united in their murky misogyny. For their part, the police - always keen to turn a blind eye to grooming gangs - have found a whole new wonderland of woman-hating in Woke.

Some of it's just silly. The Thames Valley Police appear as a partner on the website of an organization called MyUmbrella which, if you still aren't convinced of how sumptuously insane gender-warriors are, will totally make a convert of you. According to MyUmbrella, there are 371 genders; my favourite must be Tetrisgender[21] - 'A person whose gender identity builds up over time, but once they feel like they've completed their gender identity, it disappears. Just like in Tetris, where you build up blocks over time only to have the lines disappear' - though you're spoilt for choice. 'But this is just lip service - it doesn't affect the way the police actually operate!' you'll be scoffing by now.

People have been arrested, held in cells and fined for *misgendering* on social media. In 2019 Harry Miller,[22] a former policeman who campaigns for freedom of speech under the name Fair Cop, re-Tweeted a rather striking free-form poem:

> 'You're a man.
> Your breasts are made of silicone
> Your vagina goes nowhere
> And we can tell the difference
> Even when you are not there
> Your hormones are synthetic
> And lets just cross this bridge
> What you have you stupid man
> Is male privilege.'

A policeman promptly engaged Mr Miller on the telephone for more than half an hour, accusing him of 'hate speech.' When he asked if he had committed a crime, Plod replied 'It's not a crime, but it will be recorded as a hate incident.' Harry says:

> 'This is where it gets incredibly sinister. The cop told me that he needed to speak with me because, even though I'd committed no crime whatsoever, he needed (and I quote) 'To check my THINKING.' Finally, he lectured me: 'Sometimes, a woman's brain grows a man's body in the womb and that is what transgender is.' You can imagine my response. Lastly, he told me that I needed to watch my words more carefully or I was as risk of being sacked by my company for hate speech.'

From the ceaseless police coddling and propaganda on their behalf, you'd be forgiven for thinking that *trans folk* (they love to call themselves *folk* with the wholesome overtones of The Little House On The Prairie) are without doubt the most defenceless and law-abiding sector of society - sort of like Mixed Infants crossed with Amish elders. But however much mascara they may trowel on, men dressed as women seem to conform to a crime-pattern far more male than female.

Even a brief skimming of the news media from the year 2020 produces a selection of stomach-turning Troon crimes. A cross-dressing Labour councillor from Devon, Roger Spackman, walked free from court after being found guilty of possessing nearly 300,000 child pornography images 'He likes to pretend he is a young girl who will be abused,' Mr Spackman's barrister explained. Anthony Scales[23] of Derby swerved a custodial sentence for child pornography possession after his defence claimed his 'gender dysphoria' as an excuse: 'He is a 64-year-old man who now presents as a woman' - well, that's alright, then! A Blackpool *woman* was reported as accessing *her* vast collection of child pornography from a hospital bed while recovering from a heart attack - except *her* name was John Marshall; unusually, this one was jailed for a few months. But being *trans* can literally be a Get Out Of Jail card as in the case of an Iowan paedophile who sexually abused fifteen children - including a one year-old baby - but had their sentence cut short after taking hormones which lowered their testosterone levels in their bid to become a born-again law-abiding lady.

These are just a handful of many reports of Troon crimes from the year this book is being written but there are many, many more for anyone with the stomach for a more in-depth delve. Nevertheless, to hear their cavilling, you'd think that they were only ever sinned against, as with the repeated lie that we are living through some some of transgender murder epidemic. But though they identify as victims, Troons are far more likely to be involved in violent crimes as perpetrators. Since prisons made the ludicrous decision in 2016 to allow people with penises into women's prisons simply because they clicked their ruby slippers three times and said 'I'm a lady' they have carried out seven sex attacks on women in jail, being responsible for 5.6 of sexual assault despite being one per cent of those incarcerated in female prisons. Moreover, the former Prisons Minister Rory Stewart[24] claimed that there had been 'situations of male prisoners self-identifying as females then raping staff in prison.'

Aside from the obvious stupidity and cruelty of allowing violent men access to vulnerable women with literally nowhere to run, there's a less shocking but sneakier aspect. All these crimes will be recorded as having been committed by women; in future times, our descendants will look back and wonder why large numbers of women suddenly became so vile. Women make up less five per cent of the prison population, mostly for non-violent offences but this has never stopped the more misogynist type of newspaper from why-oh-whying annually, when the latest crime statistics are released, about how much more violent women are becoming. Invariably, the headline will be something like Deadlier Than The Male (question mark optional). This searingly original query also raises its head whenever a cold-blooded female killer is sighted - though, of course, the fact that we can recite the unholy canon of Myra Hindley, Mary Bell, Beverley Allitt and Rosemary West simply demonstrates how rare such women are. If we tried to recall the list of cold-blooded male killers who've been brought to justice in the post-War world, we'd still be here at the next millenium. At the turn of the century, the Daily Mail ran a piece claiming that the female prison population had doubled in five years - but even if 17% of prisoners are now women, they're mostly in for shoplifting, fraud and not paying their TV licence while men, remain steadily dependable at 83% with rape, murder and child molesting.

It won't be like this in the future, now that male crimes are recorded regularly as having been committed by women. So telling a man he isn't a woman counts as a hate crime - but lying about the frequency of evil behaviour of a whole half of the world's population for posterity is progress.

*

Women aren't children, though we were treated as much until relatively recently. Anyone who grows up as a girl gets wise early on to the various ways various men will attempt to abuse, use or screw her, given half a chance; learning to spot and avoid these situations is a lovely little *skill-set* which we are cis-privileged to absorb before we reach the age of consenting to being abused, used or screwed. But we never saw this coming; these latest strange side-stepping stitches in life's rich post-modern tapestry. We never dreamt that there would be a whole new way we could be invalidated, disrespected and gaslighted. That the day would come in the year 2020 when in Canada (a country which increasingly looks like a once-mature senile delinquent going through a mid-life crisis determined to show how Down With The Kids it can be) a six-year-old girl would go home and, in some distress, tell her parents her teacher had told her that 'girls were not real.'

Sex education in schools in always a *hot potato* - Woke-mockers like me will have greatly enjoyed the disruption of the Cloud

Cuckoo Coalition in 2019 when mainly Muslim parents were seen squabbling with same-sex shaggers (why, it's almost as if GAYS FOR PALESTINE is an absolute slice of wank-puffin paradox) outside schools across the land as they protested/promoted the teaching of homosexuality to primary school children. How much more confusing for children not yet able to spell Autogynephile (mind you, I keep having to look it up) to absorb the fact that girls and boys are figments of our collective imagination!

Of course the vast majority of paedophiles are *straight* men, if that isn't the creepiest of word combinations. But it's impossible to ignore the fact that those who argue for transgender rights do seem unhealthily keen on co-opting children into their cult in a way even the Jesuits have stopped boasting about; give a tot Drag Queen Story Time till they're seven and they'll spout bollocks about non-binary gender-fluidity for life. In 2020 another flag began turning up alongside those who saw themselves as sexual Tetris; in stripes of dark blue, light blue, dark pink, light pink, yellow and white, it represented MAPs - Minor-Attracted Person, as they now call themselves, paedophilia quite rightly being something of a dirty word.

We'd been here before, of course, when the Paedophile Information Exchange (PIE) attempted to piggy-back in on the gay liberation movement to push for such policies as lowering the age of consent to ten. Whenever the world today seems mad, remember that Time Out once had as its front page headline PAEDOPHILIA: THE DIFFICULT ONE while the National Council Of Civil Liberties[25] (led by the lily-white Labour grande dame Harriet Harman) granted 'PIE' formal affiliate status. This being the case, I can't say that I was shocked when the leading light of PIE, Thomas O'Carroll (last seen having his collar felt by the Labour Party in 2016 when it realised that its ranks contained someone even less popular than Jeremy Corbyn) popped up disguised as a new-fangled gender-fluid type crushing over the 12-year-old American Drag Queen who goes by the not-backward-in-coming-forward name of Desmond Is Amazing. His mother Wendylou Napoles, who has been happily promoting him to perform in gay nightclubs where men throw

money at him for some years, was appalled to read O'Carroll's open love
letter to her son:

> 'Desmond is truly amazing — and hot! Being a drag queen, or
> a drag princess if you will, puts it right out there in the open for
> all to see. It says loud and proud 'I am a sexy kid with sexy
> feelings. It's totally cool for grown-ups to get turned on by me.
> I love it. That's why I do this stuff.' We are getting far more
> than just a celebration of gender diversity or an innocent display
> of precocious performance talent. So why all the denial? Why
> the coy insistence that kids 'drag performance has nothing to do
> with their sexuality?'

Desmond's momager retorted:

> 'It is highly inappropriate to speak of minors in this manner.
> Just because Desmond identifies as gay does not mean he is
> sexually active or wants to be. We are just appalled at this whole
> situation.'

It's truly a surreal world when one finds oneself in agreement with
a man who probably believes that two-year-olds have tantrums because
they're forbidden to have sex with him, but in this case O'Carroll is
correct. Poor Desmond, dumb with lipgloss and blind with mascara, is
obviously a sex object to the screaming queens who drop loose change
down his sequinned hot-pants. And it's only because Wokedom has
promoted transing to a state of grace which must never be challenged that
everyone involved gets away with it.

I have many gay mates who become as outraged as any Mumsnet
member at the way Wokeness has muddied the water between the perfectly
justifiable right of adult homosexuals to go about their business in peace
(if not in public) with the distinctly weird desire of adults to leer at children
or peer at urinating women in the name of civil rights. In turn, sensing their
strength as business after business takes up their cause in the hope of
grabbing the Woke Wad as they once did with the Pink Pound, the Troon
Massive are now increasingly turning on the gay community which they
once hitched their wagon to in the hope that their outrageous demands
might somehow be mistaken for something as reasonable as the same-sex
age of consent.

Troons are bullies, so they tend to leave gay men alone - so many of those Muscle Marys are so strong from all those hours in the gym, while the transies exercise little but their wrists. But they approach the lesbian community with immense fear and loathing. Lesbian porn being the choice of the man fearful he can't measure up to the massive tackle of the male performers, Troons both desire and despise their chosen sex objects to the point that when they are not preaching to them that they are *transphobic* for rejecting *trans-women* and that a good dose of *lady-dick* would sort them out, they are referring to them as 'hairy barren lesbians' and 'saggy old dykes.'

It's ironic that whereas homophobia once came from reactionary institutions and individuals - whether it was actual conversion therapy or the unsolicited sidewalk advice to gay women that all they needed was a good seeing-to - it now comes from the section of society which considers itself the most enlightened. By way of the pornography which sustains these creatures as surely as oxygen does the rest of us, the message that all lesbians are waiting for a cock has wormed its way deep into the wizened brains of the Troon massive. We're ladies - but with dicks! Surely every porn lesbian's dream?

Growing up in the twentieth century, every young woman who ventured into Bohemia eventually met a man who believed that it was somehow seductive to leer into her ear that he was really not a lecherous man at all but rather 'a lesbian trapped in a man's body.' If our I.Q ran into double figures, we'd howl with derision and tell him he wasn't anywhere near cute enough to be a lesbian. These days, a man can say this and - in Woke circles - young women are expected to go along with it. The experience even has a suitably bed-post notch and saw-conquered-came name; the Cotton Ceiling, coined by the Canadian Troon activist and porn performer Drew DeVeaux, which with unashamed seat-sniffery refers to the gusset of what these creeps no doubt think of as *panties*. (Said no real woman ever.) The insensitivity and one-track-mindedness of these woman-hunters in shepherd's clothing is unconsciously revealed with its derivation from the phrase Glass Ceiling, referring to the age-old discrimination against women in the workplace. For some strange reason, though they repeat the mantra TRANS WOMEN ARE WOMEN with all the nuance and variety of a Dalek expressing destructive intent, Troons seem extremely reluctant to have sex with each other. It's almost as if should two *girl-dicks* touch the embarrassed owners would immediately be faced with the uncomfortable fact that they were actually just two gay men in drag all along.

Grown lesbians are tough enough to resist any phallus-waving half-wit who demands sex on the grounds it's inhuman to say no to a trapped inner lesbian and have responded with appropriate combativeness. As the small but perfectly informed group calling themselves Get The L Out[26] put it 'We believe that lesbian rights are under attack by the trans movement and we encourage lesbians everywhere to leave the LGBT movement.' But young girls who may be confused or troubled by their sexuality can be easy pickings for a new kind of predator; one who comes bearing not sweets but stirring words about being born in the wrong body accompanied by a programme of puberty-blockers. Seeking to rebel against their parents yet conform to their contemporaries, the chance to identify as *trans* must seem a merciful escape for a girl to whom the prospect of being a grown woman seems nightmarish. It's an interesting and ineffably sad aspect of the different reasons why the sexes want to swop over; men often identify as women because they are porn-sick whereas girls want to become boys because they are sick of porn.

The number of children referred to the NHS service through which all candidates for a sex change under 18 in this country are processed rose from 77 in 2009 to 2,590 in 2019. In 2007 the overall ratio had been 75% males seeking to be female; ten years later 70% of referrals were females seeking to be male. Many of these girls have mental health problems long before gender dysphoria gets its fangs into them. Everything from anxiety to autism can trigger a state of existential panic which can see *transitioning* as a cut-and-dried (literally, when one considers the invasiveness of genital swapsies) answer to what can often seem unfathomable to the over-loaded adolescent mind. And never forget the power of the herd, which is strong is the young, shipwrecked between the simplicity of childhood and the sophistication of adulthood and seeking some shelter from the storm of uncertainty. For teenage girls in particular peer groups are everything. A friend of mine who worked in a private psychiatric practice in London traced the first wave of self-harm from the top tier of fee-paying girls day schools down to the lower tier over the course of six months and said it was chilling how you could pinpoint exactly where it would strike week by week; another friend who attended the prestigious Godolphin and Latymer school once told me breezily 'This term, to be In, you need a silver A-line skirt, a pack of Marlboro Light and an eating disorder.'

These days it might be transing which is the new dangerous dance craze. In 2018 the Times reported:

> 'At Dorothy Stringer School in Brighton, the wind of gender change is blowing hard. Hailed by Tatler magazine as the coolest state secondary in town, with a "liberal vibe" to fit its progressive catchment area, Dorothy Stringer is at the forefront of something very cool indeed.'

We know we're living through strange days when 'cool' is interchangeable with 'confused' - at Dorothy Springer School, forty children do not identify with their gender and another 36 'gender-fluid' youngsters aged between 16 and 16.[27]

The combined NHS areas of Surrey, Kent and Sussex - which includes Brighton - has delivered more children with a phobia of their own genitals to the NHS gender service than the whole of Greater London combined, implying that this, like most neuroses, is a disease of affluence.

There are dissenting voices amongst the apparent desire of many health professionals to lop off anything they can get their hands on. Polly Carmichael, director of the NHS gender service for children, told the Sunday Times:

> 'Without a doubt there are some young people who are finding a community, friends and all sorts of things through joining a group who have an interest around gender. It's probably the case that [some] are caught up in something rather than it being an expression of something that has arisen from within.'

And in the U.S.A in 2018 the public health professor Lisa Littman coined the phrase Rapid Onset Gender Dysphoria to describe the wild-fire effect of gender confusion amongst teenage peer groups, speculating that it was often a social coping mechanism - like bulimia - to mask other conflicts. Her study asserted that 'among the young people reported on — 83% of whom were designated female at birth — more than one-third had friendship groups in which 50% or more of the youths began to identify as transgender in a similar time frame.'

Sometimes the children involved are shockingly young. One Brighton charity, the Allsorts Youth Project (which receives public money and runs *awareness* courses in schools all over Brighton - including Dorothy Stringer) advises 'trans or gender-questioning' children aged five to 11; the average age is nine. And it may be a minor point, but isn't it somewhat distasteful to call a charity which deals in genital confusion Allsorts? Rather like calling a charity for children with stunted growth Midget Gems.

But to give *Allsorts* (could have been worse - could have been *Dolly Mixtures*) their due, their name very much reflects the bright and breezy, theme-park thrill-ride magic-bullet that transing is now portrayed as - everybody's doing it! 'If X jumped off a cliff, would you do it too?' mothers used to ask daughters of my generation when as teenagers we copied our wild best friends in some reckless action. Now the question is more likely to be 'If X had their breasts cut off, would you do it too?' - and the answer in the affirmative.

To make the pressure more seductive, teenagers today don't just have a peer group of immediate friends to contend with but the massively influential vloggers of social media. To quote the Times again:

> 'Impressionable young people, largely girls, are told by upbeat, pretty folk, slightly older than themselves, how transitioning can be an escape route from uncertainty, autism, friendlessness, abuse, the pains of puberty, or homosexuality. Being a young lesbian is less cool.'

I have a friend with a brainy, beautiful tomboy daughter; though most people would call him a reactionary, he was unconcerned that she might be a lesbian. 'I was looking forward to her growing up and having all sorts of adventures while other girls were getting married too young and having children - we've never had a lesbian in the family but so many of them seem to have such interesting lives. I wasn't over-thinking it in a creepy way, but I felt excited for her at the future she might have being free of the usual stuff women have to go through, often due to men like me. But now

I'm scared she'll come home from school one day and ask to have That Operation.'

Sadly, he appears outnumbered by the strange parents who seem to want nothing more than to trans the gay away in a trendy, caring way. In the past people such as Susie Green, the founder of Mermaids, an organisation which exists to promote the castration of children, might have been stage-mothers furiously pushing their baffled children into the limelight in order to get attention in the absence of their own achievements. Now they arrange for them to have their cocks cut off and splurge the ensuing gender-reveal all over social media. They're a creepy cross between Mama Rose from Gypsy and Munchausen-by-proxy monsters.

It's popular for Troons to use the typically melodramatic phrase 'dead-naming'[28] when someone understandably refers to a person with their penis hanging out of their pinafore as Pete rather than Petula. But when a child is mutated into some haphazard imitation of the opposite sex, more than their name dies. Little boys who might have grown up to be great dancers and rampant homosexuals will spend a good deal of time inserting dilators into their fauxginas so they don't heal up like the wounds they are. But even sadder, considering what a short time young females have been afforded any freedom whatsoever, girls who would once have grown up to be fascinating lesbians excelling in everything from sport to seduction will now nurse their scarred chests for the rest of their days, playing with their pretend penises. They may well join the ranks of 'detransitioners,'[29] the growing numbers of young women who realise they have made a terrible mistake. One of them, Charlotte *Charlie* Evans, talked to the Daily Telegraph about it:

> 'She decided to detransition this year after the scars left by her mother's mastectomy prompted her to question why she would want to have her own healthy body parts removed. This realisation was backed up by a trip to Ghana where insisting her pronouns were respected seemed like such a first world problem. Key to her epiphany was also undertaking long-term counselling with therapists who weren't gender specialists. 'Unpicking what happened to me as a child was enough to take the edge off me feeling so uncomfortable with the body I wanted to be chopped apart,' Charlie says. 'I wouldn't have got

that if I'd gone to a gender identity clinic, because they have to
affirm your belief. There's a lack of interest in detransitioner
studies and outcomes and data, because it doesn't really suit the
people pushing this ideology to know about the bad outcomes
– even the doctors who are following a protocol with their heads
in the sand.''

And with this reversal, preferable though it undoubtedly is to having to go
through life pretending to be the opposite sex, comes more surgery and
more pain. At a time when they should be revelling in their youthful, fit
bodies, transers creep around like frail old invalids, their vigour and
vitality all dissolved down the drain of the sex-change lie.

There's a book title I love more than any other - When I Lived In
Modern Times, a novel about the recreation of Israel in the 20th century
by Linda Grant. I've loved living in modern times - but I fear they're over,
and that Woke is their undertaker. Dr Moore said something interesting to
me about what would succeed modernity: 'I saw at college how
postmodernism was a fashionable theory which meant that you could have
a kind of 'feminism' without actual women - that men could occupy every
position. Everything was either 'relative' or simply a text to be interpreted.'

In the age of cosplay, being a woman has been reduced to the
ultimate white male privilege; like Buffalo Bill from The Silence Of The
Lambs, a certain sort of man believes that he can construct a Woman Suit
from words and rob us of the privileges which he believes we have.
They're not actually murdering us in order to fashion their outfits, but they
are attempting to remove our freedoms piece by piece. And they are
leaving the bloodied body-parts of those too young to understand what
their feelings mean as their calling card.

For a few blessed decades, we decided that being different was
fine. You could dress like a boy and be a girl, dress like a girl and be a boy
and no one turned a hair - not even my dad watching Top Of The Pops, in
the end, who went on to become a massive David Bowie fan, much to my
teenage annoyance. 'Got your mother in a whirl/Cos she's not sure if
you're a boy or a girl,' Bowie sang to us in 'Rebel Rebel.' Well, your
mother will certainly know what you are now, because the moment you
show any interest in things the opposite sex *should* like she'll book you
into the castration clinic.

Wokeness took us right back to where we'd started from - back to reactionary behaviour with revolutionary rationale - as it always does.

*

And then the plague came.

As the Troons are always keen to compare their sexual pathology with the sensible requests of the homosexual community, I couldn't help comparing the energy and practicality with which the gays took on AIDS with the attention-hungry antics of the transies in the face of coronavirus. Some of it was comic; 'I don't know if anyone else is having this issue but a big part of being trans is performing my identity in public...and in isolation I have no idea of who I am' one poor thwarted show-off Tweeted. 'I need to come out to my grandad before he dies of Covid!' another cross-dresser cried. Some was tragic-comic 'I'm scared of being buried as the wrong gender'[30] one poor oofums told the BBC, which at a time when deaths from the virus were spiking seemed lacking in empathy to say the least. Some reactions were just so wonderfully bitchy that I hugged myself with glee. One bright spark carped on Twitter that as most *cis* women lied about their age - cheap gender stereotypes, anyone? - there would be uproar when females past the age of 50 were told to stay at home during lockdown and those who had been masquerading as spring chickens were finally defrocked.

But of course, it wasn't people lying about their age at all which was trounced by the coronavirus - it was people lying about their sex. The BBC reported a story from Panama where the authorities decided to reduce the number of people about during lockdown by letting men and women go outside on alternate days. Monica, a trans-woman, went out on the women's day. But when she entered her local shop everyone went silent. The owner approached her and, instead of smiling as he usually did, said, regretfully: 'Sorry, Monica. The police said we can only serve women today.'

Woke news websites all around the world warned that *trans-women* were at a terrible risk from Covid-19 - much more at risk than those moaning cis women who were privileged enough to be trapped in homes with their tormentors, the *domestic* death toll now doubled. And for once, Troon tantrum-throwing had a kernel of truth. Trans-women

**were** more at risk of dying from the virus. For the simple fact that men were twice as likely to die of it as women - and because trans-women are **men.**

Mother Nature - what a Terf![31]

*

'Alice laughed: 'There's no use trying,' she said 'one can't believe impossible things.' 'I daresay you haven't had much practice,' said the Queen. 'When I was younger, I always did it for half an hour a day. Why, sometimes I've believed as many as six impossible things before breakfast.... ''

We are all Alice now, Alice in Wokeland, down the rabbit hole with no direction home, running from the many-mawed, multi-cocked Jabberwocky, be-wigged and angry, as it seeks to erase us from our own sad, beautiful, hard-won story.

---

## Notes

[1] https://en.wikipedia.org/wiki/Widow_Twankey

[2] https://en-academic.com/dic.nsf/enwiki/679861

[3] https://www.smh.com.au/national/just-a-bloke-in-a-frock-20090603-bvod.html

[4] https://www.huffingtonpost.co.uk/entry/david-bowie-top-of-the-pops_us_5693ff52e4b0cad15e65ac86?ri18n=true

[5] https:// www.thetimes.co.uk / article / interview-the-1975s-matty-healy-on-drug-addiction-greta-thunberg-and-isolation-2mcdp5l62

[6] https://en.wikipedia.org/wiki/Sex_change

[7] https:// www.pinknews.co.uk / 2017/01/25/can-you-be-transabled-meet-the-people-trapped-in-their-working-bodies/

[8] https://isawlightningfall.tumblr.com/post/120546446112/when-he-cut-off-his-right-arm-with-a-very-sharp

[9] https://isawlightningfall.tumblr.com/post/120546446112/when-he-cut-off-his-right-arm-with-a-very-sharp

[10] https://www.youtube.com/watch?v=qiS-hvQUbDE

[11] https://www.nationalreview.com/2019/10/rachel-mckinnon-is-a-cheat-and-a-bully/

[12] https:// www.postandcourier.com / news / the - tweet -heard – round - the - world-charleston-professor-sparks-global-twitter-debate/article_4a462cda-c9c7-11e9-8134-d32dc721835d.html

[13] https:// www.dailymail.co.uk / sport / sportsnews / article-6778013 / Transgender-cycling-champion-sparks-controversy-posting-picture-Sharron-Davies.html

[14] https:// www.outsports.com / 2020 / 1 / 14/ 21062012/fallon-fox-trans-athlete-mma-courage-brave

[15] https://cinergycoaching.com/2013/10/sticks-and-stones-may-break-my-bones/

[16] https://www.peaktrans.org/district-judge-kenneth-grant/

[17] https:// www.feministcurrent.com / 2018 / 04 / 27/ trans-identified-male-tara-wolf-charged-assault-hyde-park-attack/

[18] https:// www.dailymail.co.uk / news / article-5613057 / Model-punched-feminist-smashed-120-camera-violent-brawl-walks-free-court.html

[19] https:// www.feministcurrent.com / 2018 / 04 / 27 / trans-identified-male-tara-wolf-charged-assault-hyde-park-attack/

[20] https://www.thetimes.co.uk/article/anger-over-women-s-business-honour-for-cross-dressing-banker-h0gv3l7nw

[21] https://gender.wikia.org/wiki/Tetrisgender

[22] https://www.bbc.co.uk/news/uk-england-lincolnshire-51501202

[23] https://www.mirror.co.uk/news/uk-news/sick-pervert-downloaded-child-abuse-223 51718

[24] https:// www.telegraph.co.uk / news / 2020 / 04 /12 / female-prison-officers-raped-inmates-claiming-trans-rory-stewart/

[25] https:// www.theguardian.com / politics / 2014 / feb / 25 /harriet-harman-daily-mail-argument-nccl-link-pie

[26] https://news.trust.org/item/20190412100802-6md1q/

[27] https://www.dailymail.co.uk / news/article-6426961/Fashionable-Brighton-school-40-children-not-identify-sex-birth.html

[28] https://en.wikipedia.org/wiki/Deadnaming

[29] https:// www.thetimes.co.uk / article/ the-detransitioners-what-happens-when-trans-men-want-to-be-women-again-fd22b7jhs

[30] https://www.bbc.co.uk/news/uk-52690931

[31] Alice Through The Looking Glass by Lewis Carroll

# CHAPTER FIVE

## PAINT CHART POLITICS: FRESH'N'FUNKY ANTI-SEMITISM AND WOKE ISLAMOPHILIA

Growing up as a teenager in the Bristol of the 1970s, I knew nothing about racism. I certainly didn't know that the city (which I see now from a distance was extremely beautiful but at the time considered the most boring backwater on earth, constructed solely to prevent me from achieving fame and fortune in That London) had been built on the profits of slavery. I didn't know when I saw my first ever live band - Cockney Rebel - that the Colston Hall where they played was named after Edward Colston, the slave trader, philanthropist and Member of Parliament who had founded Colston's School on this site in the early 18th century. If I had, I'd have gone home even more appalled than I already was by the mystifying gurnings of Steve Harley. Was he sexy, was he profound? Neither, so far as I could see - so therefore he was rubbish at being a pop star.

I probably wasn't best-placed to appreciate him anyway because - adolescent masturbation aids such as Bolan, Bowie and Bryan aside - I only liked black music. When I first heard punk music, I remember thinking 'This isn't music - this is just yelling' and even though I had to pretend to like it in order to become a writer (bitter irony, considering that punk songs were sub-literate to say the least, a typical tune of the time being called 'I Wanna Be Sick On You') there's only ever been one sort of music for me and that's black dance music - soul, Motown, Philly, house, handbag - call it what you will. (In later life I thought I was living dangerously when I started buying Massive Attack records, as they had one white member.) Anyway, anything further from sweet soul music than punk - totally white, male, anti-love, anti-sex - cannot be imagined. After a miserable three hours at the Roxy or the Vortex, witnessing once again The Lurkers droning or The Drones lurking, I would return to my lowly room and wipe all that aural damage away by tearing off my skintight leathers and dancing around to the Isley Brothers in my birthday suit.

I'd felt this way about black music since I was eleven and started at comprehensive school. I'd been a sensitive Mixed Infant/Junior, fond of ballet dancing and pressing wildflowers, but Baby Jekyll was born-again as Jailbait Hyde in this Bristolian blackboard jungle which both terrified and thrilled me. Once I worked it out that I'd be jostled rudely and my reading matter ripped up before my eyes by my jeering peers if I chose to spend my break-times with my nose in a book, we got along fine; I was a tall, blonde, pretty girl who could easily pass for normal while I made my inner Oscar Wilde wait a while till I made up my mind what to do with my young life. (Ideally the Three Fs: fame, fortune and that other thing your parents hope you'll never get around to.)

My schoolmates were basically British rednecks, the country-drawling sons and daughters of hired hands - but this didn't translate to racist. Had any girls ever been as glamorous as the feather-cut Fifth Years who swaggered round the corridors in their Trevira skirts (cunningly masquerading as regulation school uniform) with linked arms, bellowing their war-cry - 'NUTS, WHOLE HAZELNUTS - OOO! CADBURY'S TAKE DEM AND DEY COVER DEM WIT' CHOCOLATE!' It was an early harbinger of the Jamaican patois which many inner-city working-class white kids would adopt in decades to come - no offence meant and none taken, because we didn't have Twitter in those days, and thus no permanent class of people dedicated to wetting their adult nappies on behalf of another group of people who couldn't care less. In that innocent chocolate-praising chanting, I heard an echo of the 2020 Wokestorm when Adele got monstered for marking the Covid-crushed Notting Hill Carnival with an Instagram snap wearing a Jamaican flag bikini and her hair in Bantu knots - and a host of black celebrities rushed to her defence, pointing out that she had grown up in parts of London where it was the habit of white youth to adopt the West Indian heritage of their friends. It was a lovely moment illustrating the tone-deafness of the privately-educated

Woke when it came to the working-class melting-pot; that what they called cultural appropriation we called being mates.

Because, walking there at the front of the cool kids at my comp, there would always be a couple of ice-cold black kids - there weren't many of them at the school, but they were untouchable. There were even a few of those mythical black skinheads to be seen, the ones that frighten the bourgeois so badly; there he'd be hanging around smoking fags and catcalling girls at weekends in full regalia with his crew - like a shorn and booted Sammy Davis Jnr enjoying his special status with the Rat Pack. If one of us white girls was asked to dance by a black kid at a club on Saturday night, she'd be queen of the school on Monday. An unpopular girl's mother commenced 'living in sin' with a black man - and suddenly everyone wanted to be her friend.

Then a few Ugandan Asian girls started turning up at school - pretty and shy, they didn't have the coolness of the West Indian kids, but I don't recall we did anything bad to them apart from teaching them to swear. The black kids didn't like them much, probably as they were so studious; there was talk that the black skinheads never said no to indulging in a spot of 'Paki-bashing' but as children do, we couldn't really fathom what wasn't right in front of our eyes. Years later I would read Michael Collins masterpiece The Likes Of Us and experience the thrill of recognition:

> 'How dare the middle class preach to the working class about racism? The modern-day white working class had a more varied, more honest, more intimate experience, having known non-whites as lovers, muggers, husbands, killers, wives, victims, neighbours, rapists, friends, foes, attackers, carers. For decades, the urban white working class had largely been educated in multiracial schools, worked in multiracial environments, and lived in multiracial neighbourhoods. Many may not have wanted this, and many escaped it in the form of 'white flight' but many more accepted it - or at least didn't manifest their opposition by rioting or carrying out racist attacks.'

Because of my background, I never had to make an effort not to be racist; I hadn't really thought about it enough to worry about it - that would be for people with time on their hands, people who went to 'uni.' I still believe that the natural and desirable state is to be not racist rather than anti-racist - and there's a real difference. It might be simply and vividly summed up by the fact that when I look at a monkey, I don't see any resemblance to a black person - to me, the most simian human I've ever seen is the breathtakingly beautiful Billie Piper, and she's even whiter than me. But anti-racists are always getting into states about monkeys; in 2019 a friend of my teenage years, the similarly proletarian Danny Baker, was sacked from his job at the BBC for Tweeting a photo of the new royal baby as a circus monkey, with the clear implication that the Windsors are somewhat similar to a bunch of performing chimps. **He just wasn't thinking** that the baby would be a quarter black - because it would be 100% part of the ruling class and therefore perfectly eligible for the mockery of cocky subjects. He (like me a black music obsessive) made an honest mistake because there was no badness in him and nothing to over-think. He had no secret prejudice to examine and conceal; he is **not** racist. But whenever I see a painstaking middle-class **anti**-racist I always think 'Hmm, I wonder what **you're** hiding…because whatever it is, you're really having to shout very loudly at it.'

I first met This Sort at the same place I met Danny - the New Musical Express, where I went to work in the summer of 1976. As Jon Snow would later say of a Brexit rally, I had never seen so many white men in one place. I noticed that some of my colleagues played reggae music ceaselessly - the one sort of black music I loathed. But before you write me off as a racist old gammon like my fellow contrarian Morrissey ('All reggae is vile') I would concede that the early bouncy stuff which sounds like it was recorded in a shed was lovely, as was the ska, bluebeat and rocksteady which were the roots of reggae – some of the perkiest tunes Pollyanna could hope to meet. Of course I love Johnny Nash, Jimmy Cliff, Desmond Dekker and 'Young, Gifted And Black,' 'Uptown Top Ranking,' 'Born For A Purpose.' But that I can name all the ones I like in a sentence is proof of how much I loathe the genre – if I started naming the songs and singers in the other black genres I love, I'd die doing it.

I knew that a lot of what was wrong with reggae could be put down to the lack of an electric female presence which vivifies every other form of black music from gospel to house. When I remarked on this to the reggae-mad editor of the NME (he progressed to doing newspaper horoscopes, so the mental rigour was strong in this one) he advised me to listen to 'Lovers Rock' a reggae sub-genre so limp and twee that it makes Patience Strong look like Sylvia Plath, the musical equivalent of 'a small glass of sweet white wine for the lady.'

In acts of what would now be nobbled as Cultural Appropriation, these colleagues flagrantly smoked stinking cannabis and spoke in a frankly absurd Jamaican patois. Even I, with 'Nuts, whole hazelnuts' still ringing in my ears, was somewhat stunned by the random cries of 'Ey mon!' and 'Soon come!' which punctuated office life. I wrote it off as hippie derangement, but one thing puzzled me. I asked one of my workmates why the NME had no black writers.

He laughed!

Patronised by the Left, demonised by the Right, I really shouldn't have been so shocked when I turned on the TV in the spring of 1980 and saw black Britons rioting in my own sleepy city, in the mostly black neighbourhood of St Pauls. But I was surprised to say the least. Surely riots were what the Americans had, the bitter harvest of a black population brought there on slave ships rather than here on boats from the Caribbean, with such a positive attitude that Lord Kitchener (a.k.a Aldwyn Roberts, the Trinidadian calypsonian) would sing on the quayside at Tilbury Docks after arriving on HMT Empire Windrush:

'London is the place for me
London this lovely city…
Well believe me I am speaking broadmindedly
I am glad to know my Mother Country
I have been travelling to countries years ago
But this is the place I wanted to know…
To live in London you are really comfortable
Because the English people are very much sociable
They take you here and they take you there
And they make you feel like a millionaire…'

Next morning it was on the front of all the newspapers; the Daily Mail wrote of 'a riot-torn immigrant area of Bristol…mobs of black youths roamed the streets after nearly eight hours of violence.' It transpired that the main trigger had been the notorious 'Sus' law which allowed the police to stop, search and arrest people on suspicion of them being in breach of section 4 of the Vagrancy Act 1824; similar riots would take place the following year in black neighbourhoods of London, Leeds and Liverpool. Twenty years on from the riots Inspector Neil Smart, a local policeman, said that policing methods had changed for the better, telling the Bristol Post 'We've learned tremendous lessons since the 1980s and our methods are very different now. I like to think a situation like the riots could never take place again.'

Very few people would deny that the police habitually harassed young black men far more than they did other groups, and that something had to change. But, as often is the case, some bright spark always has to take a thing too far and spoil it for everyone - stop it from being desirable progress and mutate it into detestable pretentiousness. So before the likes of me taunted the Woke, we teased their forebears - the Politically Correct, defined by Merriam-Webster as 'Conforming to a belief that language and practices which could offend political sensibilities (as in matters of sex or race) should be eliminated.'

The first mention I could find of the phrase was in a 1934 New York Times which reported on Nazi Germany favouring 'pure 'Aryans' whose opinions are politically correct.' As with many unfortunate things (anti-Semitism comes immediately to mind) that which was extremely Right-wing could easily become something extremely Left-wing and the American commentator Herbert Kohl, observing Communist vs Socialist squabbles in the New York of the late 1940s and early 1950s, wrote:

> 'The term "politically correct" was used disparagingly, to refer to someone whose loyalty to the CP line overrode compassion, and led to bad politics. It was used by Socialists against Communists, and was meant to separate out Socialists who believed in egalitarian moral ideas from dogmatic Communists who would advocate and defend party positions regardless of their moral substance.'

By 1987 Allan Bloom's book The Closing of The American Mind had outed the phrase as being yet another signifier of the silly led by the sinister while in his 2009 publication Political Correctness: A History Of Semantics and Culture Geoffrey Hughes claimed that debate over political correctness concerns whether changing language actually solves political and social problems or simply encourages censorship, intellectual intimidation and the performance of moral purity on the part of those who practice it, inevitably pushed by a minority rather than an organic form of language change.

For people who purport to be interested in the life of the mind, it's striking how first the Politically Correct and now the Woke have such a tin ear for language. It's like they give it both too much clout ('Words are literally violence!') and too little respect. It doesn't really matter a great deal if the city council of Berkeley, California, formally changed the name of 'manhole cover' to 'maintenance hole' though it may be my dirty mind which actually finds the latter version the most suggestive. It didn't matter a great deal when in 2006 two nursery schools in Oxfordshire instructed their Mixed Infants to sing 'Baa Baa Rainbow Sheep' rather than refer to an ovis aries of a darker hue, though as the splendidly-named and no-nonsense Jill Edge of a rival nursery retorted:

> 'We sing Baa Baa Black Sheep and Baa Baa White Sheep because that's reality, that's what the children see in the fields and it encourages them to look around them. Realistically, they are not going to see rainbow sheep in the fields. There are much better ways of addressing these issues.'

Indeed - for example, in 2000 a warning by Birmingham City education department that 'Baa Baa Black Sheep' should not be taught in schools because it was 'racially offensive' was dropped after black parents ridiculed it. It is the constant drip-drip (fittingly onomatopoeic) of such incidents which makes the majority of the electorate who are more concerned with actual problems in everyday life actually dig in their heels and become far more inclined to vote for populist leaders who mock this stuff for the nonsense it is.

It is a strange dichotomy given an airing in the case of the colour-coded sheep; black is beautiful, or at least the equal of any other skin colour, yet the word black should be avoided if possible. But logic has never been a strong point of the PC/Woke when it comes to colour. Due to their social class, most Woke activists have grown up surrounded by fellow white people - and on late exposure to black people they seem to utterly lose their minds. Whether slurping at a black sole, believing that such self-immolation may make them one with the black soul, or knowing better than Martin Luther King when he dreamed that people would be judged by their personal qualities and not by the colour of their skin, they practise a strange creed which I coined Paint Chart Politics more than a decade ago. That is, the further from white, the more likely you are to be right in the eyes of the Left.

Thus democratic Israel, which gives full civil rights to women and gay people, is \*worse\* in Woke eyes than the countries which surround it, which don't but are darker. (This brand of ignorance led both to the Labour Party being under investigation for racism and to the Holocaust being described as 'a white on white crime' by a Woker.) It has given fresh life to the oldest hatred, under the banner of what I named 'Fresh'n'Funky Fascism' - this time being peddled by young Islamists rather than old white men, and therefore so much more attractive to the Woke. In a time when anti-racism is quite rightly reviled, the Jews - being \*white\* - have become the only acceptable ethnic minority to bully. It's always funny to see pasty-faced Western pro-Palestinian activists being bundled into vans by dark-skinned Mizrahi IDF, their simple Paint Chart Politics brains trying to take in the fact that Israelis can be brown- and black-skinned too. Similarly, in Darfur the Left were thrown a curveball when it turned out that the Arab Muslims were terrorising the black Christians. Um, Islam good, Christianity bad – but hang on, Christians darker here! DOES NOT COMPUTE!

In the simple-minded Janet And John world of heroic Left vs bullying Right, saintly black vs sinner white, Western society is a monolith of powerful pale-faces oppressing everyone else. The real world is so much more complicated. Whistle-blowers are accused of rape. Muslim men pimp out infidel girl children. Romanies reveal a virulent loathing of homosexuality. The BBC sacks middle-aged women in order to boost its ethnic diversity quota. Eastern European immigrants are shocked by how many black Britons there are. The intermarriage of British Asians with British blacks is objected to far more by the members of these communities than marriage to either is viewed by indigenous white Britons, who are great fans of racial inter-marriage: as Trevor Phillips put it 'My expectations of Britain are high. This is the only country in the world where a sizeable mixed-race population has come about as a consequence of love rather than coercion and slavery.'

But what happens when a group has no interest in assimilation and indeed sees other communities - both white majority and other ethnic minorities - as inferior? The black activist Darcus Howe returned to Walsall twenty years after he lived there to make a television programme about the town, where he was confront by a group of angry young Pakistanis:

> 'They told me of their violent hostility to West Indians and
> threatened to break my legs. Pakistani nationalism is their stock
> in trade. 'We are Muslims,' they said, 'and nobody likes us."

It's difficult to know how they got that idea, when the West often appears to be in the grip of what I can only call Islamophilia. The most grotesque example was of course the refusal of numerous British police forces to tackle grooming gangs for fear of being accused of Islamophobia but every week a new example of Islamophilia comes to light. It took our splendid Home Secretary Priti Patel (unhampered by wet white Wokeness when it came to minority ethnic criminals) to make a start on the scourge of modern slavery in the summer of 2020 after she named misguided 'cultural sensitivities' as the reason police and government agencies held back from tackling illegal sweatshops in Britain's fast-fashion industry lest they be accused of 'racism.' Why, it's almost like the white establishment really doesn't mind throwing women under the bus in order to suck up to Muslim exploiters. It's almost like a sex sweatshop called Rotherham never happened, with all those little white slags boo-hooing all the way to the cop shop only to be treated like trash.

Though not a race, Islam has taken on a special place in the panoply of protection and promotion. Even during the Rushdie affair there was a sustained effort on the part of the BBC to present Islam as something essentially 'joyous' and 'vibrant' - sort of like Afro-Caribbean culture, only with fasting and fatwas. As I wrote in the Guardian in 2001:

> 'The BBC's Islam Week brought us the wonders of mosques
> and Mecca, glossing over the Islamic Empire, which at its
> height was bigger than the Roman (remember: British Empire
> = bad, Islamic Empire = good), taking in - ho, ho, ho! - a
> Muslim football team and Laurence Llewelyn-Bowen's

creation of an "Islamic garden" and finishing up with Jools
Holland's Rhythms Of Islam. That's Islam, then - fun, fun, fun!
Not a mention of the women tortured, the Christian converts
executed, the apostates hounded, the slaves in Sudan being sold
into torment right now.

And by 2025, the BBC informs us, a third of the world will be
Muslim...'

You could almost hear Auntie's lips smacking lasciviously as she
anticipated the sexy subjugation of the seven veils awaiting her.

The BBC's fanatical desire to serve Islam at the expense of all
other faiths (remember the creepy 'PBUH' on their religion website) was
noted in 2019 by the redoubtable Lord Singh of Wimbledon when he
resigned from being a regular contributor to Radio 4's Thought For The
Day after the BBC had prevented him from discussing a faith leader who
had fought the conversion of Hindus to Islam in 17th century India as it
might have offended Muslims. A world in which Islam never 'converted'
those of other faiths at the point of a scimitar? Not so much Thought For
The Day as Magical Thinking Of The Day. He wrote:

'I am leaving Thought for the Day with great reluctance. But I
can no longer accept prejudiced and intolerant attempts by the
BBC to silence Sikh teachings on tolerance, freedom of belief
and on the duty we all must share to build a more cohesive and
responsible society.'

The BBC didn't learn their lesson; in the summer of 2020 their coverage
of the Muslim religious festivals was so ceaseless that one could easily
imagine one was living in the UAE rather than the U.K.

The reason for Islamophilia is often presented as wanting to
protect the underdog; a number of writers sat on the fence after the Charlie
Hebdo massacre and accused the magazine of 'punching down'[1] at a
vulnerable community. But Islam **is** the world's fastest-growing religion,
and **will** command one third of the world in five years time. When will
Islam **not** be the underdog? When half the world is Muslim? I'm sure that
the Western defenders of Islamism will have another set of excuses ready
by then. Because their defence of it isn't really down to their affection for
the underdog at all. It's fear of the attack-dog; knowing that a small
proportion of followers of this one belief system will slay them soon as

look at them when offended. They're not the proud defender of the underdog, but the school bully's cowardly little sidekick, who will egg his overlord on to stomp on as many victims as possible in the hope that the heat and hatred won't target him for one more day.

It's pathetic enough when Woke Western men do this, but at least you can see what's in it for them when they throw their puny weight behind this most misogynistic of religions. But what sort of woman wants to be less free? You can often predict who'll do it next by their track record of attention-seeking. Upon discovering that Sinéad O'Connor had converted to Islam, I was about as shocked as a Yuletide shopper hearing the opening bars of Slade's 'Merry Xmas Everybody' while picking up last-minute stocking-fillers.

A vast amount of male Islamic conversion takes place in prison - suddenly thugs have the blessing of a higher power to torture, rape and kill - but with women I think it's often an elaborate way of grieving for fading physical attractiveness: 'Look at me in my lovely special modest costume, you sluts!' O'Connor at least had talent, and did admit to being mentally ill. Lauren Booth's entirely inappropriate addiction to the spotlight, although obviously designed as one of Mother Nature's Plus-Ones, is her sole stand-out feature. A failed actress, a mediocre hack, it's pretty fair to say we would never have heard of her had her half-sister not married a man who became Prime Minister. After being evicted from the jungle during the 2006 version of I'm A Celebrity Get Me Out of Here for crimes against rap she finally found her muddled metier in Mohammedanism, working as a paid stooge for the murderous Iranian regime's television channel Press TV. A woman, choosing to act as a front for a gang of thugs who uphold the punishment of death by stoning for adulteresses - this was surely Sharia Syndrome gone gaga.

Booth converted to Islam in 2010, adopting full hijab which handily allowed her to eat as much as she wanted; perhaps that was the reason she described her newfound faith as 'this shot of spiritual morphine, just absolute bliss and joy' - **all that cake, with the hijab covering so many cakes sins!** But a sinner doesn't become a saint overnight and though Booth vowed never to show her breasts in public again, complete fidelity to truth and honour seems to have been somewhat lacking when she took a Muslim husband who was unfortunately someone else's. Sohale Ahmed's beautiful wife of sixteen years. Faiza, told the Daily Mail in 2013:

> 'She destroyed my home. You can't just put on a hijab and say you are a good Muslim woman – it's about having boundaries with men, and love and respect for women. On Eid Day, Lauren arrived home from the mosque with Sohale and other family members but no one warned me. I walked out of my kitchen and she was there in my front room in full make-up, dressed from head-to-toe in red, the traditional colour of a Muslim wedding dress. She looked like a bride. She followed me back into the kitchen and said 'I am sorry I stole your husband!' He spent all his time attending to her and they went off into the night. None of his family members said anything to him. She came into my house as my and my husband's guest and did this under my nose. Her behaviour appals me, and other Muslim women – the very people she professes to support – must now judge her.'

The odd couple - Booth's increasing girth made her diminutive mate resemble a handy portable snack when they were photographed together - were soon disqualified from holding any trustee positions after the Charity Commission found they could not account for half the money raised by their Palestinian aid charity Peacetrail, a whopping £70,000 of which had mysteriously gone missing. One word: **cake!**

What sort of woman cosies up to a religion which supports the oppression, torture and murder of women who dare to want freedom? The kind who write love letters to serial killers. It's one thing to completely lose one's mind over Muhammad (as the website Iranian.com, a voice of the country's exiles, captioned a photo of Booth in full Muslimah drag, HAS THIS WOMAN GONE MAD?) - we all do dumb things when we're in love. But imagine a sensible group of women - elected female Swedish MPs from a progressive anti-Trump feminist fair-trade gluten-free government, say - who chose to hijab-up when visiting the Iranian leadership in 2017, while all across the Muslim world heartbreakingly brave women are paying with their liberty and lives, facing imprisonment, torture and death for removing theirs, in order to break free of the shroud of submission.

A young Iranian woman wrote an open letter to Magdalena Andersson, the Swedish Minister for Finance in what boasted itself the world's first feminist government:[2]

'I am an Iranian woman and the founder of My Stealthy Freedom Campaign that has been militating against compulsory veil and in favour of freedom of choice for women. You claimed that wearing headscarf in Iran is the same as wearing a hat in Sweden. Are you serious? This is me in the picture when I was a parliamentary journalist, the cleric is trying to punch me on the face just because of not wearing a proper Islamic hijab. A hat was not an option.

Have you ever been forced to wear the hijab all your life? Have you ever experienced the brutality of the morality forcing you to cover your hair? The answer is: NO. However, for us, millions of Iranian women, this is unfortunately a daily reality of our life. That is why you probably do not understand the difference between a compulsory headscarf and a hat (which, by the way, you have worn willingly). Your comparison of both situations is downright inattentive to the daily struggles of millions of Iranian women who brave beatings by the morality police whenever they attempt to express their freedom of choice.

Yes, you can make fun of our struggle, but I would appreciate it if you understood that we are talking about compulsory hijab whereas when you show us your pictures with hats, you are actually exercising your freedom of choice. You are actually trying to blur the huge distinction between the compulsory veil that Iranians have to wear and your act of willingly wearing a hat. I am sure that you must have condemned the burkha ban in France. So did our campaign because the burkini ban as well ran counter to freedom of choice. By the same token, you never downplayed the burkini ban like the way you are downplaying the compulsory veil law in Iran.

No-one forced you to wear these beautiful hats. We sincerely wish that you have fun and stay safe. Despite your stance, we will never give up our struggle and I am sure one day you will hear our voice and our challenge against compulsory hijab. As evidenced by your act of wearing the compulsory veil when you were in Iran, it is no longer an internal matter; our government forced all of you to follow a discriminatory law. We all have to be brave and say NO to any form of humiliation. That is called sisterhood and solidarity. Let's be clear: we have never asked you to insult the laws in our country; we have merely asked you to challenge this insulting law and not to abide by it.

By showing us pictures of yourselves in hats that downplay your act of wearing the compulsory veil, you are actually insulting all women who have been fighting against compulsory hijab. By blurring the distinction between both, you are banalising what Iranian women have to endure on a daily basis. Stand by your sisters and do not hesitate to grill our rulers about this discriminatory law. History will judge all of us. By the way, we are welcoming you to our beautiful country, but please be as brave as Iranian women and challenge the compulsory hijab because if you forced Iranian female politicians to take off their headscarves upon their visits to the West, they would definitely protest. We are in favour of good relations with the West, but we would have loved to see you stand your ground and preach the feminism the same way you do it in Sweden.'

The previous month another act of mass veiling by free women took place. I like to prance around showing off in hats and shouting at men as much as the next broad but I had no desire to join any of the Women's Marches which took place in January 2017. Firstly, I was sure they would be full of 'Strong Women,' a phrase I hate at the best of times - and feel should only be used if the lady in question can tear a telephone directory in half with her bare hands - and which seemed especially inappropriate to describe a bunch of overgrown Veruca Salts having a collective temper tantrum because their side lost to Trump. Once again, we saw the regressive Left repeating the same behaviour that lost it power in the first place - namely, childishly demonising any opponent as Hitler With Funny Hair.

On a more sinister level, I found it rather repulsive that one of the organisers of the Washington march, Linda Sarsour, is a vocal fan of Saudi Arabia - '10 weeks of PAID maternity leave in Saudi Arabia. Yes PAID. And ur worrying about women driving. Puts us to shame' went one Tweet. It conveniently side-stepped the fact that as women in Saudi Arabia aren't allowed to drive, meet unrelated men or feel the sun on their bare heads, giving them permission to stay at home looking after children is about as empowering as giving a fish permission to swim.

Then we had the grotesque spectacle of many non-Muslim women voluntarily hijabing-up on the various marches. It made me recall the liberal Muslim feminist Asra Nomani who said she voted for Trump because she felt that she could not stomach four more years of apologism for Islamism in the White House. She ended up getting abuse from a white feminist who accused her of normalising 'white supremacy.' As the writer Nervana Mahmoud put it: 'Now we liberal Muslims feel alienated again. Those who are marching against Trump are selective liberals; they remember liberalism when a white man like Trump is the culprit, but happily defend the illiberalism of non-white authoritarian regimes and ideologies. My message to all social activists marching in America is simple: Feel our pain, and stand with our common values. One cannot stand against Trump's misogyny while condoning or ignoring others' misogyny as 'cultural' or 'religious.' Such selectivity is what led to the rise of Trump in the first place. Women's rights are for all, not just for American and other Western women.'

Rather as Winston Churchill said of democracy, a police force is the worst form of policing except for all the others - but by the summer of 2020 his statue had already been boxed up to save it from the somewhat basic though no doubt heartfelt artistic efforts of the mob, so we can take it that his opinion wasn't worth much in the topsy-turvy fever dream of the post-lockdown world. Covid-19 remained the big black bird of prey in the room - or in the midst of the jam-packed BLM protests - silently lining up the carrion of many who suspected they had no future and made it ever more of a literal likelihood by pressing up against each other in their thousands to demand a better life. Looking at the infection potential of the demonstrations against the killing of a career criminal, which would invariably bring about a large number of deaths of far more worthwhile lives than his in the sorely affected black communities many of the protesters would return to, I couldn't help but think of the vulgar old saw by the comedian George Carlin: 'Fighting for peace is like fucking for virginity.' Demonstrating against black deaths, in this context, would surely bring about many more black deaths.

London's mayor Sadiq Khan presided over a rise in knife crime which saw the black areas of London run red with the wasted lives of the capital's youth as reliably as the Changing Of The Guard does uptown. After ceaselessly blaming this on those wicked Tories, sobbing to the

Fabian Society that 'Nothing keeps me up at night more than knife crime' and announcing in 2019 that police in the capital would get an extra £234m because 'keeping Londoners safe is my number-one priority' this man of many faces rapidly did an about-turn in the summer of 2020 to announce that he too was going down the primrose path to police defunding by proposing cuts of £110million for the policing of London. Defunding police to end the death of black youths by knife crime is somewhat like screwing for virginity, too.

Of all the innocent black people murdered by racist white policemen, why was George Floyd chosen as the martyr of this movement? Warning bells rang right from the get-go for anyone not working themselves into a froth of half self-loathing, half self-adoring parasexual excitement, as the performative shoe-licking (like the toilet-hungry antics of the Troons) seemed more informed by pornography than politics. It was a good clue to the rest of us that the Black Lives Matter movement - such a seemingly unqualifiedly benign statement - was rotten to the core right from the start. And that, once again, women's lives didn't matter much in the wonderful world of Woke.

It was bitterly amusing to see young British Leftists who ceaselessly rail against the U.S.A import an American protest movement wholesale, like when you see moronic Islamists wearing Coca Cola T shirts. Not at all entertaining, however, for women who'd grown up with the knowledge that reporting a rape to the police was likely to prove so humiliating that many of those who did so compared the experience to being 'raped all over again' (to the point where in the summer of 2020 the Victims Commissioner Dame Vera Baird could seriously say that rape had largely been decriminalised in this country,) to see the police suddenly taking human rights so seriously that they frequently felt the need to kneel in supplication. The PC Police of the grooming gang years had become the fully-fledged Woke Brigade. It wasn't just the police; hot on the heels of clapping for NHS, caged Britons were now encouraged to crawl for career criminals all across the land. A friend living in one of England's least ethnically diverse seaside towns saw it happen on a beach by her house: 'It was a pack etc of desperate white people, muzzling their kids and kneeling on the beach in perhaps the most idyllic place in England. It was sad and weird and seemed to me to have nothing to do with the suffering of black people in the cities these people had in many cases taken 'White Flight' from. It was just another way of keeping up with the Joneses.' Indeed, the sight of so many people down on one knee all across the Western world was discombobulating in the extreme; I kept thinking that one of those mass Moonie weddings might be in the offing, when three thousand couples all tie the knot at once. Sometimes it was vile, though, and not a bit funny: a tiny white girl no more than eight, kneeling in the doorway of her humble home while holding a home-made placard with an arrow pointing to her scared little face and the words 'PRIVILEGED #blacklivesmatter.' As the commentator Raheem Kassam wrote: 'Imagine not just instructing a confused child to kneel in shame like this, but documenting the event and uploading it to social media for pathetic Woke points.'

We were living through days so strange now that they made the Doors song sound like it concerned a quick trip to Homebase; the only thing that could have added to the madness of the melee would be a few strapping blokes in skirts - who, a black American friend teased me, would be along any minute as one of the founders of BLM, Alicia Garza, was 'queer' and 'married' to a 'trans man.' That is, I thought it was teasing - but it was true. What on earth could unite a bunch of streetwise young black men and a gang of mincing mollies? Black struggle movements in the past have been extremely straight, sexually speaking — homophobic, even. Because white society has historically attempted to castrate black men - generally metaphorically, sometimes literally - it's understandable that they present as macho when they get the chance. The downside is the numerous heartbreaking accounts of the hard time given to young black gay men who attempt to come out in their own community; such is the taboo that the footballer John Fashanu claimed that his brother Justin, who committed suicide, had not been really gay but merely 'making up stories to get attention.' If black men especially find it hard to be gay, it makes sense that they'd parrot the lie 'Trans women are women' so they can enjoy penis without theoretically having sex with a fellow man.

Even so, by the autumn BLM had removed the WHAT WE BELIEVE page from their website (it's good to have the courage of one's convictions) perhaps having an inkling that the average black citizen has more to worry about than Woke ruminating:

> 'We are self-reflexive and do the work required to dismantle cisgender privilege and uplift Black trans folk, especially Black trans women who continue to be disproportionately impacted by trans-antagonistic violence. We foster a queer-affirming network. When we gather, we do so with the intention of freeing ourselves from the tight grip of heteronormative thinking, or rather, the belief that all in the world are heterosexual (unless s/he or they disclose otherwise).'

Didn't Michael Jackson have a song that went like that? A right little toe-tapper, as I recall. But seriously? So instead of actually campaigning for something which might actually save a sizeable number of black lives - like stopping the 'no-knock' police raids that killed Breonna Taylor - the whole BLM movement proposed to centre itself on the tiny number of black cross-dressers killed by their customers and/or dealers. If one wanted to derail any Woke political movement, one would only need to get inside and 'trans' it; they'd end up making a big fuss and bother about people who are in hardly any peril to speak of, and the majority of sensible citizens would see this very quickly and turn their backs on it.

It was perfect somehow that the Woke Bros and their new big bad besties would have a run-in with the Thelma and Louise of women's rights, Posie Parker and Venice Allan, a brace of broads who never saw a scrap they didn't like. They first came to notice in 2018 with the WOMAN - ADULT HUMAN FEMALE T-shirts which they sold to pay for a billboard stating the same outlandish hate-speech at that year's Labour Party Conference and then popped up all across the U.K. In stating a simple truth they revealed the full extent to which society was hurtling heading down a rabbit hole leading to an endless Mad Hat(t)er's Tea Party of Troons and macaroons. Unimpeachably feminine, they boast an extreme blend of sex appeal and mischief which rubbed not only their AGP enemies up the wrong way but also caught old-school feminists on the back-foot of their Birkenstocks. Like Marilyn Monroe and Jane Russell strutting after what they wanted in Gentlemen Prefer Blondes, there was no mistaking the glint of saucy sedition in their eyes. They are the scourge of the Woke Bros; female, fearless and most vitally totally unconvinced that feminism and Leftism are natural bedfellows - or indeed, if feminism itself is not irretrievably tainted by Wokeness. In the summer of 2020 they were speaking out at Speakers Corner when a BLM march happened by. Venice told me:

'I'd just done my speech and Posie had wrapped up the event and I was at the back, mingling and smoking, when I felt the crowd push towards me and cries of 'trans women are women!' I immediately went up front to see what was going on and protect our women, some of whom were elderly and scared of Covid. I started shouting 'Go worship your dicks!' -I'm not sure why that popped into my head but it seemed the right thing to say in the moment. Unfortunately, it was interpreted on Twitter as 'Go wash your dick!' and people were saying 'I really don't think it's great optics for gender critical feminists to be screaming 'Clean your penis' at black men!

Later, a group of young women came back to debate with us and we were pleased to have the opportunity, in the wonderful tradition of Speakers' Corner. It was frustrating talking to these women who have all the language about oppression but don't seem to understand it at all. They said they didn't believe that boys were taking university sports scholarships from girls in the US, and when we gave them examples like CeeCee Telfer, they said 'Those aren't boys, they are girls!' In the end I said there was no point in discussing any more - they lived in the land of rainbows and unicorns where nothing means anything.'

Posie elaborated:

'On our third time at Speakers Corner we were invaded by BLM - as soon as I heard the cries of 'Black trans lives matter!' and saw the signs, I started the counter chant 'Woman - adult human female' followed by 'Transwomen are men' - it was exhilarating to say these words out loud to people we know, without thought, oppose them. Their response was predictable, they were angry, aggressive and bursting with misogyny. We engaged with some of the young women in the aftermath of the heated crowd exchanges; the grooming of these women through liberal feminism has been hugely successful. They missed the basics of womanhood, our sexed bodies. It is this pivotal understanding which shapes their comprehension of all other feminist ideas. These girls are a modern version of building one's house upon the sand.'

That a march by a group whose whole ideology is based on the heinous fact of slavery should attempt to silence another group of people who suffered - and in many countries, still do - from a kind of global slavery sums up the whole hysterical horror of Woke, where waters must be ceaselessly muddied lest people wake up to the fact that it is still privileged white men - albeit posing as brothers rather than masters - who are controlling the discussion. So many atrocities go ignored because of what the Woke Bros deem more or less important. The bitter irony is that slavery is not historical, and cannot be stopped in any way by pulling down statues of dead men, however offensively pallid they may have been. Slavery is a crime against humanity which is happening right now, from the sweatshops of Northern England to the slave markets of Arabia, where today an estimated 529,000 to 869,000 black men, women and children are still slaves, bought, owned, sold, and traded by Muslim masters in Algeria, Libya, Mauritania and Sudan. But according to our old pal Paint Chart Politics, historic slavery is more riot-worthy than slavery taking place this very minute, depending mostly on the melanin levels of those doing the enslaving rather than the amount of agony which can be prevented among the enslaved.

The Hebrews were famously slaves, too, of the Egyptians - but of course that doesn't count, as we imagine Egyptians being on the darker side of the Pantone chart even though the Hebrews themselves originated in the Middle East and would have been similar in hue. Verdi even gave the Hebrew slaves their own song:

> 'Go, thought, on the golden wings…
> Greet the banks of the Jordan…
> Oh, my homeland so beautiful and lost…'

And of course the minute they seized the day and recreated their ancient homeland - rather than act as shivering victims in need of Whitey's protection - the Jews were once again fair game after the revelation of the full extent of the Holocaust gave them a few years grace.

With any complexion of politics, there's always enough spare hatred over for the Jews, hiding there in plain sight as they do with their dastardly 'white privilege.' The Tweedledum and Tweedledee of identity race politics are Islamophilia and anti-Semitism and where you find one you will generally find the other; they call anti-Semitism 'the socialism of fools' and there's no more foolish a socialist than a Woker. 'The Jews did it!' is invariably the-butler-did-it remedy with which moronic masses seek to soothe themselves - that's why they crop up in so many conspiracy theories - when times get tough and the BLM did not shirk their duty in this instance. Very quickly, as the Black Lives Matter melee played out, it seemed that the movement seemed to blame the Jews for the black condition far more than the actual Aryan Christians who had orchestrated slavery so enthusiastically with the help of the African chiefs who had so willingly sold their own people into bondage. In a glorious demonstration of how white Western Wokers have no idea of what they people they patronise actually want, in 2009 the Civil Rights Congress of Nigeria asked that descendants of those chiefs should also apologise, as many white Western leaders were doing at the time:

> 'We cannot continue to blame the white men, as Africans, particularly the traditional rulers, are not blameless. In view of the fact that the Americans and Europe have accepted the cruelty of their roles and have forcefully apologised, it would be logical, reasonable and humbling if African traditional rulers ... [can] accept blame and formally apologise to the descendants of the victims of their collaborative and exploitative slave trade.'

What a confusing day for practitioners of Paint Chart Politics that must have been!

Back at the Jew-bashing beano of summer 2020, there were the usual edifying epigrams on Twitter as BLM supporters wondered why the Jews kept on about the Holocaust as it was such a long time ago - to which Jews and their allies quite rightly responded that the Holocaust wasn't as long ago as slavery, so should we forget that first? Then the standard swill about freeing 'Palestine' (an imaginary kingdom populated by pro-gay Muslims and turkeys in favour of Thanksgiving) started up in the BLM social media feed. Then came the by now horribly predictable attacks on Jewish shops and synagogues, despite a statement by the Jewish Council for Public Affairs in which more than a hundred affiliated organisations declared themselves 'outraged' by the killing of Saint George Floyd, declared 'solidarity' with the black community and called for an end to 'systemic racism.'

Sometimes I think it is the very civilisation of Jewish discourse - like women, they have been socialised to please - which allows people to treat them like no other ethnic minority group is in the Woke world. If only diaspora Jews could be more Israeli! But here they are, the most loyal of all ethnic groups imaginable (the times I've had to grit my teeth through 'God Save The Queen' at Jewish rallies!) never failing to draw flack, being insulted by Jeremy Corbyn in 2018:

> 'British Zionists clearly have two problems. One is they don't want to study history, and secondly, having lived in this country for a very long time, probably all their lives, they don't understand English irony either. They need two lessons, which we could perhaps help them with.'

And monstered on Twitter by Corbyn's pet rapper Wiley in 2020:

> 'Listen to me Jewish community…Israel is not your country…the Star of David that's our ting…Israel is ours…there are 2 sets of people who nobody has really wanted to challenge #Jewish & #KKK…cowards…snakes…'

What a rude awakening for all those poor, duped, anti-Israel Jews who had worked so tirelessly for so many years to climb up the fundament of black nationalism, thinking they'd be snug and safe from anti-Semitic abuse there! Still, its better to know the truth than live in a fool's paradise. The liberal Jewish writer Hadley Freeman of the Guardian (a newspaper I left because of its vile level of anti-Semitism - and because the Times offered three times as much money) wrote:

> 'It was the Jeremy Corbyn era that really knocked the stuffing out of me, with people I consider political allies insisting that the 85% of British Jews who saw Corbyn as anti-Semitic were, at best wrong, at worst mendacious. When I wrote about this, I was sent so much anti-Semitic abuse – not criticism, abuse – I had to go to the police. And still, I was told to suck it up and vote for the man endorsed by David Duke.'

I remembered Hadley from 2014 when she wrote a column about me and a couple of other fans of her people with the headline 'God save us from the philo-Semitism of Burchill, Amis and Mensch' - I bet it doesn't seem so bad now! While four years previously Anne Karpf had written in the Independent:

> 'We live in postmodern times where some of what looks like anti-Semitism isn't, but, conversely, some of what doesn't look like anti-Semitism in fact is. Burchill's philo-Semitism is a form of anti-Semitism, I'd suggest, because it bunches all Jews together, as though we were a single, uniform entity. The idea that all Jews are wonderful is little different from all Jews being hateful: in both cases Jews are stripped of individual characteristics, and are nothing except Jewish — a view to which most racists happily subscribe.'

I wonder if she still prefers anti-Semites to philo-Semites? I'd guess not - but you never know with these post-modernists. Hopefully Karpf and her fellow sufferers took the fact that #JewishPrivilege trended on Twitter in the July of 2020 as a compliment rather than a diss, and didn't agree with the writer Karen Harradine when she reminded her fellow Jews:

> 'Pogroms, 6 million slaughtered in the Shoah, 1 million Jews forcibly exiled from Middle Eastern countries, Israel under constant threat of destruction. We are the most persecuted people in history. Privilege?'

From the point of view of Paint Chart Politics practitioners, yes. And using the same logic surely explains why Wiley kept his MBE after his 2020 outburst while in the same summer the 73-year-old lecturer Stephen Lamonby was sacked from his post at Solent University for remarking during a private conversation that 'Jewish people are among the cleverest in the world.' In this topsy-turvy world of Woke, hate is love and love is hate and the Colston Hall is now the Bristol Beacon. It hasn't brought any slaves back to life - and it sounds like a sexually transmitted disease clinic. Good work, Wokers!

## Notes

[1] https:// www.nationalreview.com / 2016/01/charlie-hebdos-critics-punching-down-cartoonists/

[2] https://www.government.se/government-policy/a-feminist-government/?TSPD_101_R0=088d4528d9ab200011c24d75a6a4bb2b4b1e6f227f3bd787a2c6bfb0858672a65a978e8f388a3af3083d646f3d143000bbd04b51f6ece39bbc5efdc117e1159bcd64abe1ada9aac6099c4630c069dc299af2dfc8bd0d13894c9fb6093619b8eb

# CHAPTER SIX

# THE WRONG KIND OF DIVERSITY: THE WOKE DEMONISATION OF THE WORKING CLASS

Sometimes, on one of the very rare twilights when I feel 'pensive ' - 'wistful' even - I will gaze at the crepuscular enigma that is the sea from my balcony in an Art Deco apartment block on the smartest avenue in Hove and wonder where it all went right. How did I get away? How did I come all this way? How did I get to have my dream job (upsetting people and getting paid for it) for almost half a century when I come from a working-class background so profoundly blue-collar that when my bright, attractive cousin told a career guidance bod in the 1970s that she fancied being an air hostess, he advised her to 'Come back down to earth'? I know a man growing up in South Wales at the same time whose career guidance consisted of 'OK, which pit do you want to go down?'

On such evenings, a tiny part of me believes that I should never have turned my back on my salt of the earth brethren; my factory-worker father took a real delight in refusing the offers of promotion which he believed might stop him being such a hard-headed upholder of his comrades rights, and I worshipped my dad. Shouldn't I have been more like him and dedicated myself to the selfless furthering of proletarian prosperity?

But on the other hand, he almost took a real pride in reporting the incident when one of the bosses asked him if it would be alright if his daughter was allowed to meet him briefly 'as she's such a fan of **your** daughter.' 'She asked me all these questions about you like you was important or somethin' - I didn't tell 'er you're a right little madam!' he snickered. My mother, meanwhile, was less happy with my newfound fame; 'Don't **ever** do that to me again!' she scolded me after a soap opera teenager boasted that she'd be the next me. I assured her I wouldn't, but then the following week Terry Wogan mentioned me on his radio show and we were back where we started, with her convinced that I was somehow setting up these media mentions for some nefarious reason of my own, probably just to embarrass her.

Such wistful, pensive evenings come only thrice a year, usually with a hangover. Because if I hadn't bagged my teenage career in journalism when I did, it would only have gone to some dreary spawn of the bourgeoise who'd been to *uni* and knew how to pronounce Goethe and Nietzsche. Every time I see my byline I smirk, knowing that I've robbed some privileged prat of their dream job; so, on balance, I'll keep hold of my view from up here where the air is rarified.

But rarely a week goes by when I don't think of my class-corralled contemporaries who may not have had my lucky break, talent or big green eyes but who were certainly as bright as the vast majority of their middle-class cohort I've had the pleasure of belittling. In the old days it was the working classes who made sure there was a job for their son in the print or down the mine, but these days that privilege belongs exclusively to the better-off with the better-paid jobs. If I ruled the world I would ban posh kids from getting jobs which are both fun and well-paid, say for the next decade, just to make the situation a bit less hideously unfair than it is now. And also on anyone following the same profession as their best-paid parent did; then all the over-educated, under-talented types currently nabbing these jobs because their parents were in the music/acting/hacking racket could then go and get one of the 'proper' jobs, like doctoring and teaching, which they often advocate that everyone else should be aiming for instead of being obsessed with fame.

I think this most savagely when I see the scholastic success rates broken down by sex and ethnicity - when the boys who chased me and tormented me, the good-looking, the bad-attituded and the ugly-tempered, are all shrunken down to statistics on a graph, the ones where they inevitably come in last, with only 9% of working-class white boys going to university. There's lots to like about these graphs too - Asian Females come top, followed by Black Females, followed by *Mixed* Female.

(Such is our porn-addled age that it's impossible to write even those categories without imagining some Woke PAM frantically fiddling with himself.) And come to think of it, I'm not the biggest fan of 'uni' - they're the breeding ground zero of Wokeness, if 'breeding' isn't too life-affirming a word for such a sterile and moribund belief system. Millennials still living with their parents - rueing the day they ever heard of Media Studies - are legion, whereas if they'd taken apprenticeships as plumbers or electricians they'd be decorating their second homes in Spain by now. But while gardeners and builders invariably score highest in the happiness surveys, it doesn't then follow that working-class white boys shouldn't have the same chance to watch daytime TV for three years.

Michael Merrick writes beautifully of being the first of his family to go to university in his Notes From Nowhere:

> 'I think I was 14. It was an English lesson, as I recall. And the words were delivered with the hint of a smirk.
>
> Well of course, the Sun has a reading age of eight.
>
> Innocuous enough. And I didn't know if it was true, nor much care. The truth was less important than the implication, to be honest, veracity less important than meaning. I knew what was going on, what was really being said: 'Here are people who are not like us, we clever ones, we sophisticated ones, we who can see through the ruse to the ignorance of folk. We, children, know better, are better.'
>
> I wanted to be part of the in-group. I wanted to have real status and authority, too. To be like you, Sir, all knowledgeable and self-assured and authoritative. I didn't want to be one of Them, so subtly scorned with a barbed comment and the raise of an eyebrow. So it seeped in. It became true. Those stupid Sun readers – thickos, bigots all. Only, my Dad was a Sun reader. And many of my family. And most of the folk on the council estate where I grew up. I knew this because I delivered their morning papers seven days a week.
>
> And yet, for all I was quietly rejecting them, they never rejected me. I was one of them, even if I increasingly gave the impression of not wanting to be. I was 'Our Mike' and forever would be. And as time has gone by, I realise how intensely proud I am of them, and of the great fortune it is to have been raised as a working-class kid, as one of them. This background was not an obstacle to be overcome, which is what arguments

for social mobility nearly always collapse into, but a fertile soil in which to plant the seeds of future success.'[1]

Not if the Woke have their way - to them, working-class boys are mired in both male and white privilege, and deserve to end up in dead-end jobs, from whence they will grow up to be 'Gammons'[2] (Woke went further than previous generations of over-grown, under-employed students, who had likened the police to 'pigs'[3] by applying it to a whole social class beneath them) and thus even more deserving of the disdain of those born in more privileged circumstances. As one brought up in a working-class Communist household, I must admit I was quite taken aback when I heard about the Woke concept of white privilege and felt indignant that I'd been done out of mine when I was told by teachers I'd never amount to anything simply because I attended a sink school. And that toothless old veteran living in a shop doorway that I give a tenner to every day will be made up when I add as a bonus the glad tidings that he has more privilege than the Duchess of Sussex by virtue of his skin colour.

You could also believe that white privilege is a divide and rule tactic of the Woke bourgeoise to completely draw fire away from the class privilege which has stunted and poisoned society in a way racism can only dream of - and which they benefit from, from cradle to grave.

Working-class white people are often demonised by the liberal establishment for doing things their dark-skinned brethren are easily excused. Grooming gangs and sweatshops come to mind, as does bigamy in the Muslim community; indeed, there was an astonishing case of a Muslim man who was allowed to swerve jail for dangerous driving as he was speeding due to the fact that he had two wives. In the nights following the St Pauls riots there were disturbances in two other areas of Bristol; while St Pauls received nation-wide attention and sympathy, the insurrections in Southmead and Knowle West were commented on only in Bristol. The populations of both areas being mostly white, the teenage rampages were dismissed as merely local yobs.

When working-class youngsters catch a break, it often doesn't end well. In 2019 Jessica Small,[4] a promising young PhD student at Kent University, hanged herself. In a statement her mother said 'She told me people in her lab made her life hell, that it was toxic. The underlying issue was that Jess had gone through state education and the others had gone through private education. She wasn't posh enough - she told me about being mocked for her accent and because she'd never been sailing.' Having graduated with a first-class honours degree, along with a Masters, Miss Small had received a prestigious scholarship to fund her PhD; she also taught younger students. A colleague, Dr Chris Deter said: 'I loved working with her - she was very good with the students, and she made them think.' I doubt that this situation would happen on grounds of race in modern Britain - the black equivalent of pretty, kind, clever Jessica Small would be belle of the Freshers Ball.

It's not just cold-hearted scientists who make working-class kids feel like cut-price fish out of Evian water; the arts are also guilty. I have a gorgeous gay Cockney mate, who briefly quit making a fortune in the City to train as an actor but within months had given up and gone back as he found there to be far more boorish, posh, entitled types at his drama school than in the Square Mile. 'For starters, the fees are now ridiculous, no working-class kid could ever afford to go to a drama school such as Rada or Lamda unless they won a scholarship. Government-funded grants are called DaDAs, the ultimate in patronising paternalism. The massive irony was at my school they were given to two kids, and one was the son of a millionaire. (He lied!) I'd say 90 per cent of the kids on my course had rich parents and were being supported while they studied. And whilst I made friends and some of them were sound, if you discriminate against at least half of the population, obviously the talent pool shrinks. I'm of the opinion that because only the children of the rich now can afford to indulge in artistic pursuits, whether it's acting, art, music or writing, that's the reason our cultural landscape is so bleak at the moment.'

The actress Julie Walters backed this up in 2015:

'It felt like a revolution, like being on the frontline of something. It felt like you were doing something ground-breaking, things like Blackstuff and working at the Everyman. In terms of class, yes, definitely. And that started in the 50s. Michael Caine and all those people. And it's going back the other way now. People like me wouldn't have been able to go to college today. I could because I got a full grant. I don't know how you get into it now. Kids write to me all the time and I think, I don't know what to tell you…working-class kids aren't

represented. Working-class life is not referred to. It's really sad.
I think it means we're going to get loads more middle-class
drama. It will be middle-class people playing working-class
people, like it used to be.'

Cheryl Cole[5] spent her formative years playing with second-hand Barbies.
She told the Times:

> 'I wanted to be a ballerina, And then I went to the Royal Ballet
> summer school when I was 9. Hated it. Squashed the dream. It
> wasn't me. I didn't fit in. I had to be sponsored to go there
> because me parents couldn't afford to send us there, and
> everyone else was – obviously...basically I was a bit of an
> outcast. It was the first time I'd ever felt... class. I didn't know
> what it was. I didn't understand it. I just knew it was...
> different. And that they were... looking down their noses. But
> I couldn't express it. I was out of place. I think about 9-year-old
> me, and I think 'That must have been hard.' Hard enough for
> me to go home to me parents and say 'This is not what I want
> to do anymore.''

She probably believed that such vile behaviour - social racism, no less -
had been left behind with her threadbare pointe shoes. But fame would
bring her more class-hatred, in 2011, from the privately educated
(Millfield, Bedales and Prince Charles's junior alma mater, Hill House)
pop star Lily Allen,[6] who would go on to become a rabid Corbynite and
who, if of no other apparent use, perfectly exemplified the attitude towards
the white working-class by Labour's metropolitan activists. On being
called 'middle-class' on social media she threw her rattle from the pram
and puked up this revelation:

> 'So what if w'ere [sic] middle class? Just cause your mum was
> too lazy to get her fat ass up off the sofa and make some cash, I
> shouldn't be able to make tunes yeah?'

Of course I couldn't restrain myself, and used my column in the
Independent to write an open letter to Lily's mother - sorry, 'mummy' -

> 'This week it came to light that a baby born in working-class
> Glasgow will live 28 years less, on average, than one born in a
> middle-class area. Is this because those babies mums are, to
> quote your daughter, too lazy to get their fat asses up off the
> sofa and make some cash? What DO they teach children at
> those public schools? Something called 'social racism' I fear.

Do you really believe that this filthy prejudice against the poor
should be allowed to pass without criticism? In a country with
a free press? Of course you do – you're her mum. (Or
"Mummy", or whatever you people call each other.) But I am
not. I am a professional journalist, and if I see someone who has
found fame and fortune partly by posing as 'street' saying this
I am going to call them on it.'

In previous decades, I doubt whether Lily Allen would have been
so open about her disdain for this flagrantly feckless working-class, idling
away their days on the sofa and growing their bulging bums even bigger
while siphoning off benefits to blow on online bingo. Working-class
people who'd made it against all the odds in our hideously snobbish
society had been respected at best, fetishised at worst - which is quite fun,
IMHO - ever since the 1960s. But as social mobility stalled in the twenty-
first century, the increasing credence given to the opinions of working-
class people who broke through in the arts and the media - everyone from
Shelagh Delaney to Steven Morrissey - became less important. Silly, even
- the poor creatures didn't have a clue. Political Correctness stepped in and
laid down the law that speaking in an approved way (once it had been form
that cut us out of the conversation - now it would be content) was more
important than speaking our minds, something my class have always been
best at.

Lily Allen's cultural appropriation of the Cockney vernacular
while jeering at the humble beginnings of a girl from a Northern council
estate can be seen as a dummy run of the Troon War yet to come when
Woke grabbed the baton from PC; as real women could be erased and
replaced by parodies of femininity, so could privileged people who
adopted the speech patterns of the poor put themselves forward as the real
thing. The children of the privileged were blocking up every exit from our
rat-run; as Cheryl Cole[7] noted 'If we weren't doing this, we'd be on the
checkout at Tesco.' (Times don't change; when I was a teenager in the
1970s a rich patron had described me thus: 'She's fascinating - like a very
clever Tesco check-out girl.') By the time I wrote the following column in
2012 about spoon-fed soft-lads like Keane and Coldplay cleaning up,
youth who could have chosen any career-path going crashed the only ones
we had a chance at:

> 'Fewer than one in 10 British children attends fee-paying schools, yet more than 60% of chart acts have been privately educated, according to Word magazine, compared with 1% 20 years ago. Similarly, other jobs that previously provided bright, working-class kids with escape routes – from modelling to journalism – have been colonised by the middle and upper classes and by the spawn of those who already hold sway in those professions. The spectacle of some smug, mediocre columnista who would definitely not have their job if their mummy or daddy hadn't been in the newspaper racket advising working-class kids to study hard at school, get a "proper" job and not place their faith in TV talent shows is one of the more repulsive minor crimes of our time.'

Social mobility, which just a few years back we all presumed would rock on regardless, has reversed with a vengeance, doing over the already vulnerable working class with the force of a steamroller. Yes, you chirpy Cockneys and you stoic Northerners, not only have the jobs your parents did — making things — disappeared, but the cushy jobs that a blessed few of you once might have escaped the surly bonds of the proletariat by nabbing — modelling, acting, writing for newspapers — have now been colonised by the children of the rich/famous/well-connected.

But how did they take popular music, of all things - the actual **sound** of red-blooded, straining-at-the-leash working class youth, forever fighting off the cage of adulthood on some blustering British beach? In 2013 Sandie Shaw - the 1960s pops star who resembled a Cleopatra from Dagenham - gave evidence to the Culture Select Committee of the House of Commons about this dismaying development:

> 'Finance is the biggest barrier for emerging artists... at the moment, unless you come from a public school and have a rich family that can support you, you're on the dole and you're trying to work...they cannot start because of their background. The best music comes from those in challenging backgrounds. It comes from Glasgow, Manchester, Essex. It comes from places and people that are really struggling to make some meaning out of their existence.'

Showbiz and media were always the escape hatch for bright working-class kids too impatient to wait for academic validation - I was one of them. But I probably wouldn't be today; in the case of national journalists, the proportion of those educated privately has also increased over the past two decades, with only 14% of us educated at comprehensive schools. In the light of the long odds against the likes of me becoming a writer now, would I have stayed on at school and gone to university if I was young today? Even before Covid rained on that particular parade, I very much doubt it - and it would probably have been a fool's errand anyway. Even many of those who aren't driven to suicide by snobbish classmates drop out. Olivia Fletcher wrote this in 2019:

> 'A year and a half ago, I shuffled into my lecturer's office in floods of tears. I was going to tell him that I was dropping out of university - University College London, one of Britain's most prestigious academic institutions. I had been there for six months. Since enrolling, my mental health had spiralled. I was failing most of my course modules. My bank account was empty. I missed my dog. I felt like I was the only person there who didn't like avocado on toast. More than anything, I was gravely out of place...working-class students benefit the least from graduating. We've already established that most middle-class students have access to better schools because their parents have more money. There's one more thing to add to our holy trinity: contacts.
>
> As a student at UCL I was never more than three metres away from someone who knew someone at the BBC, in Canary Wharf or in Parliament. Usually through familial networks, middle-class students tend to already have access to the career of their choosing. In comparison, even when graduating from top universities, working-class graduates face climbing a tall ladder to elite careers. After graduation, students from advantaged backgrounds will earn 16% more than their disadvantaged counterparts. Why? They know who can get them their internships, their work experience, their references and their hefty paycheck. Systematically, the odds are stacked against poorer students. From the walk into the classroom, to our first lecture and finally into the job market, we are always catching up in a race we feel like we'll never win.'

It's a vicious circle - bright working class kids drop out of university while dim privileged kids make it through, leading to the situation where the elected representatives who make our laws are supercilious strangers to us. 90% of MPs are university graduates, compared to 20% of the population overall. In fact the very name of the Labour Party seems almost a snarky joke at the expense of the many by the few these days. In the summer of 2020, Dan Hodges[8] (a disaffected Labour Party member and son of the ex-Labour MP Glenda Jackson) wrote in the Mail:

> 'Last month a group of Labour MPs, led by Ed Miliband, published their report into the collapse of the party's Red Wall in the last Election. They identified a number of reasons. The toxicity of Corbyn. The chaotic position on Brexit. The Generation Game conveyor-belt of implausible promises that constituted Labour's manifesto.
>
> But they ignored another significant factor. The liberal Left now view white, British working men and women as their enemy. And they hate their enemy with a loathing that is visceral.
>
> When I was going round the country during the Election, I quickly recognised this feeling was reciprocated. It was clear that working Britain was going to reject Corbynism decisively. But I thought that once he and his tin-pot Marxist army were routed, a process of re-engagement would begin. Labour would instinctively reach out to its lost heartlands. It's clear from the past week that it won't. It can't. Because its instinct is not to go near the working classes unless it's with a barge-pole – one that only sees the light of day at Election time.'

How the humble have fallen! It's surreal to realise how diverse the House of Commons once was, with Labour represented mostly by working men (and a few women, to be fair) and the Tories, as you'd expect, represented mostly by vermin, as Aneurin Bevan put it. In 1945, two actual Communists, belonging to the actual Communist Party of Great Britain, Willie Gallacher and Phil Piratin, were elected. Also in the first election after the War, a whopping 45 miners were elected to parliament - but miners were also MPs before the Labour Party existed, back as far as 1874. The former miner Lee Anderson got so much abuse for supporting Brexit that he changed parties and was elected Conservative MP for Ashfield when the Red Wall came down in the glorious winter of 2019.

It was a bit ironic, considering the reasons why Keir Hardie had founded the Labour Party in the first place - to represent the workers - that it took the Tories to re-prole Parliament with the new intake of Northern MPs. Gloria De Piero wrote in the Telegraph:

'Waking up on Friday 13th 2019 was a horror story I hope no Labour member or supporter will have ever have to relive. The scale of the defeat left even those who feared the worst taken aback. The seats we lost did not just represent numbers on a graph. They were seats that represented our hearts and souls. But these voters and these seats had been ringing alarms bells for years. At the last election Ashfield and Bolsover in the East Midlands saw the biggest swings to the Tories in the country and we also lost Mansfield and North East Derbyshire, which had never before been represented by anyone other than a Labour MP. We could and should have acted then. I called the Labour leader's office and offered to carry out a listening exercise in these former coalfield seats within days of the last general election. I never received a call back.

Brexit is only part of the problem. There is also a strong sense that the Labour party – or at least those who run it – simply do not share the same instincts, attitudes or worldview of the majority of voters in these seats. Patriotism and self-sufficiency are not regarded as Tory values in these areas and nor do they exist in opposition to civic pride or community spirit. All political parties are dominated by the middle classes but for a party that was formed to represent the working class, we have too few working class members.

They voted Tory, or refused to vote Labour, because they despised us. They want to come back but that will only happen if we listen to their arguments and change as a result.'

As the 2019 election approached, I became increasingly keen to find Labour MPs, preferably of working-class origin, who didn't dismiss Brexit, just to keep me faithful and stop me from what my father had always told me was a fate worse than death - voting Tory. Imagine my excitement on discovering Lisa Nandy, the young MP for Wigan (home of Northern Soul, the World Pie Eating Contest and that pier which George Orwell used as a peg on which to hang his searing account of the harsh lives of Northern working-class people in the 1930s) who resembled a mardy teenager from Coronation Street. When I discovered what she had written in her student newspaper, I truly believed I had found my proletarian politician princess:

'As I've said many times over the course of this year, there are just no fit men at this university … There's a lot of diversity in a university – virgins, slimy bastards who offer to buy you a drink but have no intention of doing any such thing - geeks, the lot! The trick is how to spot them. You can usually identify a virgin from a thousand paces, cos they'll be trendy dressers and well into dance music. The only solution is to quit the manhunt and wait till after uni when you're back amongst normal people.'

But her grandad was a Liberal Lord!

To be fair, Nandy looks like the Little Match Girl compared to the monstrous regiment of Red Princes - and the odd Red Princess, though this being the Labour Party the men get first dibs. Will Straw, Euan Blair, 'The Hon' Stephen Kinnock (that was quick!), David Prescott, Tamsin Dunwoody, The Hon Emily Sophia Wedgwood Benn…the list is shameless.

And it is a Labour problem, for some strange reason. In 2014 Sophie McBain wrote in the New Statesman:

> 'If Labour wants to convince disaffected voters that its politicians aren't drawn from a narrow, self-serving Westminster elite, it has a few problems. The latest research found that 54 per cent of the party's candidates selected in marginal or inherited seats (those with retiring MPs from the same party) for 2015 have already worked in politics or for think tanks. In comparison, 17 per cent of Conservative candidates are political insiders.'

Just as nepotism on the part of Labour seems counter-intuitive, so does the fact that it's getting worse, not better. For nearly two decades - from 1970 to 1997 - there was a run of Prime Ministers - Heath, Callaghan, Thatcher and Major - who had no inherited political connections and while often mocked by the grandees of their parties were recognised by the electorate as leaders who had made it under their own steam. But the story of Labour's abandonment of the working-class heartlands for the head-rush of Woke can be seen best in the tale of two Keirs. Keir Hardie, the founder of the Labour Party, worked in the Lancashire coal mines from the age of ten. Sir Keir Starmer, the present leader of the Labour Party, read law at Leeds University where even then a reference in the student newspaper hailed him as 'Keir Starmer – King Of Middle Class Radicals.'

In the past, the unions might have balanced out the over-educated element of the Labour Party with a sound bit of blue-collar common sense.

But in a shocking piece of political origami - the ideological equivalent of gender reassignment, with all the contortions involved - the unions have clambered onto the Woke-wagon too. In the summer of 2020 the GMB - one of the country's largest remaining unions, having more than 630,000 members composed of workers in everything from retail to local government - wrote the following letter to Liz Truss, the Minister for Women & Equalities, demanding that men in dresses be allowed to use women's spaces, which is what self-identification boils down to in the workplace especially. It included the following paragraph:

> 'As a trade union we represent all workers, including many trans workers. We know the levels of discrimination and abuse trans and non-binary people face in the workplace as well as wider society: many employers do not adequately understand trans issues, nor do a large number of service providers that trans people rely on. We know from TUC research in 2017 that almost half of all trans workers have experienced bullying or harassment at work, with under a third having their status revealed without their consent.'

What percentage of GMB members are allegedly 'trans' and 'non-binary' compared to female comrades who want to maintain their safe lavatorial space, I wonder? It's almost like having a chance to openly express their lack of respect for women is more important to them than their own survival. Additionally, as we've already seen, respect for 'trans women' often goes hand in hand with contempt for true women, and the Woke Bros certainly aren't alone in this.

Four years previously a whistle-blower had called out Unite - Britain's biggest union, with nearly £1.5 million members - by leaking an internal report which showed that more than half of female officers had been bullied or sexually harassed by fellow officials or members in their workplaces. You'd hope that comrades could learn from their brothers mistakes, yet just a matter of weeks after the merry men of the GMB had been poking their noses into ladies lavatories, an independent investigation into sexual harassment there concluded that the organisation was 'institutionally sexist' and in dire need of a 'complete transformation' after bullying, misogyny, cronyism and sexual harassment were found to be 'endemic.'

The barrister Karen Monaghan, who led the inquiry, wrote:

'Examples of sexual harassment I heard about included touching hair, leering, commenting on body shape and clothes, placing hands around a woman's waist, staring at a woman's breasts... propositioning young women, sloppy kisses, sticking a tongue in a woman's ear, touching of knees, bottoms and hips and slapping of a backside...sometimes sexual harassment is used as a form of bullying with examples given to me of men deliberately sexually harassing women in public to humiliate and embarrass them. I have also heard of more serious sexual assaults...I was told by one witness that 'It is simply expected that you'll have to suffer from being groped at events'...'serious sexual assault (rape), drug use and sexually predatory behaviour.''

The aptly-named Mr Tim Roache - Glorious Leader of the GMB since 2016 - had given up his golden throne in the spring of 2020, presumably to avoid bringing further shame on his union after being accused of running a 'sexist and aggressive casting couch culture' by a disgruntled member in an anonymous letter. Up the workers, indeed!

Not a cry you ever hear from the Woke Bros, by the way - not 'Power to the people' either. The slogan so beloved of Black Panthers and anti-Vietnam war protestors in the 1960s has fallen out of fashion in politics, last heard in a television commercial touting car insurance in 2009. The unions might be as keen in cuddling up to the Woke as surely as Roache was to his female comrades, but the Woke have no interest in unions. With the negotiation aspect of trades unionism anathema to their performative preference, they can't handle all those pale, stale males flashing their white privilege about. To be fair, they've got a point there; say what you like about the casual racism of my 1970s calf-country, but the decade gave us the magnificent 'strikers in saris,' those Asian ladies led for two years by the fearless Jayaben Desai, who reportedly told her manager at the Grunwick film processing plant as she led the walkout 'What you are running here is not a factory, it is a zoo. But in a zoo there are many types of animals. Some are monkeys who dance on your fingertips, others are lions who can bite your head off. We are the lions, Mr Manager.'

If only the working class could be exclusively BAME then the Woke would definitely be up for a bit of rainbow coalition with the type of person who can't pronounce Gstaad. But as they are, they just won't do. Like women, the working class are a majority treated like a minority, and the mediocrities of Woke are similarly wary of both; understandably for a group with so little ability, Wokers like their oppressed groups to actually **be** a minority so that their own place in the pecking ordered isn't threatened. Far safer to keep both the women and the workers 'theoretical,' as Dr Moore said, in any future struggle, as when they do speak (be they demanding the right to spend a penny without being perved over or objecting to being undercut by a people-trafficking gang-master) they confirm all the Wokers worst fears. Bolshy - not Bolshevik.

Not only were the Woke not keen on The People getting their paws on Power, but there rose up in recent years many well-bred voices both in Britain and in the U.S.A which put forward the notion that what was wrong with the world was too much power in the hands of the people. IS MORE DEMOCRACY BETTER DEMOCRACY? carped The New Yorker in 2018 - TOO MUCH DEMOCRACY IS BAD FOR DEMOCRACY whinged The Atlantic in 2019. Always altruistic, the Guardian stepped in to bleat FOR TOO MANY PEOPLE IN TOO MANY COUNTRIES, DEMOCRACY ISN'T WORKING. What a shame for Extinction Rebellion[9] - with their pipe-dream that a People's Assembly could over-rule an elected parliament on matters of climate change - that their autumn of 2019 antics shared news bulletins with the ongoing protests of the brave and beautiful young people of Hong Kong taking on the might of a monster state determined to rob them of their civil rights. (China is also of course the world's biggest polluter, - but Extinction Rebellion never let facts get in the way of a family-size hissy-fit.) With their freedom flags and solemn songs, they recall the days when protest was a matter of life and death, not of huff and puff. IS DEMOCRACY HAVING A MID-LIFE CRISIS? the BBC asked hopefully in 2018.

It wasn't democracy which started having a mid-life crisis in 2016; it was the liberal establishment which somehow believed that it would be able to tell poor people how to behave as it had throughout its history, ever since the Fabian Society openly favoured forced sterilisation of the Undeserving Poor. The BBC and the EU (the Tweedledum and Tweedledee of Metropolitan Elitism, National and International Branches) couldn't cease spluttering with incredulous outrage...AFTER ALL I'VE DONE FOR YOU! Scratch a Brexiteer and nine times out of ten you'll draw the blood of someone who'd like to break free of our BBC overlords too; they're so similar in their endless entitlement, their fake enlightenment, their crazed spending of other people's money. Their mottos - 'Nation shall speak peace to nation' (the BBC) and 'United in diversity' (the EU) - are amusingly interchangeable - and so is the bitter harvest they both must face. Institutions outlive their usefulness and at that point they change or they perish - this was the refreshing message of populism.

Of course, if Clinton and Corbyn had got elected, and if Remain had won, there wouldn't have been one piqued peep about democracy being ready for the knacker's yard. But there was one unexpected side benefit for born-to-rule liberals who'd had had repeated rude awakenings since Victory Morn, as I call the Brexit referendum result. After all that pretending to be more civilised than other people, failure freed them up and they no longer felt it necessary to set a good example. They took to the taboo taste-thrill of unabashed hatred for the lower classes with all the sensual fervour of organically-raised pigs in muck.

For people keen on accusing our side of jingoism, Remainers were awfully keen on tossing around references to our country's heroic struggle against the Nazi war machine. They saw themselves as The Few, I'd wager (true numerically, if not symbolically); when Paddy Ashdown referred to Tory Brexiteers as 'Brownshirts' the gorgeous MP James Cleverly responded 'So I'm a Nazi now, am I?' only to have the secretary-shagger respond superciliously 'Heavens! Even allowing for these over-heated times, do we really have to lose contact with the concept of the metaphor?' But as if to prove that such profound thickness was no respecter of age or ethnicity, here was the MP David Lammy, frothing that to compare the European Research Group to the actual Nazis was 'not strong enough.' Julian Barnes, an apparently sensible cove, fizzed into a masochistic froth on the subject, hoping that we would be 'well punished' by thigh-booted Brussels. But perhaps no one pushed the Woke war-boats out as far as his fellow novelist Ian McEwan. 'A gang of angry old men, irritable even in victory, are shaping the future of the country against the inclinations of its youth,' this very angry old man, very irritable in defeat, told a Remainer rally remain in 2017. 'By 2019 the country could be in a receptive mood: 2.5 million over-18-year-olds, freshly franchised and mostly Remainers; 1.5 million oldsters, mostly Brexiters, freshly in their graves.' Wishing your enemy dead? What a civilised man.

To anyone who could get past the fact that the United Kingdom not wishing to be part of a German superstate was being literally Hitler, Brexit came as a beautiful bit of insurrection - and very timely in that it came along just as the Labour Party was dying under the auspices of Jeremy Corbyn, first leader of Woke ('My name is Jeremy Corbyn, pronouns he/him' - in my house, we settled for calling him It) so that all of us comrades repulsed by nepotism and hypocrisy had a home to go to. We are often reminded of the 'hatred' the referendum 'stirred up' in our society — warned off democracy by those who would control us for our own good, as if we were wayward children eyeing the biscuit tin. What these sorrowing sad-sacks failed to add is the hate comes largely from their side. 'Too much democracy' has merely flushed the poison out. Brexit did indeed unleash hate — but the hate it unleashed was not that of the British for foreigners but rather of the liberals for the masses. There's something reminiscent of Nineteen Eighty-Four's Two Minutes Hate about it:

> 'Within 30 seconds any pretence was always unnecessary. A hideous ecstasy of fear and vindictiveness, a desire to kill, to torture, to smash faces in with a sledge hammer, seemed to flow through the whole group of people like an electric current, turning one even against one's will into a grimacing, screaming lunatic. And yet the rage that one felt was an abstract, undirected emotion which could be switched from one object to another like the flame of a blow-lamp.'

After Brexit, it was open season on the revolting masses; especially from those who had positioned themselves firmly on the side of the proles but could now enjoy the novelty of hating the humbly born. In the U.S.A, too; long before Boris advised ballerinas to become cyber-detectives in the virus-ravaged Britain of 2020, American Wokers were advising the working classes in devastated industrial cities to 'learn to code.' They voted for Trump instead.

I'm rarely shocked but in 2020 I heard the comedian Alexei Sayle - raised as a communist - talking about a job-creation scheme in some trade he disapproved of - on a radio show. The way he said 'To create jobs…' in the most namby-pamby voice, as though people had demanded golden elephants rather than a living wage, made me literally catch my breath - a life-long Left-winger, mocking the unemployed for wanting to work! Even the tame audience had to work hard to raise a titter. Woke anti-worker snobbishness had even corrupted this once-decent man, that he could, as a Jew, happily stand alongside anti-Semites in the service of Corbyn. In 2016, he wrote that while he'd been happy to mock Blair's New Labour in his act, now that Corbyn was 'reforming the party in his own image – ascetic, socialist, kindly and ethical' he would stop making jokes about Labour. No one noticed, though, as he hadn't been funny for a good two decades.

Dan Hodges again:

> 'One trade union official said to me a few months ago: 'I never thought I'd see the day when one of our members would stand up at Labour conference and plead for jobs to be a priority alongside the environment, and get booed.' Why wouldn't they be booed? They are the enemy now. Men and women who have been working all their lives and have the temerity to think they may have a more rounded grasp of life than the teenage Greta Thunberg. People who are grinding their way through the same type of dead-end job as their parents – if they're lucky enough to have a job at all – but don't feel like waking up every morning and checking their 'white privilege.' Or parents and grandparents who dare to suggest that politicians might actually prioritise their daily struggles over the plight of the Palestinians.'

Paul Embery, the firefighter and trades unionist sacked by his union for addressing pro-Brexit rallies, foresaw the fall of the red wall due to the Woke takeover of Labour in the spring of 2019:[10]

> 'The group-thinkers and virtue-signallers and woke liberals and quasi-Marxists and echo-chamber-dwellers who comprise so much of the modern Left believe themselves to be Inherently Better People than those of us from the more traditional Left.

We are Gillian Duffy and White Van Man of Rochester – ripe for votes, but not fit to be seen in public with. It is this patronising mindset that compels them to assume that ethnic minority voters cannot possibly be in favour of Brexit or opposed to free movement. Yet research shows that around a third of ethnic minority voters supported Leave, and that many of these, particularly the older generation, were hostile to free movement, not least because they considered it unfair that prospective migrants from outside the EU – in many cases, people like themselves – faced bigger hurdles in coming to the U.K than did those from inside it.

At a time when the traditional working class has never felt so disillusioned with Labour, the party's support for policies such as free movement, which did so much to alienate this group in the first place, will do nothing to win them back. Whatever their skin colour.'

As the losers like to say about Brexiteers/racists, not all Remainers are Wokers - but all Wokers are Remainers. For all their sanctimonious sermons, what Remainers really wanted, what made their cold little hearts beat faster was limitless access to cheap Sancerre and cheaper au pairs. They'd consider themselves 'caring' people on the whole, I imagine, but they didn't care that the hideous phenomena of modern slavery and sex trafficking is with us courtesy of free movement, assisted by the brotherhood of man and soundtracked with the Ode To Joy.

There's a simple reason why the working class object to immigration far more than those above them on the social ladder and it's not that they're evil knuckle-dragging bigots. It's because **their** livelihoods are impacted when the labour pool increases and when many of those newly arriving are happy to ignore the gains made for indigenous workers by their long and savage history of trades union struggle. There's a reason why the Confederation of British Industry has always been against immigration controls: it enables the bosses to bus in swathes of slave labour from Eastern Europe and then accuse the indigenous workers whose wages are going down the Swanee of being racist if they don't just knuckle under and accept it. It was this perfectly healthy - and socialistic - reaction to being played by greedy overseers which led so many working-class people to vote for Brexit.

A 2011 letter to the Independent from Graham Wright of the Vale of Glamorgan - replying to an opinion piece stating that the more immigrants we have, the better, even with millions unemployed - said it well:

> 'While the skills and training of Britons could certainly do with some improvement, the main barrier to our getting jobs are the low wages and poor conditions of service that employers are increasingly offering. Employers often favour migrant workers for their so-called 'work ethic.' We used to have this kind of 'work ethic' in Britain. During the industrial revolution it was commonplace. We haven't lost it; we fought our way out of it, largely through the efforts of the trade union movement. We are right to demand the kind of meaningful life outside of work that such long hours make impossible.'

We were always told that Britons 'wouldn't do' the jobs in catering and hospitality, which is why we needed to ship in all that cheap Eastern European labour, but when in the spring of 2020 the farming industry warned that thousands of tonnes of fruit and vegetables would rot in fields, some 35,000 Britons applied in the first few weeks. They were mostly rejected in favour of Eastern European workers who could be crammed into mobile homes on the farmers land, enabling them to dock food and housing costs - around £70 per worker per week - from their pay. It's worth remembering that cheap immigrant labour doesn't just damage indigenous people, but also the people doing it; the Chinese Morecambe Bay cockle-pickers died because they had no knowledge of local tides, unlike the local workers, who they replaced by virtue of being paid a pittance. There's a reason why 'gang-master' is such an ugly title.

This was the poisonous state of affairs - the ruling class importing a docile foreign workforce to punish the working class for daring to demand a living wage - which the Brexit referendum addressed. It was never about racism; unless, ironically, one considers the racism of Eastern Europeans, many of whom were quite open with their distaste at the number of different ethnicities they encountered in British cities. But still the Woke Remainers clung to their ego-boosting fantasies of how their fellow countrymen were racist hordes ready to run amok at the merest sniff of wodzionka; imagine their dismay when the Guardian published the following findings in the spring of 2019:

'British people are more persuaded of the benefits of immigration than any other major European nation, according to a global survey which has also found that almost half of Britons think immigrants are either positive or neutral for the country. The findings contradict the assumption that Britain is more hostile to immigration than its European neighbours are while many argue concerns over immigration were the key driving force behind the Brexit vote.'

The Woke desire to see hoi polloi as semi-human was nothing if not a shape-shifter. Luckily for them, soon after it became obvious to even the most rabid Juncker-sucker that Brexit couldn't be undone, there was a plague just around the corner. The Woke had called the working-class stupid when they voted for Brexit in 2016, and again when they voted for Boris Johnson in 2019 - what better way to start a new century than telling them once again that they were unable to grasp the situation, gaily super-spreading their way through the summer? It was those chavs what done it - drinking their beer on the beach rather than sipping wine at a pavement cafe. It's funny how the Woke refer to the workers quite like the way Rudyard Kipling writes of the native in The White Man's Burden - 'Your new-caught sullen peoples/ Half devil and half child.' - when it's their highly unattractive petulance which has been so strikingly consistent. The Big Sulk - 'Le Bouder Grand' - was an expression I coined in 2020 referring to those who both refused to accept the result of the Brexit referendum and also refused to engage with its outcome in any constructive way. It could be seen again during the plague year when for some people literally nothing the government did was good enough.

Hypocrisy is nothing new. We're used to seeing people in power being hypocrites. There's a whole rationale for it; de La Rochefoucald's old saw that 'Hypocrisy is a tribute vice pays to virtue.'[11] You could get away with this in a culture of deference which had no mass media, where the peasants could be scared into believing that they'd burn in Hell if they even contemplated misbehaving themselves as their betters did. But as populism in general and Brexit in particular showed, we no longer live in forelock-tugging times.

Because this plague was a whole new thing, we weren't ready for the same old double standard. Teachers who happily availed themselves of the labour of working-class people all summer long but seemed to think that they were too special to go back to work - 'JJ Charlesworth' on Twitter said it well: 'There was never any lockdown. There was just middle-class people hiding while working-class people brought them things.' Government advisors preaching lockdown and getting around like something out of a Beach Boys song. The sneering on social media at the people licking Mr Whippies on Southend beach which wouldn't be aimed at some snob swanning around Sandbanks, even though those who bore the brunt of the patronising fury were far more likely to be on furlough, freshly unemployed and/or stuck in a small home without a garden. Clapping for the frontline workers went stale after awhile (those lorry drivers probably voted Brexit anyway) and there was about to be a new, exotic dance craze in town.

As if the coronavirus wasn't discombobulating enough, the fetishisation of our black population which took place in the summer of 2020 was both entertaining and enervating. Vicky Pollard had once been the only television character to have a black baby - and she was strictly a figure of fun. But by the summer of 2020, every single relationship in the TV commercials featured a a beatific bi-racial couple and their adorably 'vibrant' children. As Trevor Phillips pointed out, the British working-class had been miscegenating for years for decades; a black American musician said to me in the 1970s 'You English girls sure do mix - not like American girls.' I like to believe that the popularity of 'Devon' as a black American Christian name may stem from happy memories of the welcome their grandads got from our women when they were stationed there in World War Two: 'One thing I noticed here and which I don't like is the fact that the English don't draw any color line,' said an American lieutenant at the time. 'The English must be pretty ignorant. I can't see how a white girl could associate with a negro.'

But apparently it had only just occurred to the chattering classes - and they went overboard with the zeal of a con-man convert. 37% of ads featured BAME people, even though they make up 3% of the population. It was amusing to see how the advertisers tried to outdo each other - and when the attractive lesbian couples started rocking up in car adverts, one did start wondering whether some poor PAM was bringing his hobby to work. One Christmas commercial featured a Sikh, a Muslim woman in a burqa, and a gay couple with an infant daughter; 'Perhaps this year they'll 'go for gold' and put them all in the same room,' smirked the commentator James Maker.

It wasn't just the shillers of ad-land who caught Woke fever in that plague summer - of course, the BBC caught it worst of all. One was used to Radio 4 presenters being posh; writing in the Radio Times, Michael Buerk pointed to the imminent bailing of John Humphrys from the Today programme to note; 'All four of the regular presenters will now have been privately educated, like a quite remarkable proportion of other people working for the BBC on both sides of the microphone.' Never mind, Auntie knew how to put accusations of class-prejudice that right in one fell swoop: DIVERSITY - NOW WHITEWASHES FASTER THAN ANY OTHER SOFT SOAP! (Until this point the BBC appear to have understood the word 'diversity' as meaning you could pay young women less than young men and sack old women more than old men.)

In the summer of 2020 Michael Crick[12] wrote in the Spectator:

'The BBC has announced plans to invest £100 million pounds in 'diversity' for its television output. Bravo. I'm a great believer in diversity. A thriving, vibrant democracy needs as much diversity as possible in public discourse – a plurality of voices, of outlook and of background. But I suspect that the BBC is thinking of 'diversity' in only the narrow, fashionable sense of today – in gender, race and sexuality, but little else. Until the BBC definition of 'diversity' entails a lot more emphasis on the elderly, on people who didn't go to university, on working-class people and the poor, and people from outside the big conurbations, then the Corporation will never understand its whole audience. It will grow ever more out of touch with the have-nots, the left-behinds, and the people who voted leave the EU.

I love the BBC. It employed me for 21 years. I would hate to see the Corporation weakened or destroyed. But if the BBC sticks to a narrow, liberal, academic, middle-class definition of diversity it will be severely handicapped in the looming Battle of the Licence Fee. If large parts of the population – the old, the less well educated. Unless the BBC adopts a genuine commitment to true 'diversity,' its £100 million proposed investment could end up costing a lot, lot more.'

To wake up in the summer of 2020, as a woman of working-class origin who had been listening to Radio 4's RP for more than four decades, was to wonder both a) what kept them and b) what time the bodysnatchers had landed. Every other person speaking suddenly had a black or Asian name, and it was refreshing and lively - but on the other hand, there were still no white working-class voices. Perhaps we were just being given the silent treatment by our betters to remind us of our white privilege?

I wish I'd known I was privileged all those years - I'd have been even more of a diva. No matter, because here on the radio is the Guardian writer Afua Hirsch (Wimbledon High School, Oxford, Doughty Street Chambers) explaining to me why Meghan Markle is one of the wretched of the earth. Here is a young black lady horse-riding in Brixton. Here is another, rambling in the countryside and wishing it was more 'inclusive.' (Doesn't she know that farmers hate everybody equally?) Here is a young black lady talking about 'coding' - having to speak differently in order to make the middle classes understand you're not thick, because of course that never, ever happened to the kids I went to school with. Here is an extremely charming and bright black girl reporting on 'the working-class experience of being a student during the pandemic.' Here is a new portrait of Queen Victoria's African goddaughter Sarah Forbes Bonetta unveiled; 'Black history is part of English history and while we know we have more to do, we at English Heritage is committed to telling the story of England in full.' The young lawyer Hashi Mohamed presents Radio 4's Adventures In Social Mobility, quite rightly celebrating his remarkable career after arriving here aged nine, an unaccompanied child refugee with hardly any English. But last year's The Trouble With Social Mobility - presented by a white man - suggested that social mobility was not in itself a good thing. Because there's **so many of them** - and who will clean our offices now the Somalians are going to law school? Just as Woke prefers *women* with cocks, they seem only to recognise the worth of working-class people if they're black. Otherwise, they might be racist.

I felt genuine glee on hearing these different voices. But I wonder how truly diverse an organisation can claim to be when all these different voices parrot the same views on everything from Israel and why icicles are melting so fast - it's like saying that marshmallows represent a balanced meal because some are white and some are pink. By championing racial diversity the Woke ruling class has happened upon a smart way of swerving the far greater injustice which exists in this country - the class system, which wastes more lives than any other form of oppression ever invented. So you'll hear a beautiful Bajan accent reading the BBC news - but never a pleb Brummie. Despite those expensive educations, the Woke ruling class don't understand what the uneducated UnWoke working-class ask of them, simply because they talk differently; to not be dismissed as a chav, gammon or Karen, in a milieu which would rather cut out its tongue than dehumanise any other group so, and thus have 99.9% of all life opportunities stifled at birth.

Middle-class white children are already **eighteen months** ahead of white working-class children before they start school. Maybe it's not even the fault of the privileged Woke that they are so tone-deaf — maybe they just don't hear. In the autumn of 2020 a study by University College London and Yale University in the US claimed that holding a conversation with someone from a different social class requires more brain power than speaking to someone from a similar background. The Daily Mail reported:

> 'People's prejudice towards those who are richer or poorer than them even makes basic small talk more taxing, a study has found. The study, published in the journal Social Cognitive and Affective Neuroscience, involved 12 minutes of conversation for every pair. People aged 18 to 44 were given conversational topics at random, including autobiographical subjects such as what they did last subject, and objective ones, such as one person telling another how to bake a cake. The pairs, who were strangers to each other, were well matched in terms of age, sex and race, but 19 of them were hugely different in terms of their backgrounds. They ranged from people who had left education after school to university-educated people, and from those whose families had an annual income of less than 50,000 dollars (£38,659) to those from family incomes of more than 150,000 dollars (£115,978). Professor Joy Hirsch said: 'The message from our research is that people might want to spend more time with people different to them, and engage this part of their brain more. The more you use certain pathways in the brain, the more efficient they become. These interactions might get easier if people practise them.''

But the Woke won't be practising, as they can bear only to be with their own kind, lest someone point out that the emperor has no sustainably-sourced clothes and that their holier-than-thou kingdom is nothing more than a supersized house of cards which will soon come tumbling down. It's not that they don't hear - it's that they really are as foul as they seem. The word 'ignorant' has two meanings - the first indicating lack of knowledge, the second lack of civility - and when a Woker accuses a non-Woker of the first, they cannot do so without proving themselves the second.

We see this strongly in the new improved model of what my mum would have called a 'Lady Muck' - a woman who is convinced she is better than others with no evidence to show for it, no beauty or wit or humanitarian acts. Once most obviously found among the Tory ladies of the shires, they have now found a new lease of Woke life, more common in Shoreditch than Surrey and can be identified by their clean-eating habits and 'blessed' hashtags: anything that sets them above the rest of us. In 2017 the artist Hetty Douglas posted on Instagram a photo of three men in building site gear queuing in McDonald's with the caption 'These guys look like they got 1 GCSE.' And in the summer of 2020, a BBC podcast featured two youngish women called Charlotte and Amelia who launched an extraordinary attack on 'Karens' - the new diss-name for lower-class white women. Brendan O'Neill wrote brilliantly about it:[13]

> 'Wokeness increasingly looks like class hatred in disguise. 'Karen' is a female version of 'gammon' - just as Corbynista trustafarians refer to working-class men who support Brexit as pigs, so now the same constituency look upon lower-status white women as 'Karens.' 'Educate yourself' said Amelia, 'Read some books' and giggled as she said it, no doubt the endorphins of moral superiority kicking in. Charlotte said white women 'should try not to be defensive about your whiteness' and instead 'should think critically about your identity and privilege.' 'Get out of the way' she concluded. 'Yeah, basically leave,' agreed Amelia, and they laughed. It's hilarious, you see; educated middle-class women telling lesser women to fuck off. Indeed, that two white women can sit around talking about the problem with white women tells us something about what the phrase 'white people' means these days. It isn't just a physical description of those born white. It's a class indicator. 'White

people' typically refers to the lower orders, the insufficiently educated, the 'unaware.' Only working-class white people and lower-middle-class white people are reduced to their race, to their whiteness. It's a way of dehumanising them, in order both to delegitimise their opinions and their values (all of which are said to originate from their whiteness) and to ripen them up for lecturing and social interventions by cleverer, more socially aware white people like Charlotte, Amelia and an army of Woke academics and public officials.'

These revolting excuses for human beings, these seat-sniffers and bed-wetters, these Hetties and Lotties and Amelias have had their fun - but they should be careful now, though, as those they mock will increasingly have literally nothing to lose as we plunge into the free-fall of an unprecedented economic depression. Better get yourself back to Mummy and Daddy in their cosy gated community while you can, because there are some things you can't hide from behind the Wokescreen. And no matter whether you understand what the masses are trying to say to you or not, they probably won't be suffering in silence this time around. G.K Chesterton said it well in The Secret People:

'We hear men speaking for us of new laws strong and sweet,
Yet is there no man speaketh as we speak in the street.
It may be we shall rise the last as Frenchmen rose the first,
Our wrath come after Russia's wrath and our wrath be the worst.
It may be we are meant to mark with our riot and our rest
God's scorn for all men governing. It may be beer is best.
But we are the people of England; and we have not spoken yet.
Smile at us, pay us, pass us. But do not quite forget.'

As I look down from my bijou balcony, I think of the others easily as bright as me (well, almost) who never got a chance, now being passed over for a smaller group who will not have the numbers to dismantle the master's house - no matter how many statues they tear down - and may therefore be humoured and indulged. When I see the Woke media supplicating over minorities for their own narcissistic and performative ends, I foresee the nihilism of white riots to match the black ones. Because the trouble with identity politics is that you make being white an identity too. And if you split yourself off from others of your class because of their colour, dismissing their lived experience as privilege, blaming them for things they haven't done, eventually those people will say 'OK, you win. I'll talk to, live among, and vote only with my kind.' So though I'm looking at Brighton beach, I'm seeing Dover Beach as Matthew Arnold described it:

'For the world, which seems
To lie before us like a land of dreams,
So various, so beautiful, so new,
Hath really neither joy, nor love, nor light,
Nor certitude, nor peace, nor help for pain;
And we are here as on a darkling plain
Swept with confused alarms of struggle and flight,
Where ignorant armies clash by night.'

In such turbulent times, who can help us make sense of the supreme bond of humanity (while honouring our unique journeys, of course) which unites us? Where is our Martin Luther KIng, our Mother Theresa? Lucky for us, the First Couple of Woke were there to lead the way to a better place - in a private jet, naturally.

## Notes

[1] https://togetherforthecommongood.co.uk/stories/notes-from-nowhere

[2] https://en.wikipedia.org/wiki/Gammon_(insult)

[3] https:// www.noiseomaha.com/resources / 2021/7/1/a-brief-history-of-the-word-pig-as-slang-for-police

[4] https:// www.kentlive.news/news/kent-news/exceptional-university-kent-student-26-3714903

[5] https://www.thetimes.co.uk/article/cheryl-cole-girl-interrupted-fqh3dhjgkjz

[6] http://www.mtv.co.uk/lily-allen/news/lily-so-what-if-im-middle-class

https:// www.independent.co.uk/voices/columnists/julie-burchill/julie-burchill-word-advice-lily-don-t-listen-what-people-me-say-about-you-2291858.html

https:// www.belfasttelegraph.co.uk / opinion / columnists/archive/julie-burchill/dear-lily-dont-listen-to-what-people-like-me-say-about-you-28627519.html

[7] https://www.thetimes.co.uk/article/cheryl-cole-girl-interrupted-fqh3dhjgkjz

[8] https:// www.dailymail.co.uk / debate/article-8514095/DAN-HODGES-liberal-Left-view-white-British-workers-enemy.html

[9] https://unherd.com/2019/07/dont-be-fooled-by-citizens-assemblies/

[10] https://www.spiked-online.com/2019/03/26/many-ethnic-minority-voters-backed-brexit-too/

[11] Francois Duc De La Rochefoucauld, Reflections or Sentences and Moral Maxims

[12] https://www.spectator.co.uk/article/the-bbc-has-lost-touch-with-real-diversity

[13] https://www.spiked-online.com/2020/07/07/what-they-mean-when-they-talk-about-white-people/

# CHAPTER SEVEN

# THE GRABDICATION: WOKE COMES TO WINDSOR, HOLLYWOOD HANDMAIDS AND THE GREEN, GREEN GRASS OF WOKE

When most people fall out of love, they can easily dismiss their bout of lubricious lunacy with the simple spell 'I never loved them!' before deleting them on social media and moving on. For a writer this doesn't work - it's all out there, smeared all over cyberspace like a particularly attention-seeking Dirty Protest. This is how I see my rather embarrassing crush on Meghan Markle, which lasted from 2017 till 2020. In the winter of 2017 I scribbled thus for the Spectator, no doubt dotting the letter i with hearts whenever it appeared:[1]

> 'Prince Harry is a lucky man to have found a companion who is so definitively un-princessy – even though she is as beautiful a woman ever to have walked the Earth... It would be nice to think – for reasons of spite and scandal – that Meghan Markle is that splendid thing "an adventuress: a) a woman who seeks dangerous or exciting experiences: b) a woman who seeks position or livelihood by questionable means" (Merriam-Webster). But I think the far more wholesome if less thrilling truth is simply that she is a young woman in love.'

There's worse to come. Whenever I post my newspaper columns on social media, I always add the warning: 'REMEMBER WE HACKS DON'T WRITE OUR OWN HEADLINES!' Well, in this case I did; the headline was 'MEGHAN MARKLE HAS RESCUED HER PRINCE' and was indeed inspired by the final line of passionately purple prose: 'Meghan Markle has never waited soppily for some prince to rescue her. In fact, it seems far likelier that it is she who will rescue the prince.' CRINGE! As the youngsters say.

Thankfully, by the summer of 2019 I was thoroughly disillusioned: 'Harry and Meghan took four private jets in eleven days after a summer of lecturing us about climate change; this followed shortly after the prince's jaunt to the Google climate change summit where he is also thought to also have taken a helicopter, as he habitually uses them to fly short distances whereas the Queen makes do with a train. Having Elton John rush in to defend them didn't help, but only further established that the Sussexes saw themselves as international stars rather than one nation's public servants.'

Shortly after hearing that Meghan planned to semi-retire from royal duties in order to spend more time with her merchandising, I coined a fabulous phrase - The Grabdication - and now my rehabilitation is complete. The Grabdication was another Woke event (along with the GRA and the Remoaner refusal to accept Brexit) which while appearing to be liberal was actually reactionary. The Grabdication told peasants that princes may do as they wish with no regard to public opinion, the Gender Recognition Act that men may do as they wish with no regard for the opinion of women and a second vote on Brexit that the ruling class may do as they wish and ignore the voice of the people. On social media I espied some sore loser opining that they suspected a good deal of *crossover* between Leavers and loathers, presumably as all Leavers are racists and only racism would lead one to criticise someone who took four private jets in eleven days after a summer of lecturing us about climate change. There may well an overlap - but only in that critics of both Brussels and Sussexes are united in despising a bunch of money-grubbing hypocrites who dress up their meretriciousness with snippets of the Desiderata.

We'd been on this do-as-I-say-not-as-I-fly bumpy ride before of course; Prince Harry's father, Prince Charles (perhaps the grand-daddy of Woke, with his Malthusian mutterings and Islamophiliac slobberings) has long exemplified my observation 'It's no wonder than the wealthy are friends of the earth - it's been a damn good friend to them.'[2] The idea of a pre-industrial Eden, the rich man in his castle, the poor man at his gate, has fuelled the righteous fury of aristocrats against capitalism since the 1969, when Friends Of The Earth International was founded with a donation of half a million dollars from one Robert Orville Anderson, an oil man with rich parents and a guilty conscience. In the 1970s and 80s, the Green Party was guided by the rather charming and telegenic Sir Jonathon Espie Porritt, 2nd Baronet and old Etonian; another Etonian, Zac Goldsmith (or Baron Goldsmith of Richmond Park as his friends call him) proved that super-rich and sexy Conservative MPs could be as rabidly pro-planet and anti-humanity as any smelly old unelectable loony with his extensive championing of ecology issues over the past two decades. The well-born travelling the world in order to gather evidence as to why the humbly-born should stay at home and treat themselves to a lovely staycation in Slough – which Goldsmith felt so strongly about that he resigned as a Conservative MP when the government approved the construction of a third runway at Heathrow Airport in 2016 - was to become the blueprint of all the little XR Zacs still wowing their Montessori teachers with their finger painting all over the more affluent hoods of England.

Goldsmith is believed to have inherited between £200 million and £300 million after his father Sir James Goldsmith's death in 1997; some tax experts have speculated his income could amount to as much as £5 million per year from the trust left to him alone, making him the second richest man in Parliament. (He currently occupies a characteristically cushy billet in the House of Lords.) But his undeniable sweeteners of charm and beauty makes his hypocrisy go down easier than that of the relatively poor bore George Monbiot who is such a steaming Marie Antoinette that he once wrote of Ethiopia:

> 'In the poorest half of the poorest nation on earth, the streets and fields crackle with laughter. In homes constructed from packing cases and palm leaves, people engage more freely, smile more often, express more affection than we do behind our double glazing, surrounded by remote controls.'

Male life expectancy is 42 years - obviously, like those early-expiring porn stars, Ethiopians are dropping dead of sheer molten happiness. Then there's Baron Melchett, who ran Greenpeace for 12 years;

another Old Etonian, scion of the founder of the British Steel Corporation and heir to his great-grandfather's fortune from the chemical giants ICI. Melchett owns an 800-acre estate in Norfolk and has spoken of his Greenery as 'part of a family tradition of trying to do the right thing.

But none of these Green hypocrites could hold a hand-poured soy vegan Highgrove candle to their kingpin, the Prince of Wales, who in 2007 flew First Class to the U.S.A - with an entourage of 20 people - to collect an environmental award. And then two years later used a private jet on an 'environmental' tour of South America, costing approximately £300,000 over a 16,000-mile trip. Say what you like about Prince Harry's parentage, he certainly seems a chip off the old blockhead in this department. Prince Charles has an actress chum, too - and far from Meghan drawing ire for her hue, it's hard to think of any actress with royal connections who was so mocked as the very pale Emma Thompson[3] (the grandmother of Woke) who flew in First Class from Hollywood to join the Extinction Rebellion protests of spring 2019, a 5,456-mile transatlantic flight between LA and London stomping out a three-tonne carbon footprint. Extinction Rebellion, which demands that flights be used only in emergencies, simpered that Dame Emma's jaunt was 'an unfortunate cost in our bigger battle to save the planet' but the splendid David Blunkett was having none of it, asking during a parliamentary debate on that pesky old third runway at Heathrow:

> 'Does the minister agree that investing in alternative fuel sources for flights in the future would be more beneficial than people who use airlines regularly preaching to other people that they should stop using them to go on holiday or for commercial purposes – particularly when they have the comfort of flying First Class?'

In short, Green - like Wokeness itself - is the first socio-political movement in which every single mover and shaker ranges from well-off to filthy rich. Hearing the over-privileged half-wits of Extinction Rebellion talk about economic growth as if it was child abuse, you can sense real contempt towards people who believe that working at a job in order to make money and pay the taxes which keep society civil is a desirable thing to do. But perhaps this is understandable when you consider that no protest movement has ever featured so many double-barrelled names or Instagram skiing trips as this one, while demonising air travel for the masses. It's a bit rich Woke Blokes like Jon Snow[4] smirking how he's 'never seen so many white people in one place' at a Brexit rally when Extinction Rebellion are so white they make the Last Night Of The Proms look like Reggae Sunsplash.

Ecology is politics for people who don't like people and are miffed that the masses are now free to travel cheaply, rather than being hooked up to a plough or doing laundry in a creek. Just like the politicians they decry, there's one rule for them and another for the rest of us – as when their leading lights, Rupert Read,[5] took a taxi to a radio interview because he was in 'a terrible rush' while his crusty comrade, one Robin Boardman-Pattison, flounced out of another interview after it was pointed out that the skiing trips he had posted on social media are hardly the 'emergencies' that he wants flying to be confined to.

That the silly would be led by the sinister soon became evident in the ranks of the Green goons. The silly contingent were easily picked off by their own frenzied desire for attention, which was too time-consuming for them to concentrate on anything seditious. A dozen topless XR women chained themselves to the railings of Parliament; this, following XR's mass dance-in outside Buckingham Palace, made me wonder whether a high proportion of these extraordinarily performative protestors were frustrated 'resting' entertainers, with even more time on their hands than usual now that Theatreland was dark. The sinister showed their hand a few months later when XR targeted printing presses and left a nation without newspapers the next day. The tired old rationale was nothing new; the usual claim that the 'mainstream media' is controlled by a small number of people, and that news corporations are guilty of consistent manipulation of the truth to suit their own personal and political agendas. (You could also see AND THE JEWISH-CONTROLLED MEDIA reluctantly scratched out by one of the more sentient Sinisters.) Amusingly, the protest meant that thousands of Sun readers were unable to read an exclusive interview with Sir David Attenborough in which he explained why he supported Extinction Rebellion - and what Sun readers could do to help reduce climate change.

While all this was going on, James Lovelock[6] - founder of the Gaia Hypothesis, which claims that living organisms on the planet interact with their surrounding inorganic environment to form a synergetic and self-regulating system that created, and now maintains, the climate and biochemical conditions that make life on Earth possible - celebrated his 100th birthday. I'm not an environmentalist, believing that life will always find a way, but this is a hero with a hinterland so much bigger than scrounging off the state and going on holiday. From a working-class rural family, he was a maverick from the start; working on ways of shielding soldiers from burns, he refused to use anaesthetised rabbits and exposed his own skin to heat radiation instead. Always ready to change his mind when facts contradict theories, he registered as a conscientious objector at the start of World War Two, then tried to enlist after hearing of Nazi atrocities but was told that his medical research was too valuable. In 2004 he caused a sensation by declaring that 'only nuclear power can now halt global warming' and in 2012 he stated that he had been 'alarmist' about climate change, warning:

> 'The green religion is now taking over from the Christian religion – it's got all the sort of terms that religions use. The Greens use guilt. You can't win people round by saying they are guilty.'

The true divide in Green politics was not between the sinister and the silly, it transpired, but between overgrown children who know little of life versus a centenarian scientist of vast experience. But two people who wouldn't be choosing sides any time soon were Meghan and Harry, who from the fall of 2019 to the spring of 2020 were fully occupied in staging an updated version of Where's Wally Simpson? After stropping off from Frogmore Cottage, the Sussexes shipped out to neutral Canada, the ideal billet with historical ties to the monarchy and a super-Woke leader in ultimate dope-legalising, immigrant-embracing, Troon-spooning Justin Trudeau.

It was a common Woke celeb boast from Trump's first presidential campaign in 2016 that they would leave the US[7] in protest if the orange horror won - everyone from Snoop Doggy Dogg to Barbara Streisand pledged they'd be on that Greyhound bus northerly. 'I know a lot of people have been threatening to do this, but I really will,' Lena Dunham swore 'I know a lovely place in Vancouver and I can get my work done from there.' And Chelsea Handler would be on the seat beside her! Or not, as soon after Trump's first triumph, she addressed her weeping worshippers from her balcony: 'Yesterday, my staff reminded me that platforms and voices like mine are needed more than ever; leaving the country is quitting.' During the 2020 campaign Bruce Springsteen (who had previously promised to move to Australia but appeared to have forgotten about it, and this time picked Ireland with his blindfold, pin and map of the world) and Tommy Lee (probably too drunk to get on the plane to see his threat through) performed a similar mental Hokey-Cokey. But Trump or no Trump, Meghan couldn't keep away from the U.S.A, and it soon became clear exactly why she had left her husband's home country, dragging the poor sap behind her. She didn't want to be out of the limelight - she just wanted a different kind of limelight. Of course she still wanted to be looked at - but from a respectful distance. A cat may look at a king - but it musn't take a selfie with their Royal Highness, even accidentally, as happened with tennis fan Hasan Hasanov who was told off by her security squad for inadvertently photographing Her Highness at Wimbledon 2019 while going for a snap of Roger Federer. The bewildered grandfather told the Sun:

> 'I honestly couldn't really care less about taking a picture of Meghan, Harry or any of the royals — and, if I did, I'd ask first. I was much more interested in getting a video of Roger Federer in action.'

The American-born, London-based royal commentator Ashley Pearson provided a piquant comment which certainly rung true considering the peevishness which emanated from the pair as soon as the honeymoon was over: 'She had no idea how un-glamorous it really is to be a royal and, when she found out she would be a civil servant in a tiara she was, like 'No way.'' The Sussexes fervently-stated desire to pay their own way was admirable, but even the most meretricious bride would be gobsmacked by the 'bottom drawer'[8] that Meghan had amassed by the time she made a run for it. More than a hundred items - including pencils, socks and bookmarks - had proudly born the trademark 'Royal Sussex'[9] ever since the summer of 2019, bringing in a lovely bit of loose change to add to their estimated £34million private fortune.

It must have occurred to the Sussexes once they were safely ensconced in their gated community in California that they weren't going to quit their private jet habit anytime soon, now that they had to keep up with the Jenses: Lopez, Aniston and Lawrence. By the summer of 2020 they had shut down their charitable foundation and were instead touting an 'eco-tourism' scheme called Travalyst[10] (though considering the incessant keening of the Sussexes 'Travailist' might have been better) 'with ambition to change[11] the impact for travel, for good.' But this was a mere bagatelle. Another Woke crusade was rocking up - one far more dramatic and glamorous than diligently separating one's recycling every week. Black was the new Green in the fever-dream summer of 2020, when the death of a career criminal would make the rich and famous - who had previously been spending a great deal of their incomes on security to protect them from people like George Floyd - comprehend that some people led miserable lives. Once viewed as 'civilians ' now they couldn't get out there quick enough to mix and mingle while Babylon burned. Well, if not actually in the flesh (though Cara Delevigne and her fellow model Kaia Gerber were reported to have cuddled up[12] at a Black Lives Matter rally) then they were certainly going to stand up - or kneel down - and be counted via inspirational online encouragement to those disaffected citizens intent on burning down the businesses of their neighbours to prove that Martin Luther King did not die in vain.

It's not unusual for ambitious people to reframe their own story of scrabbling up the social scale in order to make them selfless epics - hence the popularity of the 'journey' trope in which our own perfectly understandable desire to have a cushy life can be presented as something spiritual. In this Incredible Journey (coincidentally the name of a film I loved as a child in which Luath the Labrador, Bodger the Bull Terrier and Tao the Siamese cat journey 250 miles through the Canadian wilderness to return to their home - a far more convincing perambulation than the Sussexes going 'home' to Frogmore Cottage or Vancouver Island) a woman with an expensive education and a passion for social change could have worked in any of the caring professions but chose to exploit her beauty instead, including a stint as 'Briefcase Girl'[13] on the game-show Deal Or No Deal. The actress who never quite made the first division would now be reborn as a dark Diana to a boy who idolised his mother and lost her at an impressionable age.

When I wrote that Meghan Markle had rescued her prince, I wasn't aware of how sinister my silly words were. She has certainly rung rings around a man born to privilege far greater than hers, remodelling him from a boy who thought nothing of using the word 'Paki'[14] or dressing up in a Nazi uniform for fun to a man genuflecting to the Obamas and embarrassingly eager to be 'educated' about racial politics. One must note here that whereas 'educate' once meant to 'lead out' Woke has changed the meaning to 'shut in' as fools who need to be told what to think prostrate themselves before their Woke Bros jury. It's similar to the form of breaking-down brainwashing beloved of the Scientologists when they 'audit'[15] a member; 'a process whereby the auditor takes an individual through times in their current or past lives with the purpose of ridding the individual of negative influences from past events or behaviours.' It's also poignant that 'educate' stems from the word 'ex' meaning out of and 'ducere' meaning lead - from which we get the word 'duke.' This was a Pygmalion in reverse, a cult of two in which the junior member had forsaken his very un-Woke cocktail of choice, the 'Crack Baby'[16] (vodka, raspberry liquor, passion fruit and champagne) in favour of fervently glugged Kool-Aid.

Of course it's good to realise that Nazi uniforms are bad, but it's a shame Prince Harry should demonstrate yet again how easily led he is by declaring loyalty to a new - albeit minor - cult of race hatred. It didn't help that he was having sex with a deliriously attractive demagogue. A useful friend told the Daily Mail:

> 'Meghan said her work as a leader is more important than ever right now and that she's been speaking with Oprah and other community leaders on how she can be part of the solution. Meghan feels like her mission goes far beyond acting. She said she wants to use her voice for change...she hasn't ruled out a career in politics.'

How long ago it seemed, in the spring of 2019, that Meghan had been scribbling inspirational messages on bananas for sex workers[17] at a Bristol charity which helped hookers exit their dangerous and dismal lives. And they weren't nice grateful prostitutes, even, like Julia Roberts in Pretty

Woman or Shirley MacLaine in Irma la Douce; instead, surveying the unfortunately phallic fruit bearing the heartfelt missives 'You are special,' 'You are brave' and 'You are strong,' one 'Nikki' complained 'People out here struggle to eat and sleep and she gifts us some words on a piece of fruit. She has the means to help us more than that. It's offensive.'

How much better to preach to the young and malleable - and, whisper it, one's own kind. In the summer of 2020 Meghan made a video address to graduates of her former Los Angeles private high school, though it seems unlikely that such a privileged cohort needed a pep talk more than inner city youngsters. It was quite a contrast with Michelle Obama's dignified visits to impoverished London schools, of which she said in 2018:

> 'I almost felt myself falling backward into my own past. You had only to look around at the faces in the room to know that despite their strengths these girls would need to work hard to be seen. There were girls in hijab, girls for whom English was a second language, girls whose skin made up every shade of brown ... they'd need to fight the invisibility that comes with being poor, female and of colour.'

Compare this to the unhinged cheerleading of the Duchess:

> 'Because George Floyd's life mattered and Breonna Taylor's life mattered and Philando Castile's life mattered and Tamir Rice's life matterered...and so did so many other people whose names we know and whose names we do not know. We are going to rebuild and rebuild and rebuild until it is rebuilt...you are going to lead with love, you are going to lead with compassion, you are going to use your voice in a stronger way than you've ever been able to. I know you know that black lives matter, so I am already excited for what you are going to do in the world. You are equipped, you are ready and you are prepared.'

Except the pretty ones, who would be best off going into show-business, marrying a rich man and leaving the heavy lifting to the others.

Of course no one is saying that actresses should be barred from talking about politics. Who doesn't thrill at photographs of Bacall and Bogart standing up for free speech against the witch-hunting weirdos of the Un-American Activities Committee? But once again, Woke ruined a beautiful thing; whereas Bacall and co wanted as much freedom of expression as possible, the Woke entertainers of today seek to shut it down. Hollywood was then Right-wing, and a politically liberal actor or writer could easily find themselves without work, on the notorious 'blacklist.'[18] Today, Hollywood is liberal, and espousing liberal politics is to conform rather than rebel.

Once upon a time the majority of entertainers came from humble backgrounds. Unschooled they may have been, but they had the common sense to understand that an entertainer complaining about attention is like a flasher complaining about voyeurs. But now that show-business is no longer something scandalous, nepotism has run riot, and stars live in a bubble far more than they did in the Golden Age of Hollywood. For instance, you could find Marilyn Monroe's number in the New York City phone book; she had no personal security apart from the self-styled Monroe Six, a gang of worshipful New York teenagers who looked out for her. Can we imagine any of todays stars trusting their fans to be their bodyguards? On the contrary, they spend a great deal of their time and money hiding from them.

In their gated compounds, wrapped up snug in their luxury beliefs, it's the easiest thing in the world for entertainers to espouse the misanthropy of the Woke for the masses. After all, aren't they themselves part of the wretched of the earth? 'It's so hard. There's all this scrutiny and social media. I wouldn't choose it,' whined Angelina Jolie.[19] It's probably the one thing she and Jennifer Aniston[20] have in common, when the Human Haircut bleated: 'There are times when you don't want anyone to see you, or you don't want to be photographed, or even go out of the house.' People who have monetised their very being, and are living a life of which most people can only dream, warn 'civilians' – as Liz Hurley memorably called non-entertainers – that it's hard out here on the frontline of fame. The dafter ones use war metaphors: Gwyneth Paltrow[21] claimed that reading nasty things about herself and her friends was 'almost like how, in war, you go through this bloody, dehumanising thing.'

Showbiz kids are always keen on saving the planet; private jets don't count, because everybody knows that only dirty commercial flights cause pollution, like food not really having calories if you eat it standing up. In 2016 Leonardo DiCaprio flew 8,000 miles from France to New York and back to accept an award on climate change. But it is the Troon crusade - the first ever protest movement which is about demanding applause for pretending to be something you're not rather than in winning respect for what you actually are, which also sums up the actor's craft - which has really struck a chord in Olympus-on-Burbank. Actresses seem to find it particularly easy being reborn as trans-maids; the same emotional illiteracy which had Kristen Stewart comparing being papped to being raped found a perfect echo in the Troon delusion that 'Misgendering is literally violence.'[22] It's almost like having renounced being bullied by one group of men - the Weinstein Woke wolves - they're desperate to be oppressed by a new group of males. Think of Emma Watson, snarking at J.K Rowling - 'Trans people are who they say they are and deserve to live their lives without being constantly questioned or told they aren't who they say they are. I want my trans followers to know that I and so many other people around the world see you, respect you and love you for who you are' - when if not for the Sainted Joanne the bed-wetting 'self-partnered' muppet wouldn't have two pennies to run together. Think of the ghastly Lena Dunham - the Wallflower of Woke - boasting in 2017 about how she had two American Airlines workers sacked after she over-heard and reported a conversation in which Troons were mentioned in less than reverent terms. Mary Katharine Ham wrote brilliantly in The Federalist:

> 'How could the world be a good place if flight attendants are allowed to talk to their friends at work in any way that gives this rich, famous public emoter a sad? What have we become, as a country, if millionaire, private-school progeny of Brooklyn art-scene families can't have their exact conception of acceptable conversation reflected back to them during every minute of a flight delay? As she is wont to do, Dunham reflected on this experience publicly. 'For those who followed my airport saga yesterday, here's my takeaway: these days it's the little things. A smile. Offering a seat. Respect,' she wrote....The little things, like having a conversation with a coworker on a break without a super-rich bully trying to get you fired.'

The U.S.A has Hollywood; the U.K has the BBC. The harlot of the golden West may seem the furthest thing imaginable from the staid-sounding British Broadcasting Corporation' but they both share the Woke wangle of frantic virtue-signalling to cover up the slithering vipers nests beneath. In recent years the BBC has attempted to become Woke judge and jury of the nation - when it was about as pure, high-minded and profoundly hypocritical as the Catholic Church, especially where sex with children on its hallowed premises was concerned. Jimmy Savile's paedophilia was both an open secret and a running joke at the BBC; it wasn't until a few brave survivors came forward to testify that the corporation — which, remember, is funded by us — seemed inclined to do anything about it. Then in 2012 the BBC were revealed as actively engaged in helping their highest-paid 'talent' pay as little tax as possible. To lose one moral/ethical compass could be an accident, to lose both looks like total bankruptcy.

Hollywood and the BBC both fetish diversity of colour while quashing diversity of views, as Woke always does. It was announced in 2020 that the BBC were to spend £100 million on *diversity* - while sending out hired heavies to menace low-income women for the licence fee. Ross Clark wrote in the Spectator:

> 'TV licence fee-evaders are evil-doers who are failing to contribute to Gary Lineker's £1.75 million salary and they deserve the full weight of the law descending upon their heads...of prosecutions for TV licensing evasion, 72 per cent are against women. They are soft targets. They get snared because they are poor and struggle to keep up with all kinds of domestic bills. The difference is that with any other bill they will first receive several warning letters and only then will the debt-collectors be set on them. Fail – or even just forget – to pay your TV license and you are straight on the wrong end of a criminal prosecution.'

One Woke fetish which Hollywood has swerved is anti-Semitism, probably because Hollywood itself was created by the can-do under-dogs of the Jewish diaspora. No worries; the BBC has enough for both of them. I've already written about the corporations's slobbering Islamophilia and inevitably this goes hand-in-hand with a bias against the tiny state of Israel while the bigoted states which surround it are allowed to literally get away with murder. So consistent was criticism of their Middle East coverage that in 2004 the BBC commissioned an investigation and report on the subject - on delivery of which they refused to release it.

If anything, the BBC has become even more a cheerleader for the forces of anti-Semitism since then, ever keen to jump on a youthful bandwagon and thus thrilled by Woke's espousal of fresh'n'funky fascism masquerading as Palestinian rights. As part of its diversity pledge, the BBC offers a warm welcome to Jew-haters, some of whom are so confident that it's always open season on this white-privileged media-running money-grubbing minority people that they can even tell the kind of race-based jokes about them which would have them out on their ears on the Portland Place pavement if they mocked any other ethnic group. The BBC is so rich in state-sponsored, seat-sniffing, laughter-vacuums that it's tricky to pinpoint the very worst Woke comedians they inflict on us, but special mentions should probably go to Stewart Lee[23] for mocking the name of the Jewish MP Tom Tugendhat because a) it's really pathetic to make fun of foreign names because they don't sound 'real' like his cited 'Fisher, Cook, Smith — derive from ancient trades' and b) he'd never dare to make fun of a Muslim name and would have all sorts of names ready for anyone who did. And of course to that giant of a man, the barely-human Frankie Boyle who occasionally breaks off from bullying handicapped children in order to bully Jews; in future, he might consider simply bullying Jewish handicapped children instead, and thus make his set more streamlined. Vulgar abuse is never the answer but I feel that at least I was engaging Mr Boyle on his own level when I Tweeted him in 2020:

> '@frankieboyle you are a state-sponsored BBC-approved comic, not an outlaw, you ugly pig. Never believed that women actually freeze dog-shit and stick it up them for fun - but that's surely what your mother did to have you.'

Even more than harbouring a dirty little anti-Semitic secret, the mark of a Woker is a rabid, parasexual obsession with 'trans' rights at the expense of all others - especially women. For the BBC, the rise of the Troons was a glorious dawn, and they fell over themselves not just to peddle transgender clap-trap to children but to be predictably namby-pamby about harping on pronouns, asking staff to declare their preferred pronouns in their email signatures, be they 'she/her' 'he/him' or 'they/them.' Or they could just save time and have all BBC employees use the instantly understandable pronoun 'parasite/piss-takers.'

To be fair, it's not like BBC didn't have anything to work with; an internal survey from 2018 revealed that Auntie had more than 400 transgender staff on board - one in fifty of the workforce, about four times higher than the proportion in the population at large. The BBC's 'director of diversity' Tunde Ogungbesan (now there's a name for Stewart Lee to conjure with - except he wouldn't, because he'd get the boot from the Beeb) promptly launched a major reform to make the corporation more 'trans-friendly' following the findings; but with that proportion already working there, surely it's friendly enough already? And Mr Ogungbesan does have time for real women, as he said that 'more lesbians' were needed[24] - but that's what all men say, the beasts. To give him the benefit of the doubt, maybe he was finally attempting to save some of the licence payer's money for once? Knowing the BBC's historic lack of regard for female equality, there might be method in their madness of scouting for Troons; count them as women and you can pay them less and sack them faster. No flies on Auntie!

The same desperation to be down wiv da cancel-culture kids can also be seen on the retail front, especially in the 'journey' (an appropriately Woke word for their hurtling trajectory along Shit Creek without a paddle, shrieking shareholders hanging on for dear life) of poor old Marks & Spencer. Like the BBC, M&S saw itself as occupying a National Treasure position which blurred somehow with sainthood, and whose integrity could never be questioned. But like the BBC, M&S is simply a slack-jawed, money-grubbing corporation which has outlived its usefulness.

Turning one's back on one's loyal customers and chasing the Woke Wonga is another symptom of the malaise they share. Woke is something of a mid-life crisis for commercial enterprises; they know that pursuing the youth is bad for them and doesn't have any money and will be cheating on them - but, o, they make them feel young again! M&S had been on the rocks for a while, alienating their core of regular shoppers with store floors resembling TK Maxx after an earthquake. It was shocking though not surprising when in 2018 they started flogging hijabs - not any old hijabs, but hijabs for tots from the age of four; in the light of encouraging pre-school girls not to reveal their ears lest some poor mullah be driven mad with lust. M&S next gaffe was counter-intuitive but no matter, it was the next station of the Woke cross which must be knelt before - making the private spaces of women open to men calling themselves Mandy on a Monday: 'As a business, we strive to be inclusive and therefore, we allow customers the choice of which fitting room[25] they feel comfortable to use, in respect of how they identify themselves.' Though maybe they aren't so different; Islamism seeks to erase women physically from public spaces and trans-gender activism seeks to erase women figuratively from public spaces. Didn't see this unholy alliance coming when we were living it up back in the day throwing ourselves under racehorses, did we, ladies!

But never fear - the one good thing about Wokism is that just when you thinking they have a chance of winning at making over our strange and beautiful world in their own monotonous and malevolent image, they start squabbling amongst themselves. It's that Purity Spiral thing; give Woke an inch and they'll take offence. M&S must have thought the cool kids would be queuing up in the spring of 2019 to try their LGBT[26] - lettuce, guacamole, bacon and tomato in rainbow-coloured packaging - sandwich, especially as the profits would go towards a charity helping LGBT youth. Nevertheless, many found it hard to swallow: 'I felt so enraged I left the shop. Basically equating us to a sandwich? Can't imagine them doing this with other marginalised groups.' Really? Have these people never enjoyed a Midget Gem?

In the summer of 2020 a shopper at Marks & Spencer espied a brassiere which seemed insufficiently sensitive to the death of George Floyd. Kusi Kimani of East Sussex noted that while light-coloured bras bore such tempting titles as 'Fudge' and 'Cinnamon' the darker one was called 'Tobacco':

> 'I saw it about two weeks after George Floyd's death - it was particularly raw to see at that time. Why not call it cocoa, caramel or chocolate – sweet dessert items? To see that 'tobacco' is for their skin tone will make young girls feel unwanted by society. Tobacco is referred to in society as bad, unhealthy, and highly likely to kill.'

Predictably M&S[27] snivelled:

> 'We have more to do and more to learn...we liaise with our store colleagues on a regular basis to determine which colours

we need to offer our customer and we are also working with our
BAME colleague network to receive their input too. As part of
this, we are reviewing our ranges, supported by our BAME
network, to ensure we have lingerie items that are flattering and
suitable for all customers. We are changing the name of the bra
colour and are writing to Kusi to confirm that, and let her know
that we're sorry for not moving faster.'

The difference between insurrectionary pre-Woke women and insipid
Woke women in a nutshell; we burned our bras to show we didn't need
establishment approval, this lot get their knickers in a twist because a tit-
sling looked at them funny.

By the summer of 2020, BLM had replaced a BMW as the thing
every advertising man worth his pure pink Himalayan salt wanted to get
next to; black lives were the new white lines. Watching Kendall Jenner
offer a policeman a Pepsi - whereas young Americans had once stuck
flowers down the barrels of National Guard guns in the course of
protesting against the Vietnam war - was virtue-signalling's perfect
moment, Woodstock and Altamont rolled into one. Her tearful apology -
'I feel really bad that this was taken such a wrong way…it feels like my
life is over' - appeared heartfelt, but the solemn young multi-millionairess
was already on a suspended sentence for crimes against Woke after
wearing an Afro for a Vogue shoot. It runs in the family; if you Google
'Kardashian' and 'apologises' a whole world of self-flagellation pops up.
Queen Bee Kim is the alpha apologist; accused of cultural appropriation
for wearing braids (twice), wearing a traditional Indian head-piece, being
so tanned that she was accused of using 'blackface' and using the word
'kimono' for her underwear range. The latter was changed when the mayor
of Kyoto urged her to reconsider; rather than telling him to zip up and
think of Pearl Harbour, she Tweeted that she was 'committed to listening,
learning and growing.'

But maybe they were born to be Woke; they are after all the most
nepotistic dynasty since the Imperial House of Japan (albeit with ruder
kimonos) acting out the old vaudeville cry 'Everybody works!' by
incorporating three generations of Kardashians into their business-show.
(Even the plug-ugly brother Rob does a nice line in cashmere socks and
revenge porn.) Nepotism - and the inevitable closing off of career

pathways to bright working-class kids - has run roughly parallel with Wokedom not merely by chance. Unlike other movements which claim to desire social justice, there is no mention of social mobility in Antifa objectives; Wokers have no interest in meritocracy. Indeed, knowing that they have their privilege by dint of birth rather than merit, meritocracy scares them. And after all, if you have objectified more than two thirds of your society as gammons, chavs, deplorables, with their white privilege and black hearts, then obviously they shouldn't be allowed to have easy, enjoyable, well-paid jobs; scratch a snowflake and you're more likely to find a socialite than a socialist.

Thus jobs which were once a way for bright working-class kids to make money and have fun doing so (journalism, modelling, acting) are increasingly colonised by the SADS; the Sons And Daughters of the rich and famous. The brats grow up to be predictably horrible, exhibiting the deforming effects of real rather than rhetorical privilege. In the summer of 2020 Honey Ross,[28] the 23-year-old daughter of Jonathan, appeared on Instagram announcing to a waiting world that she was 'in love' with herself and her body; a 'fat activist' whose contribution to society appears to be posting selfies in her underwear, she also apparently moonlights as one of the Woke Police. After she had harangued her father for daring to find J.K. Rowling's stand on women's rights 'both right and magnificent' he revised his views: 'Those who know me will concede I try to be thoughtful and not a dick. Having talked to some people (OK, my daughters) re my earlier Tweet, I've come to accept that I'm not in a position to decide what is or isn't considered transphobic. It's a wildly sensitive subject. Let's keep talking.'

And then there's Bono's daughter Eve Hewson, who on the occasion of landing her first leading role smugged:

> 'It was easier for me to get in the door. Some of the friends I went to drama school with are the most talented actors but have found it difficult to get an audition. That's never been a problem for me, and I think that's because of my family. That's not the way the system should work, of course, but if the door is open, walk through the door.'

Contrast this with the ineffably sad words of the beautiful and gifted actress Gemma Arterton, daughter of a cleaner and a welder:

'It's such a taboo to talk about but I still feel very working class. Of course, I'm not anymore - I've moved up to London and I have nice things - but I am in my soul...My Cockney accent is practically gone now and I do feel sad about that - a bit fake maybe. When I'm around my family, they sound so different to me...before drama school, I didn't care what people thought of me - I ate what I wanted, spoke when I wanted. Then I got to the school and someone told me to try not talking because it would create more mystique. So I'd go up to the canteen and just sit there, eating my lunch in silence...'

We quite rightly hear so much from gifted young people from ethnic backgrounds being held back and feeling that they must change their accents in order to succeed. But I don't think I've ever heard of one who was afraid to open their mouth lest they be mocked - on the contrary, there's no escape from the likes of the BBC dribbling all over the half-witted likes of Wiley, MBE. I remember as a tot seeing working-class people in television dramas and comedies and they weren't stupid, or racist; they were simply individuals, as various as any other group. It's different now; working-class voices are patronised at best, reviled at worst. And a lot of this may be because we hear so many middle-class actors performing working-class roles and lacking shade and nuance, like a white actor blacking up and rolling his eyes while exclaiming 'Shamone!' Consider the sorry spectacle of public schoolboys such as Guy Ritchie making films about working-class sociopaths when his mother is a Lady, his sister is a Tabitha and he obviously got that impressive-looking scar by falling off his pony and landing on his silver spoon.

So why can't working-class actors be chosen for working-class roles rather than being passed over for someone who the director was at *uni* with? Why are over-privileged people allowed to play under-privileged people when white people aren't allowed to play, say, Puerto Rican people? After being judged 'too white' to play the Puerto Rican at the 2018 BBC Proms, the singer Sierra Boggess recanted in a positively Orwellian fashion after social-media monstering:

'It is crucial to not perpetuate the miscasting of this show. I apologise for not coming to this realisation sooner and as an artist, I must ask myself how I can best serve the world, and in this case my choice is clearer than ever: To step aside and allow an opportunity to correct a wrong that has been done for years with this show in particular. I have therefore withdrawn myself from this concert and I look forward to continuing to be a voice for change in our community and our world.'

As did Scarlett Johansson after being cast as as 'trans' man in 2018:

> 'In light of recent ethical questions raised surrounding my casting I have decided to respectfully withdraw my participation in the project. I have great admiration and love for the trans community and am grateful that the conversation regarding inclusivity in Hollywood continues. While I would have loved the opportunity to bring this story of transition to life, I understand why many feel he should be portrayed by a transgender person, and I am thankful that this casting debate, albeit controversial, has sparked a larger conversation about diversity and representation in film.'

Has anyone noticed that one of the main actions which women appear to play in Woke's Rich Tapestry is ceaseless apologising? Saying sorry for their TERF words, their cis privilege, their sheer taking up of space in a world where cocks in frocks demand access all areas? It's a wonder we ever got the vote – imagine the Suffragettes today, going around apologising to racehorses for being insufficiently sensitive to their shared cultural oppression.

Here's a thought. Sex workers have a rotten time – let's not be whorephobic, let's only allow actresses who've been hookers on their way up to play prozzies. That'll be fun! And where does it end? As someone smirked recently, 'As an actual geologist, I deeply resent unqualified actors playing geologists in disaster movies.' And how ironic that at a time when performers are being told they must only perform that which they directly know, we are being lectured ceaselessly that men can actually be women even when they cling on fiercely to their penis and testicles. A world in which actors must have strictly drawn limits - but where in real life you can be the gender you want just by saying so.

The Oscars were already a sumptuous smorgasbord of virtue-signalling, wherein individuals who had the same chance as everyone else to become doctors, nurses or firefighters but chose instead to go into the business of playing pretend and reaping vast financial rewards lectured the rest of us about how to be better people - yes, You People Over There with the bad teeth and the boring jobs who voted for the funny orange man. In 2019 the Academy announced 'diversity guidelines' which films will have to fulfil to be considered for an award, such as that the film must 'centre on women, LGBTQ people, a racial or ethnic group or the disabled.' Nowhere in this self-congratulatory circle-jerk was there any mention of social class, of course, which remains the greatest dictator of whether or not people will have a decent quality of life. I always find it 'challenging' to 'root' for any British nominees, as a whopping 60% of 'our' Oscar winners over the past twenty-five years have been privately educated whereas only 6% of the population have had the privilege – so much for the 'plucky' Brit underdog.

It's the same with music. Even the music business - the last bastion of the sweet and tender hooligan determined to swerve the nine to five - has become a bourgeois endeavour, filthy with public schoolboys, and where you find the youthful bourgeoise you find the foul breath of Woke. The older generation is meant to deride the youth because their music is indecipherable and decadent - but I loathe the soundtrack to Woke because it's transparent and wholesome. It's the difference between Jim Morrison (dead at 27) and Ed Sheeran (30 and I live in hope) – all that sex, sass and swagger replaced by music which crooks its pinky rather than gives the finger, which extrapolates rather than fascinates.

Bring on the girls! On second thoughts, don't bother because this lot were surely born to be session singers and have somehow ended up in the spotlight. I call them the Jejeune Jessies; Jess Glynne (was working as a brand manager when she signed her first contract, mother in A&R), Jessie Ware (went to the select Alleyn's School, once amusingly known as Alleyn's College Of God's Gift) and Jessie J (Colin's Performing Arts School, musical theatre in the West End from the age of 11). They're just so nice; Jess Glynne lives with her parents, and Jessie Ware does a cookery podcast with her mum. Even Jessie J, who seemed pleasingly conceited at the start of her career, has become one of those Nervous Nellies who believes that banging on about mental health issues is a feasible alternative to making good records. Interestingly, all the Jessies are on record as having anxiety – we all know it's good to talk but just as homosexuality has gone from being the love that dare not speak its name to the love that won't STFU, anxiety has gone from being taboo to mandatory if you want to drive home the fact that you are A Good Person.

The house-band of Woke, Little Mix, started out on a TV talent show in 2011, brassy and bold and revelling in the bodies the Lord gave them like a cross between toddlers and lap-dancers. As the hits kept coming (50 million records sold, £28 million made) you'd have thought that these infinitely fortunate girls would have spent the next decade turning into confident women. But no. The Woke way isn't to shrug off the brickbats and catch the bouquets that life brings your way; if one did that, one might not get every last drop of the attention which is one's drug of choice in an age when youngsters steer clear of Class A stimulants. On the contrary, if you are rich, famous and doing a job you love for a vast amount of money, it is more important than ever to show your hurt feelings, exhibit them as medals like a veteran on Remembrance Day. Validation is perpetually required in Woke World; if it ceases for a moment, the feelings-haver reserves the right to talk about their emotions till the narcissistic supply is forthcoming once more, the milk of human kindness flowing freely through the media teat into the parched mouth of the poor little rich star. In interviews the three serving members and the departed Jesy Nelson appear as proud to display their weaknesses as children bringing a pet to school on Show and Tell Day. Thus we have Jesy (trolled over weight), Perrie (ongoing struggle with anxiety), Leigh-Anne (felt 'invisible' for the first three years of Little Mix due to racism, though how invisibility can be achieved when one is the best-looking, the best singer and the best colour in a band is a mystery to me) and Jade (believes that people with penises can be women - no cure for stupidity) posing under the headline ALONE WE'RE VULNERABLE - TOGETHER WE'RE A FORCE though vulnerable to exactly what (except bad wardrobe choices and crazed make-up artists) is hard to grasp. Am I cruel and heartless to find the sight of rich, well-nourished women describing themselves as *vulnerable* somewhat creepy? And despite Little Mix's frequent bleating affirmations that they seek to *empower* young women, isn't advertising oneself as vulnerable the most blatant way of sucking up to men? 'Hey boys - we may be rich, famous and beautiful - but we're no threat, we're **vulnerable!**'

It's that Wokescreen again - call yourself vulnerable, hashtag #bekind and you can get away with diva antics that would make Mariah blush. 'Our innocence has been taken from us' bleated the young multi-millionairess Jesy; it's not just the gripe of one ungrateful show-biz show-off but a real Woke belief, that there was some lovely life out there before capitalism, when actually what there was was blood, sweat and tears with a side order of semen. But as young women of working-class origin, the pre-Industrial Revolution Little Mixers wouldn't be romping through some sunlit glade without a care in the world - they'd be toothless hags, picking potatoes in the driving rain before dying in childbirth. And then, like the rest of their snowflake sorority, they'd have something to moan about. Then they'd be vulnerable - as millions of women and girls in this very world still are.

Jesy may well be bullied online for being bigger than her ex-bandmates, but even so she comes nowhere near being the biggest jessie of all - that would be Sam Smith, poster boy for Woke in all his bawling glory. Before the Covid, I'd seen him merely as a minor irritation, with a voice variously described as 'a bride breaking down during her wedding vows' and 'a fire in a pet shop.' In 2014 he came out as gay - big deal, metaphorically and literally, because show business is the only milieu where being gay pays more than being straight by giving white men a bite of the Diversity Donut where they might otherwise be elbowed out. (The great David Sedaris wrote that it was only being gay which stopped him from getting 'cancelled' as in every other department - white, middle-aged, rich - he was non-diverse.) Accepting his Grammy award for Record Of The Year for 'Stay with Me' Smith dedicated it to the model Jonathan Zeizal, who apparently had not taken heed of the title: 'I want to thank the man who this record is about, who I fell in love with last year. Thank you so much for breaking my heart because you got me four Grammys!'

You'd think that four Grammys was enough attention for anyone - but the narcissist needs novelty in their supply. (And while not all narcissists are Thems, all Thems are narcissists.) By the autumn of 2017, Smith had come out as 'genderqueer' and revealed to a retching world 'I feel just as much a woman as I am a man...I have girl breasts and girl thighs.' He then declared that he wished to be addressed as They, not Him, but presumably not one of Them - that's either homophobic or a young Van Morrison. They were obviously in such needy mode that They quickly became not just a regular car crash, but a car crash involving a police car, an ambulance and a fire engine, sirens screeching non-stop. And then, alarmingly, in in autumn of 2020: 'I want to be with the kids and I want to watch them grow and be with them every day. I want to be mummy.'

Anyone who had seen the video clip which They posted of Themselves having what my dad would have called 'the screaming ab-dabs' on social media in the early days of the spring lockdown, having selflessly put themselves into self-isolation at their £12 million home on Thursday, while by Friday they were weeping like a girl (sorry, like an *assigned at birth cis female*) because they were already bored with their own company might believe that They should start small in Mummy mode, with a hamster perhaps. Unsurprisingly They confessed 'I hate reading!' - the moral being is that if one has no life of the mind one will always be a bad friend to oneself (even if you do refer yourself in the plural) and may very well end up sending oneself to Coventry.

But the lifting of lockdown did little to cheer Them. Those of us who suspected that announcing oneself as *genderqueer* after already trumpeting the fact that one is gay is the equivalent of a flasher complaining that you're not getting his best angle - go on, have another look from this side! - were proved right when Smith hilariously complained that there are **no spare gay men in London**. 'I'm going to work my ass off and then hopefully find a boyfriend — but they're absolutely nowhere to be found anywhere in London...I've been searching all over the place. Honestly, I've been on the frontline now for a good three years and it's exhausting.' But hopefully They will have even more time to devote to winkling out the one gay man in London in the future as in the autumn of 2020, after a long hot summer of acting like a pre-school birthday girl who has consumed too many E numbers the Daily Mail could barely conceal their glee when they announced:

> 'Music industry bosses have been left baffled after Sam Smith sold just over 20,000 copies of their latest album in the first week - a fifth of sales for their last release. Last year Smith came out as non-binary, admitting they 'feel like a woman sometimes' and has considered a sex change.'

As my mum would have said as she slapped my legs 'Now you've got something to cry about!' Amusingly, Smith is cousin to Lily Allen, the reigning Woke cry-baby crooner until Them stepped up, now temporarily out of the blame game, happily posing in a dress costing £1,600 while talking of how she fell in love with with her husband because he has the words KARL MARX tattooed on his hand for lucky readers of the Sunday Times Style section, which she and Smith both bagged the cover of. It's the fashion magazines which illustrate best how the clothes industry tried to stay relevant while the little fires became big conflagrations. In the year of the plague their whole risible raison d'être - selling suckers things they don't need to impress people they don't know - collided with the fact that showing off and spending cash was suddenly curtailed. So, fearful of going broke, fashion tried to go Woke.

The environmental impact of the fashion industry is calamitous. Knowing this, and not wanting to lose a generation in thrall to Greta Thunberg, fashion had already attempted to cover its back with a lot of flim-flam about sustainability. But more than any other business, it depends on built-in obsolescence and the casting off of perfectly wearable clothes at regular intervals – how can this ever be sustainable, let alone ethical? People were catching on to this even before Covid; there's a reason even online clothes retailers were suffering, while one in eight shops stood empty even before lockdown, as we finally clocked that 'retail therapy' (the sexual intercourse of the unorgasmic) solves nothing but creates more problems, from personal debt to ceaseless landfill fodder. All new clothes are the Emperor's New Clothes now – and the only green that fashion will ever really care about is the colour of money.

This hasn't stopped fashion journalists from virtue-signalling like it was going out of style ever since the spring of 2020. Or indeed lest they themselves got the heave-ho from Sunday Times Style, an early adopter of the Woke Hack - Wack? - style which would be rolled out all across Rupert Murdoch's[29] print empire later that year. In this purge, journalists would sign up to 'diversity and inclusion objectives and training' while papers would be forced to appoint 'diversity specialists' while agreeing to 'a process for internal and external content review to track sentiment and coverage' and following a new 'style guide.' Helpfully, the human resources team privately described the readerships of The Sun, The Times and the Sunday Times as 'predominantly anti-diversity and inclusion.' This was the topsy-turvy vision of Woke in every arena from M&S to the BBC; define, insult and lose your audience.

Hundreds of seasoned hacks who were not considered suitable candidates for Woke-washing - not sufficiently pliable to offer up their cojones on a plate in order for them to be fashioned into non-binary earrings for the erstwhile owner to wear as proof of their fealty to this new order - were thus disposed of and the newspapers rendered even less attractive to a readership already defecting in droves to the rolling broadcast news media on their wrist. The Style writers were the worst, being the least substantial to start with, and accustomed to drowning in freebies they had little integrity to shed. But it served as savage amusement to see their desire to be Woke struggle with their inherent shallowness. Cheerleading for female candidates of colour in the 2020 American election, they ended up drooling over **Power Plum - The New Political Colour.** Acknowledging soberly that lockdown was 'a tough time to justify sexy fashion' they were soon slobbering over a £700 pair of pink satin stiletto sandals. Much had changed in the year of the pandemic, but if the fashion mags could make sure that young women racked up thousands of pounds worth of debt buying pointless tat on tick - so long as it was sustainable, organic tat - then at least one branch of commerce would see business as usual.

The doyen of all fashion magazines, Vogue, has always specialised not in showing women what they can have but showing them what they can't have and making them get a masochistic kick from their exclusion. The junior American branch, Teen Vogue, had been lurking behind the Wokescreen for a long time, acting creepily like a well-groomed groomer, with polemics on Black Lives Matter jostling with tips for swinging schoolgirl sodomites so eye-wateringly explicit that one could barely read them without the dawning realisation that it might be smart to buy shares in adult nappies in ten years time.

By its very nature Vogue bars 99.9% of the population from its lifestyle, which requires serious money and/or beauty; being **exclusive** gives it its cachet, as it does to the brands whose advertising takes up so many of the hallowed pages. (Think of how distressed Burberry became when 'chavs' started wearing it!) No other branch of retail would see women gleeful at being added to a waiting list of 15,000 souls for a handbag (Lady Bracknell voice). This is not about buying something; this is about paper-thin self-esteem. How can such white fragility (to use the phrase deservedly for once) deal with a world where inclusion is the new exclusivity?

To Edward Enninful (OBE) who became editor of British Vogue in 2017, the answer was diversity. (The answer to everything these days; I fully expected it to be proffered by the NHS as the cure for cancer soon.) The models within stopped being hangry white girls and the cover stars followed suit; Beyonce, Oprah, Rihanna and Judi Dench (85 and newly tattooed.) No longer can we complain about models being young, thin or white; now a far larger demographic of women can be objectified - rejoice! But not such great news for the likes of the black women who featured in a Washington Post survey in 2012 which found that while black women are heavier than their white counterparts, they have higher self-esteem and a better body image - 66% to 41%. It was thought that their very lack of representation in fashion media made them dismissive of it, and more likely to seek their self-esteem from something more solid than being able to squeeze into a body-con dress. So much for the eternal 'when you look good, you feel good' - which would have come as news to Marilyn Monroe.

Woke-speak, especially on matters of race, robs people of their individuality and reduces them to ticks and ciphers. Who would you think EE was gushing over here? 'A powerful black woman in her prime, unencumbered by the strict gender binary rules of the past.' I'd have reckoned perhaps a Sociology supply teacher in the process of going from him to shim, but no - it's Rihanna, the baddest, boldest bitch in Christendom. I'm sure that Enninful had the best intentions in the world when Vogue's July issue bore the cover line THE NEW FRONTLINE - CELEBRATING COURAGE IN THE FACE OF ADVERSITY. I'm sure his heart was in the right place when he put a handsome black male train driver on the front cover - with a pretty ginger female midwife and an attractive female Muslim supermarket worker on the lesser fold-outs.

Someone obviously had the Woke Top Trumps out in that editorial meeting, but there was one unappreciated frontline worker missing; the pale, hungry Vogue intern who puts in a full day's work five days a week but is only given travel expenses, thus rendering the position impossible to achieve for all but the affluent London-dwelling youngster. Tanya de Grunwald of Graduate Fog, a campaigner for fair internships who has named and shamed similarly stingy Woke designers from Vivienne Westwood to Samantha Cameron, actually reported Vogue to HM Revenue and Customs, which monitors payment of the national minimum wage. Imagine the rending of silks when the Customs clerks came to call in their man-made fabrics! She told me in 2020:

> 'If Edward Enninful wanted to change things he could give fashion brands a six-month warning that Vogue will stop working with brands who use unpaid interns. But 'If you won't work for free then you obviously don't love fashion enough' is the message the interns get. It's probably not a coincidence that fashion was one of the first industries to start using unpaid internships, so will be one of the last to let go. It's endemic - baked into the culture and structure.'

She's right - but fashion is only being true to itself here, red in tooth and claw and soles. Fashion by its very nature is only true to itself when it works completely outside the moral framework of society. To expect it to be moral is as silly as expecting the stock market to be moral – it's the nature of the beast. That beast is John 'I Love Hitler' Galliano showing a 'Homeless Chic' collection in 2000 which would inspire Zoolander's 'Derelicte' line a year later. It's Andre Leon Talley, the very first black man to be creative director of American Vogue, coming from great poverty, actually comparing his sacking by Anna Wintour to the killing by a policeman of George Floyd: 'I couldn't breathe!' he shrieked to an admirably straight-faced Emma Barnett in the summer of 2020. In short, as a profession which can hope to be ethical any day soon, fashion stands somewhere between abattoir management and pimp.

To give Vogue credit, they appeared to have clocked this by the time A/W rolled around. The summer seemed so far away; that summer when we finally understand what applause was for, not pandering to the privileged but showing gratitude to the anonymous. But it was no longer the faceless and thankless everyday heroes without whom society would regress to a swamp in a season who Enninful was crushing on by the December issue; it was none other than the Prince of Wales. Just as fashion mavens will always return to black and dogs return to vomit, Vogue had reverted to its old stuck-up self, where slobbering over monarchy never goes out of style. As if I'd needed even more persuasion that Woke was inherently reactionary, it was quite the sketch to see these two men at the top of their twin hierarchies wallowing in their luxury beliefs, telling the poor not to buy cheap clothes and the rest of us to rejoice that the natural world had 'healed' a little. The Prince was promoting the Modern Artisan Project - a fashion training programme co-founded by the Prince's Foundation - which was about to launch a 'sustainable' clothing collection and featured a cardigan costing £500. Let them eat cake has become let them wear cashmere.

It's strange how those Wokers who howl over recompense for the sins of Empire appear to have given the monarchy a free pass. (We shouldn't be surprised, as a whole slew of Left-wing actresses from Vanessa Redgrave to Emma Thompson have had a tendency to tug their forelocks when in the presence of royalty as enthusiastically as teenage boys tug their foreskins when alone.) The old Windsor saying 'Never complain, never explain' has been given a re-boot, so now the royals are constantly complaining (about everything wrong with society except themselves) but never explaining. Be it Prince Charles lecturing about how the poor should behave, or Prince William lecturing the BAFTA audience about privilege or Prince Harry lecturing about how it's everyone's duty to anti-racism to pull a really hot mixed-race girl, they employ the very best in smoke and mirrors when it comes to their own shameful history. Because explaining the shady past of any given throne would invariably prompt an apology in these days where apologies are the currency of this virtue-signalling world. And our monarchy, although built on and exercising the ultimate in white privilege, are never called on to apologise for their own sins, rather than spread the blame on the rest of us.

Why, you could almost believe that the lily-white hands of British monarchs had never grasped any of the bounty that resulted from the greatest empire the world has ever seen; more than a third of the world's land-mass and population. Starting with Gloriana's enthusiastic support for the slave trader John Hawkins in the 1560s (after his profitable second voyage, she honoured him with a coat of arms featuring a naked African bound with rope) and carrying on right up to abolition, British monarchy has benefitted from slavery to a revolting degree. In 2020 Brooke Newman wrote in Slate:

> 'In Britain, as in the United States, anti-racism protests that have erupted since the police killing of George Floyd in late May have reinvigorated campaigns for reparations for slavery. Having only recently acknowledged their historical links to slavery and the trans-Atlantic slave trade, British universities and London financial institutions are facing calls to make amends for past injustices and pay reparations to the descendants of enslaved people. But one institution has remained silent: the British monarchy. Officially acknowledging that the royal family both fostered and profited from the enslavement of millions is the very least the present-day British monarchy owes to the descendants of enslaved people.'

It never seems to occur to Woke mobs to attack symbols of monarchy when on one of their rampages - they'd rather desecrate monuments which honour millions of working-class men killed in the course of defending that very monarchy. You get the feeling that the dull-bulbs believe that empire and exploitation was only ever the idea of some shady counter-jumper upstarts (probably Jewish) who just went ahead and exploited a third of the world's population behind the innocent monarch's back. In the way that those Woke handmaids who laughably call themselves feminists find everything to do with the treatment of women offensive apart from things which are actually offensive - pornography and prostitution - somehow monarchy has been given access to a souped-up version of the Wokescreen. They may not be bright, but they're crafty, and so profoundly privileged that they've managed to convince many of their subjects that they're not privileged at all - the ultimate luxury. Thus we can all unite in sneering at the vile capitalist Philip Green whooping it up on one of his yachts while his similarly parasitical family is nowhere as rich as the Windsors - **and** people had a choice about paying for his goods. 'We must not let daylight in upon the magic' Walter Bagehot famously said of monarchy; a sentiment which was interpreted as respectful at the time, but in retrospect seems somewhat skeptical.

Which brings us right back to the Grabdication, when a heady blend of wealth, celebrity and Wokeness reached its shining peak, and it was briefly Camelot for Meghan and Harry, the fraudulent monarchs of a fraudulent movement, the First Couple of Woke. From the September 2019 issue of Vogue edited by none other than Me-Again herself to the moment they were revealed as the only people apart from Greta Garbo ever to move to Hollywood because they wanted to be left alone, they could do no wrong. And then the Grabdication went bust, and was revealed as being as morally bankrupt as the monarchy, the celebrity and the Wokeness which had spawned it, with a whole nasty level of its own because the three belief systems had never been seen in the same place before. Their more-in-sorrow-than-in-anger faces stopped selling magazines, as we shied away from yet another showboating photo op of them handing out food to the poor. (No inspirational bananas, sadly, this time.) Their popularity plummeted, with a YouGov poll which saw them only marginally more popular than Princess Anne's corgi-killing dog Dotty. And then, unforgivably, Prince Harry appeared to turn his back on the Invictus Games - the sporting event for maimed soldiers and veterans which he had created in 2014 - in favour of commentating from the sidelines of the Victimisation Olympics.

Never mind - they'll have their multi-million dollar Netflix deal to keep them warm until the Americans realise that there's nothing special about them without the musty tinge of monarchy, which will surely evaporate quickly when that blinding Pacific sunshine is let in on upon the magic. Will they outstay their welcome once Woke has been spurned for a new taste thrill by a Hollywood grown tired of wearing sackcloth and ashes on the red carpet? Maybe they'll move to France, as that other exiled prince and his American Achilles Heel did. They need to take care, through - maybe see which way the wind is blowing from the Bastille before they decide to lecture yet another country on How To Be Good. Because never mind the Anglo-American namby-pamby playpen-revolution of pulling down statues - the French had the right idea about monarchy. Now that **is** a street mob screaming for social justice I could get behind. Vive la guillotine!

## Notes

[1] https://www.spectator.co.uk/article/meghan-markle-has-rescued-her-prince

[2] https:// www.independent.co.uk / voices/columnists/julie-burchill/julie-burchill-so-the - prince-of-green-hypocrites-is-going-on-tour-thank-god-i-ll-be-abroad-2055351.html

[3] https:// www.thetimes.co.uk / article / racking-up-air-miles-emma-thompson-joins-climate-rebels-hc6980vg9

[4] https://www.standard.co.uk/news/politics/jon-snow-says-i-ve-never-seen-so-many-white-people-in-one-place-during-report-on-probrexit-rally-a4105051.html

[5] https://www.thetimes.co.uk/article/is-extinction-rebellion-a-big-oil-conspiracy-256cq3hl0

[6] https:// www.nbcnews.com / news / world / gaia-scientist-james-lovelock-i-was-alarmist-about-climate-change-flna730066

[7] https:// www.theguardian.com / world / 2018 / jan / 22 / move-to-canada-celebrities-donald-trump

[8] https://www.phrases.org.uk/meanings/bottom-drawer.html

[9] https://www.dailymail.co.uk/news/article-7868315/Prince-Harry-Meghan-Markle-trademarked-100-items.html

[10] https://travalyst.org

https://www.express.co.uk/news/royal/1391526/prince-harry-news-travalyst-charity-sussex-royal-meghan-markle-royal-family-spt

[11] https:// www.independent.co.uk / travel / news-and-advice/prince-harry-travalyst-sustainable-travel-greenwashing-tripadvisor-skyscanner-meghan-markle-a9139646.html

[12] https:// metro.co.uk / 2020 / 07 / 16 / cara-delevingne-kaia-gerber-cuddle-march-together-black-lives-matter-12999535/

[13] https://www.dailymail.co.uk/femail/article-5126699/Meghan-Markle-suitcase-girl-Deal-No-Deal.html

[14] https://www.independent.co.uk/news/uk/home-news/prince-harry-called-a-fellow-soldier-his-little-paki-friend-1299804.html

[15] https://en.wikipedia.org/wiki/Auditing_(Scientology)

[16] https:// www.standard.co.uk / hp / front / harry-brawls-while-wills-drools-7277660.html

[17] https:// www.dailymail.co.uk / femail / article-6664845 / Meghans-messages-inspiration-written-bananas-branded-offensive-sex-worker.html

[18] https://en.wikipedia.org/wiki/Hollywood_blacklist

[19] https://www.pressreader.com/uk/daily-mail/20191010/281681141631749

[20] https://www.news18.com/news/movies/there-are-times-when-you-dont-want-to-be -photographed-says-jennifer-aniston-2347115.html

[21] https://www.dailymail.co.uk/tvshowbiz/article-2642110/Gwyneth-Paltrow-likens-negative-online-comments-bloody-war-hits-haters.html

[22] https://everydayfeminism.com/2017/01/misgendering-trans-people-is-violence/

[23] https:// www.timeslocalnews.co.uk / tonbridge-news / mp-tugendhat-accuses-comedian-of-anti-semitism-over-name

[24] https://www.dailymail.co.uk/news/article-5911581/Why-does-BBC-care-diversity-complaints-sex-violence.html

[25] https:// www.dailymail.co.uk / news/article-7638497 / M-S-sparks-gender-neutral-fury-telling-customers-use-whichever-fitting-room-want.html

[26] https:// www.dailymail.co.uk / news / article-6996097 / Backlash-shoppers-Marks-Spencer-launches-LGBT-sandwich-years-Gay-Pride.html

[27] https://www.standard.co.uk/news/uk/m-s-apologises-racist-bra-colour-names-a452 3981.html

[28] https://unherd.com/2020/06/when-will-we-stop-fetishising-youth/

[29] https:// order-order.com / 2020 / 10/27/exclusive-news-uk-hacks-to-be-forced-onto-diversity-inclusion-training/

# CHAPTER EIGHT

# WAKING UP FROM WOKE: BAD EDUCATION AND HOPE FOR A PROGRESSIVE FUTURE POLITICS

Cancel-culture started at the universities and as they lay empty in the time of Covid, that nihilistic zeal spilled out onto the streets and the mindless mob rushed around witlessly tilting at any old windmill which looks like it might have been built before quinoa. Places which had once been about helping young people to grow into adults seemed now intent on turning back time, Benjamin Button style, so that students went in as young people and came out as monstrous toddlers, the perfect breeding ground for a temper-tantrum masquerading as a crusade. It's hard not to think that we're living through the very messy afterbirth of the pandemic, in which putative *uni* students robbed of the promise of cheap union-bar booze are angry that they've been robbed of the three years of time-wasting which is every middle-class white kid's human right.

When I was a child, students looked so wild and free to me, protesting about the Vietnam war and obviously practising 'free love.'[1] But some individualistic, impatient impulse in me made sure that I swerved this thing which might make me less myself - and whereas gentler-natured working-class kids might feel a little phantom pain where their further education might have been, I've always seen in as yet another arrow to make the bourgeois quiver, especially those in the business of paying me. On my first job, at the New Musical Express, I found that though my leather and swearing didn't frighten my colleagues - both were practically mandatory - the one way I could freak them out was to get out a can of Tizer and drink it very deliberately while maintaining eye contact with the chosen bourgeoise. How it flustered them - one accused me of 'flexing your roots' - and I knew that this was because they were eternal students, forever fearing the rough *townies* who might have mussed their mortar boards way back when. Then in Manchester a punk boy gave me a badge saying I HATE STUDENTS, YEAH! (I lost it when I was knocked down by a police horse in Lewisham at 17, after being a bit too showy in my bid to taunt the National Front marchers - back before I became 'literally a fascist' of course) and that completed my uni-scaring uniform. I didn't really hate students - as I said, I admired them as a tot - but I was certainly mystified by them. Of course if you're training to **be** an actual **thing** - like a doctor or an archaeologist - but 'Media Studies?'[2] You could be out there making your way in the big bad beautiful world - but you want to put it off for three precious years and let sharp-elbowed counter-jumpers like me push in front of you?

But as it turned out, students weren't just killing time - they were killing culture. We've seen how the actual word Woke meaning politically aware originated in the singer Erykah Badu's 2008 song 'Master Teacher' where it was, if rather po-faced, used at least in the course of creating. But something got horribly lost in translation and by the time Woke arrived in white academia from the black ghettos, the well had been well and truly poisoned. Now destruction was its only aim as a generation of students who had been told by their parents that they were never wrong united with a generation of lecturers who believed that Western culture was never right.

It's hard to know what came first - the chicken student or the coddled egghead. Whatever, the days when young people went to university to have their beliefs challenged in an atmosphere of rigorous debate and get wisdom after hearing all sides of an argument seems a thing of the past now, as archaic as antimacassars. Many of them go there to live in the same bed-wetting liberal bubble they were raised in; as Mary Beard[3] put it 'The world has turned upside down. It's meant to be the young who are risk-takers and the elderly worried about controversy.'

Generation Snowflake grew up in a world in which there was no religion but in which crusading urges were still strong - especially the urge to condemn. Universities became little universes in which the bullying conformism of teenagers could find a worthy-seeming political focus without actually having to leave the campus and mix with the common people. Trigger warnings were started with the best of intentions; genuine concern for the few people with actual Post Traumatic Stress Disorder, especially rape victims. It's quite reasonable to warn an audience which might hold someone who was abused as a child that child abuse will be discussed. But, once trigger warnings were established as a thing, everyone wanted to be special - until it got to the stage where audiences must be warned that they may simply hear an idea that they might disagree with. Brought up to believe that all must have prizes - and being so mediocre and lazy that even the smallest rewards evade them - Generation Snowflake finds comfort in the Victimhood Olympics mantra that all must have bruises.

This desire not to be offended on the part of the students formed an unholy alliance with the desire of many lecturers to spread their message to a captive audience. Baffled by the rise of populism in the U.K and the U.S.A, Left-wing lecturers turned their backs on Marxism - ungrateful proles, why can't they do as they're told! - and embraced post-modernism. You'd think that a philosophy which basically maintains that anything goes would have made campuses even keener on free speech - but the vested interests made sure that the opposite happened, with the ultimate condescending bourgeoise belief in 'false consciousness.' If the masses start to vote against people who know what's good for them, then all must be done to to stop the free movement of ideas. In a world where there is no truth there are no lies and the only permissible facts are those that your tribe endorses; it's all power play so since the idea of truth is an illusion everything is about power and persuasion - at which point of course you'd want to deny your opponents the advantage of a platform.

I frankly cannot comprehend how many modern academics could be trusted even to mind a hamster over a Bank Holiday weekend, let alone leave their imprint on impressionable young minds. Dr Alyosxa Tudor of the School of Oriental and African Studies won the 2020 Feminist Theory's essay prize by claiming that 'gender as a category comes into existence through racialisation and colonial expansion.' As Rod Liddle said:

> 'It is remarkable to think that before Cecil Rhodes we didn't
> have men and women, isn't it? I hope that students who
> attended the event were also given a good grounding in how to
> enunciate properly: 'Would you like fries with that?''

Meanwhile over at Oxford University, in the spring of 2020, Dr Emily
Cousens was fervently hoping that the institution she had spent a decade
studying and subsequently teaching at would **not** find a cure for
coronavirus:

> 'So why was my initial relief at hearing Oxford and Imperial
> are racing away to develop the vaccine followed by worry?
> Researchers at Oxford are doing vital, life-saving work. But
> races have winners and losers. If my university is the first to
> develop the vaccine, I'm worried that it will be used as it has
> been in the past, to fulfil its political, patriotic function as proof
> of British excellence.'

Thankfully, Ms Cousens academic field is 'vulnerability and gender' so
I'm sure she can come up with a lovely non-binary gender-fluid vaccine
soon, putting her imperialist science colleagues to shame. Or maybe she'll
just sit around moaning as this type of highly-educated half-wit prefers to
do.

When I was a schoolgirl, we always suspected that some teachers
were mentally deranged. There was always the weird games mistress who
lingered a tad too long when a dozen steamy teenagers were showering or
the biology master who gave every appearance of taking a kinky delight
in seeing how long he could make the word 'Sperrrmmm' last. But those
charged with educating - remember it's 'I lead out' in Latin - a nation's
youth really shouldn't be boasting about the fact that their minds are as
closed as any old golf-club bigot, as Professor Sunny Singh of the London
Metropolitan (Elite!) university does:

> 'I get regular invites to debate on various platforms. I always
> say no. Because debate is an imperialist capitalist white
> supremacist cis heteropatriarchal technique that transforms a
> potential exchange of knowledge into a tool of exclusion &
> oppression.'

When adults at universities attempt to behave like adults, and
suggest to their feverish charges that hearing different points of view was
one of things universities were useful for, the reactions bear all the

hallmarks of a giant toddler whose parent had mistakenly put their comfort blanket in the wash. There's an extraordinary bit of 2015 footage of students at Yale University berating a professor, Nicholas Christakis, whose wife Erika, also in the faculty, had the nerve to suggest that students could be trusted to choose their own Halloween costumes after it was suggested that there should be an approved list lest any UnDead take offence at any cultural appropriation aimed at their community. As her husband attempts to reason with the baying mob of students surrounding him, one of them, a young woman, screams a truly amazing thing at him:

> 'It is your job to create a place of comfort and home for the students that live here! It is not about creating an intellectual space! It is not! Do you understand that? It's about creating a home here!'

Not surprisingly, the Christakises soon moved on from this snivelling snake-pit to pastures new. It's tempting to dismiss such antics as American hysteria. But at Oxford in 202 - city of dreaming spires, and now of drivelling spite - Professor Selina Todd felt the need to to hire a brace of bodyguards to accompany her to classes after receiving death threats. Over at the University of Reading, Dr Rosa Freedman[4] was waylaid by a male student who declared her a 'transphobic Nazi who should get raped.' Kathleen Stock, a professor of philosophy at the University of Sussex, has been fighting off a constant campaign against her for years now, with complaints from students and hostility from colleagues: 'It is quite a strange situation to work somewhere where people make it clear that they loathe you,' she told Times Higher Education with admirable self-restraint.

What these three women have in common is that they have seen fit at some point to state the simple truth that biological men cannot become biological women, any more than clownfish can become clowns or seahorses can become horses. How telling it is, surveying the suffering of so many millions of humans in this world, that the issue which that gets the juvenile joint jumping every time is the self-imposed angst of handful of half-wits not sure whether they're Nigel or Nigella! But looked at closer, it makes surreal sense. The students are overgrown toddlers who have rarely heard the word 'No' and thus have come to believe that world orbits around them and their feelz; similarly awash with hostile hormones and similarly disinclined to buckle down and put in the work which might win them attention for actual achievements, teenagers and transes are a match made on the Naughty Step. Then there's the magical-thinking transmogrification angle so appealing to youngsters who only recently put away childish things and J.K Rowling books (awks!). If men can become women simply by saying it's so, then a spoon-fed private-school bed-wetter can become a dashing street-fighter, just by pulling on a bandana.

As we saw when Lena Dunham got those stewardesses the sack for daring not to agree with her views on biological sex, the witch-hunter is strong in these creatures. Though they yell a lot about being kind, empathy appears to be a foreign word to them, and one they seem to swerve, perhaps not wanting to risk cultural appropriation of the Greek lexicon. In the autumn of 2020, Cambridge students called for a porter, Kevin Price, to be suspended from his job because he had resigned from his role as Labour deputy council leader for refusing to support a Lib Dem motion which began with the sentences 'trans women are women,' 'trans men are men' and 'non-binary individuals are non-binary.' Standing down, he said that the inclusion of those sentences would 'send a chill down the spines of many women' and that it was 'foolish to pretend that there are not widely different views or concerns about women's rights.' For this simple statement of fact he was accused by the student union of showing 'a brazen contempt for the rights and dignity of trans and non-binary people' while the LGBTQ+ Officer Frankie Kendal took a break from their alphabetti spaghetti to huff 'We have a small but vibrant trans and non-binary community that should not only feel safe but feel celebrated.' So it's now the job of a working man not just to fetch and carry for these entitled brats, but to treat them like they're Mariah Carey coming down a sequinned staircase too. As Alice Sullivan, a professor at the college beautifully Tweeted:

> 'Students at Clare College Cambridge are trying to get a college porter fired, purely because he has expressed support for women's rights in his role as a Labour Councillor. The class politics of gender identity extremism laid bare for all to see. I hope Clare College will show some backbone and some

decency and support Kevin Price. These privileged young
people trying to get a worker fired should be utterly ashamed.'

A working-class man being persecuted by a bunch of white bourgeoise
students because he stood up for women's rights - what monstrous aborted
approximation of social justice is this? And the irony is that while these
yappy little Yorkies were snapping at everyday people's ankles over
imaginary slurs to themselves and their invisible non-binary mates, there
was a whole world of misery right under their stuck-up little noses.
Privileged students could actually have stood up for the whole swathes of
the student body for whom university had never been a safe space.

For starters, working-class youth have the system loaded against
them when it comes to entering higher education at all; in 2017 the number
of students from poor neighbourhoods enrolling at the college which
boasts of being one of the most diverse in the U.K, the School Of Oriental
and African Studies, was exactly zero, very much illustrating the fact that
'diversity' now means people of different colours thinking and saying
exactly the same thing. But they are often treated vilely if they get there.
In the autumn of 2020 Lauren White, a student at Durham University,
demanded action after if transpired that she and fellow Northerners were
subject to 'toxic' behaviour from both classmates and tutors due to their
accents and backgrounds. She told the Guardian:

> 'At first when they mocked and mimicked my accent, I sort of
> went along with it, even laughed, but then when I persistently
> became the butt of jokes about coal-mining and started to get
> called feral because I was local it started to feel malicious. I
> wrote an article about my experience and it snowballed and I
> got inundated with messages from other students saying they
> had experienced the same as me and some even said they were
> too scared to speak out in seminars for fear of being ridiculed.'

A student from Liverpool backed this up:

> 'I had the most horrendous time there. I'm from a working-class
> background. I was reminded of this every single day. I was told
> repeatedly that the only reason I was at Durham was because
> my family were on benefits - my family have worked all their
> lives. I was accused of stealing, I was told I would never get a
> job because of the way I speak, I was told that I was a waste of
> a worthy student's place. I received this from students and staff

> alike. Another thing I remember is 'rolling in the muck' - it was
> a thing a lot of students would say referring to them sleeping
> with a northern working-class.'

The university finally launched an inquiry 'after wealthy prospective freshers reportedly planned a competition to have sex with the poorest student they could find.' Substitute 'black' for 'working-class' and imagine the fireworks - but behind the Wokescreen, no one can see you sneering.

Another group of students who could use some solidarity from their perennially peevish peers would be Jews, who despite their alleged white privilege have had a right old time of it in England's groves of academe. No sooner had the musty right-wing prejudices against them been overcome by the 1960s (with quotas on the number of Jewish students accepted into the top universities, sprung from fears that this cleverest of peoples would trounce the dullard spawn of the Gentile ruling class) than what I've previously coined Fresh'n'Funky anti-Semitism was there to take the weasel wheel under the guise of being pro-Palestinian. What the students who espoused Boycott, Divest and Sanctions against Israel lacked in knowledge they certainly made up for in enthusiasm, and this went for the U.S.A too; when 230 Berkeley undergraduates were asked which conflicts in the world they were most interested in and how much they knew about the region, most of them claimed to 'care deeply' about the occupation of the Palestinian territories although 75% of them could not point to those territories on a map and 84% could not name the decade - let alone the year - in which that alleged occupation began. But still, you could sort of see their point of view; they weren't in it for the good of Palestine, they were only here for the Jew-bashing.

The first wave of bannings of Jewish societies started in 1975; disgustingly, considering the Jewish experience of fascism, this was at a time when the National Front was perceived as a threat and thus many student unions adopted policies of 'no platform for racists and fascists' which, in the wake of the UN passing the 'Zionism is Racism' resolution, they mired Jewish societies too.

Many Right-wing racists will deny being racist and try to keep their views on the down-low, but there is something in the peculiar nature of anti-Semitism that makes certain twisted souls feel the need to **perform** it. (Think of Corbyn saying in front of that packed hall of toadies, knowing he was being filmed, that those nasty foreign Zionists don't understand irony.) During the course of the 2002 University of Manchester's motion to declare that anti-Zionism was not anti-Semitism, and that Israeli goods should be boycotted, a leaflet was produced by Union of Palestinian Students and handed out to students lining up to vote, which described Jews as, among other things, 'vampires' who 'enslave countries and destroy their economy.' When the motion was defeated, a brick was thrown through the window of one Jewish student residence and a poster bearing the words SLAUGHTER THE JEWS stuck to its front door with a knife.

Basically, Jewish students in Britain have been systemically bullied since the founding of the very first universities right up to the present day - interrupted for a brief period after the War, when anti-Semitism was considered a bit of a faux pas. It's still open season on the oldest of hate-objects; as recently as the autumn of 2020, the Education Secretary Gavin Williamson sent a letter to vice-chancellors at English universities, accusing the universities of ignoring the persecution of Jewish students. But as we've seen of the Woke, they'd far rather get their knickers in a twist about imaginary victims than real ones. One of the oddest features of Wokers is their apparent fear of human hands; in 2015 student unions first instituted the use of 'jazz hands' rather than clapping, which was said to be 'traumatising' while in 2017 students at an American university, Evergreen State College, surrounded the president and screamed at him to keep his hands hidden in his pockets when he spoke. This chirophobia (fear of hands) came to a ludicrous climax when Imogen Wilson, a student at Edinburgh University, was cautioned for making 'inappropriate hand gestures' when she disagreed with speakers during a BDS meeting. She told the Telegraph:

> 'Later on in the meeting, someone threatened me with a second complaint because I was shaking my head – but when I was addressing the room about my worries about Jewish students, there were plenty of people shaking their heads and nothing happened. I totally do believe in safe space and the principles behind it, but it's supposed to enhance free speech and not shut

it down, and give everyone a chance to feel like they can contribute.'

Poor innocent child - only 22 and already living in the past, where free speech and heedless hand-waving was an everyday part of campus life! That Miss Wilson is an attractive girl would have doubled her offensiveness in the eyes of the Woke Bros who dominate BDS when not abusing themselves over online BDSM. To such PAMS their fellow students who are female will be seen as fair game rather than sisters in the socialist struggling - unless, Owen Jones' little friend, they are willing to 'suck dick' for it.

After the white working-class and the unapologetic Jews, no Woke target practice would be complete without spirited women, and they've certainly set about it on campus where the Wokescreen has enabled them to preach about safe spaces while invading that of women whenever they get the chance. Post-modernism was never going to be a day at the beach for women, when we consider such statements as Jean Baudrillard perving on about the transcendent beauty of the idea of taking a woman into the desert and 'sacrificing' her. (Imagine if he'd said this about a 'trans' woman - buy shares in Pampers!) Though women were finally accepted into some universities in the 1920s, as late as the mid 1980s there was a campaign among the students of Magdalene College, Cambridge to stop the admission of women, the argument being that the enrolment of these dense creatures could have an effect on Magdalene's position in the academic league tables.

But if colleges had to admit women, why not have some sport with them? In the autumn of 2020, sexual abuse at English and Welsh universities was 'a public scandal' with around 50,000 incidents every year. Sara Khan of the National Union of Students, said that their 2018 research claimed that two in five students experienced sexual attacks, of which one in eight was perpetrated by staff: 'Two years on from this, we would have hoped to see universities taking concrete action, and for the problem to be shrinking – however this is clearly not the case.'

The student body being too busy fussing over pronouns and sombreros, presumably.

Not all students suck, of course; I've been lucky enough to meet quite a few young people from university Free Speech societies, and noted despite myself that their extreme level of attractiveness does back up my theory that most student Wokers are wallflowers who couldn't even get laid in Freshers Week and are thus cross at their cuter classmates. At Sheffield University, asking Japanese students about sushi and mistaking bananas for plantain had already been declared 'micro-aggressions' so it's hardly surprising that the infant Free Speech societies was told that it was a 'red risk' (making it sound all the more desirable to anyone with gumption) and that it must submit applications to the students' union three weeks in advance each time it invites a speaker, for whom approval would be needed in order for the talk to go ahead. And not all lecturers are po-faced Peeping Toms. Who with a sense of fun did not applaud the Goldsmiths University academic Dawn Mellor, revealed in 2019 as having been hiding in plain sight as her non-binary alter-ego 'Mx Tippy Rampage' before revealing that the whole thing had been a satirical persona in the course of an academic study on social media? The outrage of her (sorry, their) hoodwinked students was hilarious to behold as they 'called her out' with all the conviction of Wee Jimmy Krankie accusing Mel Gibson's Braveheart of not being authentic, the basic premise of their play-acting having been rumbled. Namely, that no one not working 24/7 at being Woke could really see the difference between claiming to be non-binary for a skit and claiming to be non-binary for attention, except that one could laugh **with** the first and laugh **at** the second - but hey, laughs are laughs!

That Ms Mellor managed to keep her performance going for so long was an indicator of the sheer surreal silliness of Woke, which picked up pace as the springboard of 2020 became the Summer Of Shove. This season segued nicely into the fall of common sense and the winter of discontent. Let's summon up that Day In the Life cacophony again!

In June 2020 a charming photo of a pretty young black woman and a twinkly old white man sitting chatting on the grass after a BLM protest went viral, garnering hundreds of thousands of likes and shares on social media. It seemed a lovely snapshot of how anti-racism could bridge the generation gap, the old man holding a placard reading RACISM IS A

VIRUS - WE ARE THE VACCINE. But regrettably, the twinkly old man was Jim Curran, a known Right-wing activist and Holocaust denier; even more regrettably, when this was brought to the attention of the young woman, Rosie Smith, she seemed to like him even more:

> 'He is an activist and a beautiful man. Spoke some real deep truths…his words brought me to tears. He said the genocide the news went through was nothing on slavery and what black people endured and are still enduring…I judge him on our convo and from his vibe…the jews are not innocent, #israelosnotinnocent.'

While the pro-EU Best for Britain, defended their decision to promote the image on their Facebook page by saying:

> 'Some people have identified that the old gentleman in the photo is a Holocaust denier. We believe that this fact makes it even more important to share this image. It is worth applauding the fact that these two people from different generations have found common ground, and had a friendly conversation in the middle of a day of violent protests.'

No matter that the common ground was anti-Semitism, apparently. Black and white, unite and fight for the right to Holocaust deny, to misquote the old Rock Against Racism line.

July 2020, civil servants complain that they 'do not feel comfortable' with a room at the Treasury being named after Winston Churchill. In the same month, the new Scottish Hate Crime bill is revealed, which could make it a crime for actors to portray racist or homophobic characters. Also in July, an antifa mob in Portland, Oregon, set fire to a statue of an elk; also in Portland in August, a BLM mob beat a raccoon to death with baseball bats to protest against police treating black people like animals. (They're not fans of our four-legged friends in Portland.) In August the first 'Pride Train' (with a rainbow livery including the pink, blue and white of the transgender flag, as well as black and brown stripes 'to signal racial diversity and acceptance' and staffed entirely by LGBTQ people) made its maiden voyage from London to Manchester - though 'maiden' is probably 'transphobic' now that female words are verboten, so better call it 'theyden.'

In September Scotland proved itself once more to view free speech as a rather frilly thing which may well appeal to the frivolous English but can safely be left on the side of the plate by those sterner souls north of the border. The Hate Crime and Public Order (Scotland) Bill states that *inciting hatred* must be a crime, including personal observations taking place over the dinner table. The justice secretary Humza Yousaf said that there should be no 'dwelling defence' and that children, family and house guests must be protected from 'hate speech':

> 'Are we comfortable giving a defence to somebody whose behaviour is threatening or abusive which is intentionally stirring up hatred against, for example, Muslims? Are we saying that that is justified because that is in the home? . . . If your intention was to stir up hatred against Jews . . . then I think that deserves criminal sanction.'

Apart from the sheer impracticality of this - Thought Police bursting in upon to interrupt robust table talk between Celtic and Rangers fans in the style of Monty Python's Spanish Inquisition - it ill behoves a Muslim to use Jews in this manner when a certain amount of modern anti-Semitism is indulged in by some Muslims; those in glass mosques shouldn't throw stones, even though they may look fondly on doing so to adulterous women. The bill has understandably been condemned by critics including the Scottish Catholic Church, academics and artists; even the police, for once, generally so keen on stopping and searching for possession of a deadly pronoun, warned that forcing them to 'police what people think or feel...will devastate the legitimacy of the police in the eyes of the public.'

September 2020 saw selected postboxes painted black to honour black Britons from Mary Seacole to Lenny Henry; also in September, the dreary television variety show Britain's Got Talent features the black dance troupe Diversity performing a dance supposedly illustrating the death of George Floyd. Leading, in October, to a black personal trainer called Matt Simpson, (obviously believing that if high-kicks are an appropriate way to condemn racism then burpees must be too) advertising his sweaty wares with the social media post 'Slavery is hard and so is this. Entitled '12YearsOfSlave' this is our workout of the month designed to celebrate Black History Month.'

Words Are Literally Violence is a familiar Woke Mantra, but during the October inquest into the 2017 Islamist bombing of the Ariana Grande concert which killed twenty-two people, many of them children, we saw how it is too little speech, not too much, which takes us by the trusting hand and walks us into the darkness, murmuring softly of the lovely things we'll see if we just stay obedient and quiet. An 18-year-old security guard, Kyle Lawlor, earning £4.24 an hour, told the inquiry that he didn't draw the attention of his superiors to the suspicious behaviour of the bomber, Salman Abedi, because:

> 'I did not want people to think I was racist…it's very difficult to define a terrorist. For all I knew he might well be an innocent Asian male…I did not want people to think I am stereotyping him because of his race. I was scared of being wrong and being branded a racist if I got it wrong and would have got into trouble…I wanted to get it right and not mess it up by over-reacting or judging someone by their race.'

And so twenty-two innocent people, mostly children, were blown to pieces - but at least no one was racist that night.

November 2020, and the dead poet Ted Hughes is outed posthumously by the British Library as tainted by slavery, descended as he is from one Nicholas Farrar, who was involved in the slave trade 300 years before the late Poet Laureate's birth. On the same list are such famous tyrants as Lord Byron and Oscar Wilde, - both due to slavery-related activity by their **uncles.** (Why not great-uncles, or step-cousins or someone they once had a drink with in a hotel bar?) Also in November McDonald's is accused of cultural appropriation due to their new Chicken Jerk Sandwich. No doubt feeding one to a child will soon constitute abuse, but of course where there is real child abuse - such as stuffing 12-year-old children with hormones, fattening them up for a lifetime of unsatisfactory sex with fetishists as surely as a goose is force fed to produce foie gras for the decadent and discerning palate - there is Woke silence. Those who once could be trusted to look out for children, such as Barnardo's, the biggest and oldest charity of its kind, were too busy finding out that Words Are Literally Violence and thus in November blowing a sizeable chunk of their donations (and of course child abuse, like all 'domestic' crimes, shot up during the lockdowns of 2020) in producing **WHITE PRIVILEGE** -

**A GUIDE FOR PARENTS,** thus making a charity founded out of sheer colour-blind compassion focus on what divides us rather than unites us.

No one escaped the dead hand of Wokedom in 2020, the year which promised us perfect vision and instead made sure we had blinkers to match our muzzles. In November students at the University of Manchester demanded that the word 'black' be banned from textbooks and lectures when it held any negative connotations, such as 'blackmail' 'black market' and 'black sheep' - yes, it's our old friend Racist Baa Baa Black Sheep who we thought we'd seen the last of in the local council purges of the late twentieth century. It would be irritating enough for the babbling bubble of academe to circle-jerk themselves stupid to such dumb ideas, but as we've seen, the terminology of the terminally thick has a habit of seeping out into the real world and infecting previously sensible people. In the winter of 2020 a hairdresser told me that it was now impossible to order certain items for his salon if they had the word black in the colour. How long before they come for our innocent toe-tappers - Beige Is Beige, Paint It Puce, Young Gifted And All The Colours Of the Rainbow?

Though most Wokeness has a debilitating effect on even the most Pollyannish of people, prompting even the phlegmatic Brit to roll their eyes and mutter 'Doomed, doomed, we're all doomed!' there are some silly interludes which give us a chance to get the popcorn in and sit back to watch Wokers get their scanties in a state. Consider the 'purity spirals' which I wrote of earlier, when Wokers turn on each other and in some extreme circumstances even on themselves, or simply become blatant figures of fun due to inconsistency or kow-towing.

The crippled colossus that was Marks & Spencer spent 2020 bouncing from one misjudged midlife-crisis suck-up to people who never shopped there anyway after another, to add to its exotic roster of everything from toddler hijabs to bisexual sandwiches. Giddy with Woke - though going broke - they managed a crafty bit of land-giveaway when they sold globes renaming the Falkland Islands 'Islas Malvinas.' Quite understandably, some of the less spineless among us considered this something of a craven cringe to a quasi-fascist power, not to mention a slap in the face to those of our soldiers who fought, were injured or died there, as 255 did. 'This is a decorative item' a spokesperson peeved;

because nothing says 'decoration' like propagating the land-grab fantasies of a military junta which regularly tortured children in front of their rebel parents.

When weary of the marketplace, there is always the life of the mind to lift us to a more elevated level - where Woke mishaps are equally frequent, luckily. When F.Scott Fitzgerald wrote in The Crack-Up 'I avoided writers very carefully because they can perpetuate trouble as no one else can' it's almost as if he foresaw the antics of the Twitterers, where virtue-signalling and vice-shaming were only 280 characters apart. In the summer of 2020 in Canada, that chilly hot-bed of Woke, a group of 'indigenous' writers called out the trans poet Gwen Benaway for pretending to be indigenous - that they were also pretending to be women was par for the course, of course. At the same time in London a right right-on rumpus broke out on the sedate panel of the Booker Prize when the philanthropist and deaf activist Baroness Emma Nicholson was removed as vice-president of the award her late husband had founded due to accusations of homophobia by the gay writer Damian Barr for daring to vote against gay marriage back in 2013, following the dictates of her Catholic faith: 'As a gay writer I feel very concerned that a person who is actively and publicly propagating homophobic views holds a position of such power and prestige,' he Tweeted. But a quick ferret through Barr's own annals would have revealed a series of breathtakingly transphobic Tweets, from 2009 -'Tittering sickly @ story of 6'5' tranny who failed to hang herself from 5ft balcony this wknd. How many failures can one person take?' - to 2013 - 'mad tranny going through my recycling bin.'

In the world of Woke, women are invariably the soft targets for the male witch-finders to whip themselves up into a parasexual frenzy over. And so the Booker Prize trustee Lord Willetts who as a Tory MP had voted against making the age of consent for gay men equal to that for heterosexual couples, against allowing same-sex couples to adopt children and to delay the repeal of the notoriously homophobic Clause 28 act was left unmolested while the deaf octogenarian Baroness Nicholson was left out to dry. And Barr, with all the self-adoring slipperiness of an eel on Ecstasy, went on to be bigged up by his literary agent for his 'fearless determination to call out all forms of prejudice' and to keep his job with

the BBC and to be retained as 'Literary Ambassador' for the Savoy hotel
group and then in the winter of 2020 to announce breathlessly:

> 'So here's some news I never imagined sharing. Today I've
> been made a Fellow of the Royal Society of Literature. Some
> days I still can't believe I get to be a writer: to have my books
> on shelves with names who change the world and how I see
> it...and thanks most of all to my Mum for showing me
> everybody has a story.'

Unless they're a mad, suicidal dumper-diving 'tranny' presumably, in
which case they're just snigger fodder for the London literary set.

There were more trannies in varying states of irate
discombobulation than even Mr Barr could shake his stick at engaged in
the purity spirals of 2020, turning on each other so variously that
sometimes it was hard to keep up. (But then, all bed-wetting men in bad
wigs look the same to me.) Students, predictably, got first dibs when in the
autumn of 2020 Aberystwyth's LGBTQ society condemned 'drag socials'
as 'a mockery of trans women and the trans femme experience' - that drag
queens are inherently involved in mocking women seemed completely
immaterial, in true Woke Bros style. At a time when blackface is quite
rightly unacceptable, drag gets bigger by the day; you'd have to be living
in an Amish community not to have heard of RuPaul's Drag Race, while
Channel 5's Drag Kids follows a process which we squares call
'grooming.' Yet no one turns a hair. I've said it before and I'll say it again:
if the Black and White Minstrels are insulting and reactionary, why aren't
drag queens with names such as Malesta Child?

But so weird are the Woke wars that one found oneself, a full-on
rad-fem, cheering on the likes of Cheryl Hole simply because drag queens
at least appear to gain pleasure from what they do while the Troons seem
to view the ideal female state as having a nervous breakdown while
working in a barnyard sex brothel. 'Ru Paul's Drag Race unveiled its new
crop of contestants for season 12 last week,' moaned The Advocate 'and
once again, the cast is composed entirely of cisgender men.' When Ru Paul
hitched up his ballgown and got stuck in - having already been accused of
'transphobic' language - there could only be one winner (especially when
a trans contest from season 3 went on to compare him to Hitler, always a
sure sign of an argument sailing up the Swanee) even if, to paraphrase the

line about the Falklands war being two bald men fighting over a comb, this was about two men wearing skirts fighting over a tampon.

What hyped up the squabbling in the cross-dressing community was probably the fact that there were big rewards now in store for the more attractive and convincing Troons; one of them, pretty Paris Lees, managed to reinvent themselves from being a teenage boy jailbird to a model flogging shampoo, a trajectory worthy of Malcolm X - or in their case, Malcolm XY. The ideal female high-fashion body had long been tall, skinny and flat-chested; with the availability of trans models, the notoriously pussy-scared king-pins of the rag-trade could now show their over-priced tat without even having to touch the female form. Quoth Susan Stryker, author of Transgender History: The Roots of Today's Revolution:

> 'Increasingly trans has come to signify a certain Wokeness or hipness that it has not always had. To show somebody trans in a positive light as something that is desirable or normal or acceptable, that is like a marketing use of a subcultural chic, to sell shampoo or soap or tequila or what have you.'

Probably best not tequila, though, lest it trigger the sensitive student demographic who cry over small sombreros.

If the pandemic caused great panic in the paper-thin world of fashion, then how much greater was it in the half-cocked world of the rag mags, who gamely played the role of flea community barely making a living off the mangy old dog of haute couture as they chased the ever-dwindling advertising dollar. Grazia magazine in particular had shown great devotion to committing non-stop verbal analingus on male fashion designers since its inception, the fact that they were 'gay' protecting them from the usual charges of white male privilege (sodomy apparently conferring an injection of integrity) and it now doubled-down chasing the elusive Woke Wonga. But they were to become the latest casualty of the purity spiral self-pity-party in the autumn of 2020 when they gave the holier-than-thou heave-ho to one Stephanie Yeboah, their recently-recruited 'body positivity' (aka 'fat') activist (but not that active, judging from the size of her) who had promised to 'fight for diversity, inclusion and women's rights' but seemed just as keen on poking fun at the Shoah on Twitter:

'Every Jew has an attic but not every attic has Jews...AUSCHWITZ Gas Chamber Music LMAO SMH (laughing my arse off)...there have been bigger and more horrific genocides bu they happened to brown people, though, so I guess it doesn't matter, huh?'

Don't know about BLM - this particular creature seems more troubled due to a sky-high BMI and a room-temperature IQ, IMO.

Before long the inevitable divergence of a school of thought which believed that sustainability was the be-all and end-all and an industry which wanted people to chuck out perfectly good clothing three times a year took place during London Fashion Week of 2020. XR activists staged mock-funerals which saw crusties carrying caskets through the streets of the capital to the sites of the shows to 'mourn' the fact the event was taking place, followed by a request that the British Fashion Council 'stop the fashion industry's exploitation of planet, people and animals.' Another war of the Wokers, this time resembling two eunuchs fighting over a condom when it comes to winning favourable public opinion; the Guardian, always keen to see anything which brings pleasure to people possibly coming to an end in the foreseeable future, covered this spat with relish. But such was the velocity of purity spirals in 2020 that they barely had time to wipe the smirk off of their collective face before they too were fingered for being built on the proceeds of a cotton plantation which used slaves and then went on to back the Confederates against Abraham Lincoln, of whom a leader column spluttered: 'It was an evil day both for America and the world when he was chosen President of the United States.'

Sometimes it seemed that people would do anything in their quest for the Persecution Prizes. Ever since the start of the internet there had been the phenomena of silly children who bullied themselves online in order to get attention rather than actually put the effort in at achieving something; a 2013 British film called Uwantme2killhim? told the true story of a teenage boy who planned his own murder in chat rooms in order to feel important. (This was before schoolchildren could claim to be non-binary for the same effect.) When the gay black actor Jussie Smollett decided at the start of 2019 that the $100,000 per episode he was paid for his role in the television show Empire was not enough, he hired two

Nigerian brothers to tie a noose around his neck, all the while shouting racist and homophobic slurs, with the odd 'You deserve to be paid twice as much as Terrence Howard!' thrown in. To add the cherry on top, Smollett subsequently accused Chicago police of malicious prosecution, claiming he was the victim of 'mass public ridicule.'

Abusing oneself ('harrassturbation') as a way of joining the wretched of the earth became quite the thing during the era when President Trump was Woke Enemy Number One. Many of the charges were tinged with farce; a Muslim women accused a drunken white man of trying to set her hijab on fire ('Liar, liar...') and a church organist who desecrated his own place of worship by spray-painting a swastika and HEIL TRUMP on it and a Muslim student who wrote anti-Muslim graffiti on his own door, inspired by a Jewish neighbour who had suffered the same offence. Probably my favourite was the imaginative Oregon politician Jonathan Lopez who sent himself a hate-filled missive full of racism and homophobia, telling himself that his type were not welcome and that he would probably be killed - and signed, thrillingly, 'Sincerely, America.' Talk about dreaming big! It all ended happily when he took to social media to state that he had 'no resentment for whomever wrote this' proving conclusively that to love oneself to the point of 'harrassturbation' is surely the greatest love of all.

Almost as fun were the apologies forthcoming from showbiz shillers severely suffering from absence of applause in the plague year. The actor Leigh Francis apologised for wearing grotesque latex masks of black celebrities to make people laugh, though not of course for wearing grotesque latex masks of female celebrities to make people laugh. Jessica Mulroney, best friend of the Sainted Meghan, apologised for talking trash to the black social media influencer Sasha Exteter. The potty-mouth rapper Cardi B apologised for appropriating Hindu footwear. The mixed-race broadcaster Maya Jama apologised for saying that dark-skinned women with shaved heads resembled Michael Jordan - and then had to apologise for the apology, after anger that her first apology was directed towards 'all women' rather than dark-skinned black women. (No time for inclusiveness here!) But in a action which surely all human beings could unite in approval of, preachy tosser Jameela Jamil (one of those pretty girls who starts out as a presenter on TV pop shows and goes on to be an Insta-influencer banging on about world poverty and climate change featuring on devotional prayer candles sold online by 'Mose Mary And Me!') took to Twitter to apologise for being a preachy tosser after throwing stones at Kim Kardashian's bum. (Not literally, because that would be a police matter, but metaphorically, which **should** be a police matter **because as everybody knows WORDS ARE LITERALLY VIOLENCE!**) George Orwell surely foresaw the future when he wrote in 1984:

> 'There will be no curiosity, no enjoyment of the process of life. All competing pleasures will be destroyed. But always there will be the intoxication of power, constantly increasing and constantly growing subtler. Always, at every moment, there will be the thrill of victory, the sensation of trampling on an enemy who is helpless. If you want a picture of the future, imagine a boot stamping on a human face — forever.'

Additionally, it will be everyone apologising to each other, forever - but they won't mean it, and it won't work and it will just make people paranoid and narrow, with no curiosity or enjoyment, as the power of Woke constantly increases.

There was actually the one obvious thing that rich and famous Wokesters might have apologised for; being so vastly over-rewarded for doing jobs they loved, and thereafter arranging for their excess wealth to go to charities, as the young Labour MP Nadia Whittome did after her election in 2019 when she kept only the average worker's wage of £35,000 and gave the remainder of her £79,000 salary to the poor people of Nottingham who she represented. But the Hollywood mob, outrageously rich as they are, couldn't do that - for the simple reason that they all believe deep down that they're Very Important People and that, as the L'Oreal ad has it, they're worth it. It was unintentionally hilarious that when the Matinee Idol of Woke, George Clooney, revealed in 2020 that he'd given a million dollars each to fourteen of his closest male friends, they often turned out to be fellow showbiz high-rollers - truly the wretched of the earth.

To distract the mob from a level of wealth which can make Donald Trump look like Mr Bojangles (think of Elton John spending £293,000 on flowers in less than two years) showbiz liberals often make silly shows of themselves by grasping at the first rager against wicked Western ways who attracts their masochistic magpie eye. Thus in the summer of 2020 Chelsea Handler - who had become rich and famous for embodying the ultimate uppity woman - shared a thirty-year-old video of the Nation of Islam leader Louis Farrakhan ranting on about white devils, gushing 'I learned a lot from watching this powerful video' while famous Jennifers from Aniston to Garner queued up to throw their organic cotton knickers at the demented demagogue and Jameela Jamil took her preachy tosserdom to new heights of stupidity by ululating 'Someone please tell me the name of this extraordinary man who so perfectly sums up white fear in under a minute.'

Sadly for the Jewish Miss Handler and the 'queer' Miss Jamil, Farrakhan was on record as calling the Jews 'Satanic' and 'termites' with a side-dish of 'degenerate crap' for homosexuality. Within a few days, the comedienne found herself sucking up not to the section of society she had sought to suck up to, but to the ordinary Americans she had sought to vilify by siding with a bigot who just happened to be black:

> 'I want to sincerely apologise for posting the video of Louis Farrakhan…I didn't consider the context of his anti-Semitic and homophobic rhetoric that is of course contrary to my own beliefs and values. Part of the process of educating ourselves during this pivotal time is recognising and working through our mistakes. This was definitely one of mine. I was wrong. It was offensive, and I apologise.'

When in the autumn of 2020 Japan unveiled a giant humanoid robot which could not only walk but take the knee, you'd think that mankind would figure we'd gone far enough down the road to a perpetual round of accusations and apologies and that things might just start to go back to normal again. But no sacrifice was enough now - the fire fuelled itself and the cancelling continued. Sometimes the velocity seemed so voracious that people jumped onto the tracks of their own free will, eager to get it over with. Sheffield Cathedral announced that it was disbanding its choir so it could make 'a completely fresh start…with a renewed ambition for engagement and inclusion' which considering the current state of the Anglican Church is something akin to a dehydrated man crawling across a desert refusing a bottle of water because it isn't Evian. One wonders what future Christmas services may sound like once this engagement and inclusion has been consolidated; 'O Come All Ye Pagans' perhaps or 'Once In The Prophet Mohammad's City' with a final rousing version of 'God Rest Ye Non-Binary Gender-Fluid Polyamorists.'

The television show Countdown has long been a favourite of under-employed Woke Bros taking a well-deserved break from threatening TERFs with sodomy on the internet as they demonstrate the point of not having left education until the age of twenty-two by guessing the word a second before a working-class contestant who left school at sixteen. Was this the demographic which the resident lexicographer Susie Dent, 56, was hoping to kowtow to when she agreed that Millennials may well be right about full stops being aggressive? She was definitely being something with six letters and two vowels, which starts with a W and ends with R. And perhaps hoping to hang on as long as possible till the day when Countdown is deemed 'abelist' by dyslexics and cancelled.

The fear was even in Shane McGowan, whose 'Fairytale Of New York' had become the potty-mouthed Internationale of freethinkers. As recently as 2019 he remarked 'I've been told it's insulting to gays. I don't understand how that works. Nobody in the band thinks that's worth a second's thought.' But by the winter of 2020 it was freezing cold outside, and a new generation needed wooing to spare a few pennies for a fake Irishman's - born in Canterbury, educated at Holmewood House and Westminster - back catalogue. When someone calling themselves 'Harrison Brock' Tweeted this - 'Fairytale of New York' doesn't bother or offend me. But straight people being so angry & outraged at its removal and literally fighting and arguing for the right to sing it bothers me deeply' - and the Pogues re-Tweeted 'This,' that one little four-letter word was more obscene than anything the snowflakes might have got all melty over. MacGowan has had a good innings as a man of the people, but in the end proved that an expensive private school education will out.

Those who didn't jump were pushed, in the blinded year of 2020, as everyone from Sue Barker to Morrissey was 'let go' in the face of the many-mawed idol called Diversity. But this was just a more ruthless version of pensioning off people once they'd been round the block a few times, those generally unaccomplished types who do the hiring and firing wanting to be seen to be down wit da kidz in the absence of any real talent. The fun started, though, when the objects of Woke ire were just too good, too clever, too hot to care, as happened in the cases of young women as different as the 23-year-old Nobel Peace Prize winner Malala Yousafzai and the 27-year-old Emmy winner Jodie Comer. Malala dared to support her friend, a Conservative hoping to be Oxford University president, only to find herself described as a 'disingenuous careerist...had my doubts about her from early' (@hxmzaliy - a Corbynite political commentator) and an 'imperialist' amidst calls for her to be deported. 'So my hate for her all this time was wasn't unprovoked...' Tweeted a hijabed young woman residing in Camden Town; I'm always loathe to say that anyone I disagree with politically is Hitler, but if you can hate a girl who was shot in the head at the age of 15 and left for dead simply because she wanted girls to have an education, you've definitely provided me with one of the best examples of fascist thought I've ever seen. As Dr Rakib Ehsan of the Henry Jackson Society summed it up: 'The disgraceful attacks on Malala Yousafzai demonstrate how sinister some elements of the Left are. A Nobel Peace Prize-winning female empowerment icon who was shot by the Taliban, being called a 'disingenuous careerist' on the grounds of having a Tory friend. So mean-spirited.'

This could also sum up the Woke-hunt which hounded a young woman who had merely pretended to be a cold-blooded assassin rather than been the victim of one. When it transpired that Jodie Comer was dating an American sportsman who might be a Trump supporter, the malevolent masturbators of Woke went berserk. The very idea that a young successful self-made woman might want to date a young successful self-made man without submitting her mate of choice to an approval panel first! Maybe it's the extreme level of Miss Comer's beauty, but it was in her trolling that the sky-high level of sexual frustration among the Woke really emerged, and these creatures were revealed in their full impotent fury - 'cancelled' in the context only means they no long think of her when masturbating at their mum's house, as people certainly aren't going to stop hiring her. They used to call socialism The Politics Of Envy - but it was so much more than that, even if it did always end in tears. Cancel culture really is; vile overgrown toddlers trying to pull down people better than them. It's interesting how many of the targets are self-made women, too; while the Woke Bros wank their lives away on Pornhub, these uppity females are getting the work and wealth they believe should be theirs, because their doting parents always told them they were kings when they were dullards all along. Wokeness is the one stage on which they will ever get attention.

Though the Woke are stupid, they can be wily. When their latest demand isn't immediately obeyed they compare their inane requests to those of truly persecuted groups. The Troons in particular are keen to compare their mucky and mindless manifesto to the simple human rights which homosexual people struggled for in the recent past. But what did gay people ask for? Simply the same rights as every else. Gay men didn't want to barge in on women's sport or shortlists. Gay women didn't call straight women homophobic for not fancying them. They wanted equal rights and that one little word - gay, a word which had completely fallen out of use in its original meaning, no matter how much reactionary hacks fumed over this great loss to their lexicography. It was recycling of the kindest kind.

They certainly didn't want to shut down a language, as Woke wants, envious of those who can make it jump and prance and illuminate. Everyone sentient being has their one Woke moment which makes them suddenly aware that we are truly dealing with an existential evil here and mine was when Sam Smith said airily:

> 'When people mess up a pronoun or something it kind of ruins conversations, ruins moments. It's really difficult. So, I've had to just go into myself and try and deal with it in a real kind way and just know everyone's working on this. It's going to take time. We're changing a language here...'

**We're changing a language here.**

From a man who also said 'I hate reading...'

**He hates reading...**

Do the Woke read books? Apart from children's book - a sure sign of a moron. Do they have an intellectual hinterland? Unlikely, considering their raw terror at any view different from theirs. But for some reason, they believe they have the right to change a language - to abolish perfectly good words like 'woman' and replace it with 'Terf' and 'Cis.' Who died and made them Dr Johnson?

If grown adults want to stick their fingers in the ears and sing 'La la la' that's their look-out. What is not an option is for them to put muzzles on the rest of us, to make some words unsayable and to change the meaning of others. In the decade I defined as the Troubled Teens, many words have changed their meaning. Brave - once meant rescuing orphans from burning buildings, now means talking about one's troubles in public. How is it *brave* to have a miscarriage? It's sad - but *brave*? If miscarrying is *brave* what are firefighters? Diversity - once meant a pleasingly wide range of viewpoints, now means a selection of variously hued people all parroting the same liberal establishment platitudes. Activist - once meant getting out and about to help others, now means staying indoors on the internet screaming at people who think differently from one. Community - once meant a cheery group of neighbours getting together for street parties, now means a posse of peevish wallflowers going for gold in the Victimhood Olympics.

In line with Woke magical thinking, these words in the Orwellian mode of 'Doublespeak' (never actually used in 1984 but a hybrid of 'Newspeak' and 'Doublethink' which are) now mean the opposite of what they did before people discovered the pleasures of self-applied blue hair dye and self-righteousness as a means of sexual arousal. They're lovely words, too, so it's a loss to the language we all share simply because a few short-tempered tossers can't be arsed to think up some new ones.

It's bad enough that these half-witted Wokers have access to computers but when one considers that many of them work in publishing, it's like finding out that Johnny Depp runs a women's refuge. I remember publishing in its heyday; the drunken bonhomie, the three hour lunches and the road to L (L'Epicure, L'Escargot, L'Equipe) being paved with good intentions. The idea of anyone who worked in publishing being 'offended' by their writers was as risible as a lap-dancer fainting because she glimpsed a builder's bum-cleavage. But now the Pod People appear to have got their hands on this last bastion of rollicking and roistering, with junior members of Penguin Random House 'confronting' senior staff over the putative publication of the next Jordan Peterson. When I say 'confronting' I mean crying, the go-to move of Cry Bullies International; as Peterson himself had pointed out in a previous book 'Anger-crying is often an act of dominance and should be treated as such.' One dear snowflake claimed that Peterson had 'radicalised' their father, while another fretted about the effect the book might have on their non-binary friend.

A thought; might it not be easier for those easily offended by differing ideas and viewpoints not to seek employment in arenas which deal with differing ideas and viewpoints? Flower stalls are lovely places to ply one's trade; soft furnishings too, with emphasis on scatter cushions - no sharp corners! But publishing? Did the long and splendid story that began with Johannes Gutenberg inventing the printing press in 1436 - and changing as many lives intellectually as the wheel changed lives physically - really have to end up here; with publishing employees - who would be happier burning books than editing them - crying because they didn't like words? But I can't believe it will end up here, of course, because the impulse that drove both the printing press and the wheel drives the human race. Curiosity and creativity, peppered with language's lightning strikes, takes us forward into the future, despite the pull of those who for their own silly and/or sinister reasons wish to take us back into the past, into a Dark Ages masquerading as an Enlightenment. 'He who controls the language controls the masses' said Saul Alinsky, a true activist. But the masses are notorious for fighting back.

Yes, it seems bad right now, like we're living in every dystopian book and film we ever thrilled to, and which made us righteously determined to stand up to Fascist oppression. We were so into our roles, we didn't see that the threat to freedom was coming from left-field. The Hunger Games, The Handmaid's Tale, Fahrenheit 451, The Plot Against America, Brave New World - and of course 1984. 'How many fingers am I holding up, Winston?' the torturer O'Brien asks Winston Smith. 'Four.' 'And if the party says that it is not four but five - then how many?' 'Four! Four! What else can I say? Four!' Smith screams as he is electrocuted. The TERF-torturers in training, who boast every day of the torments they wish to inflict upon free women, are now holding up their nasty penises on the internet indefinitely until we all give in and call them 'girldicks.' But we will never give in. We didn't come all this way to be bested by a bunch of bed-wetters in bad wigs, as I pointed out all those years ago.

We really are in the midst of the Woke Trials now; the red shoes have captured the body politic and are whirling us into a dizzying danse macabre in which we have no idea of where we'll end up. It's possible that the worst of the Right and the worst of the Left will end up in some sort of civil war; add that to the Depression left in the wake of the virus and we can safely assume the next decade will not be a day at the beach. I never foresaw that I would be living through such an age of barbarism and hysteria; McCarthyism appeared to have taught us our lesson about the stupidity of witch-hunts, but those who do not learn from history as they're too busy spending three years getting a degree in Queer Studies are doomed to repeat it. It's a great time to be a writer - and an awful time to be a decent human being who just wants to live a quiet life. (Luckily, that's never been my problem.)

This book has taken quite a while from inception to publication - two years - as I was cancelled by my first publisher, ludicrously, for being a racist and then had to part with another publisher who allegedly turned out to be connected to an actual racist organisation. Back and forth I went, like a Wokey Hokey Cokey - third time lucky.

But the advantage to the delay is that I can end with an up-to-date roll-call of the Woke lunacy that has taken place between 2019 and the autumn of 2021, as I write this. As per Woke, the beautiful word 'education' reminded one more and more of the ugly word 're-education.' Worcester College apologised for hosting a Christian Concern event after 'distressed' students complained - despite the event taking place outside of term time. Cambridge dons were warned that they would be reported to the appropriate authorities if they raised an eyebrow when a black student or member of staff was speaking; they 'could also be committing a "micro-aggression" if they give backhanded compliments, turn their backs on certain people or refer to a woman as a girl,' the Telegraph reported. A Canadian academic announced that she was now part of 'the lowercase movement' and would no longer use capital letters 'except to acknowledge the Indigenous struggle for recognition.' Students at Kent University were instructed to fill in a four-hour 'Expect Respect' form which included such examples of 'white privilege' as having 'pleasant neighbours' (doesn't this imply that an unpleasant neighbour is non-white?) and 'wearing second-hand clothes' (which will come as a surprise to many of the impoverished people of all hues who buy their clothes in the charity shop where I have worked for the past six years.) But the greatest crime against learning surely occurred when Scottish schools were encouraged by a campaign group called Zero Tolerance to 'audit' their libraries, singling out The Tiger Who Came To Tea as reinforcing gender stereotypes because the tiger is male and waited on by the female characters. That the real crime was a tiger being encouraged to come to tea when surely he would eat anyone in his path, male or female, didn't seem to bother them.

Women continue to get the worst end of the spiky Woke stick, of course. In June 2021 a Scots woman, Marian Miller, was arrested and charged with hate crime for Tweeting a suffragette ribbon which a notorious social media cry-bully claimed was 'a noose.' *Feminist* *thinkers* (it's hard to choose which seems the least sarcastic description) Sally Hines and Laurie Penny announced that reporting rape was often unfair to men as it was often just bad sex (Hines) and that if a female child was faced with the exposed penis of a grown man, the correct thing was 'not to stare at other people's genitals without their permission, as it's rude' (Penny). With rape convictions at an all-time low and rapists being housed in female prisons in increasing numbers, it was surely a relief for incarcerated women that in the September of 2021 - in 'National Inclusion Week' - Her Majesty's Prison on the Isle of Wight (alumni include the Yorkshire Ripper and Gary Glitter) Tweeted: 'In preparation for National Inclusion Week our equalities team have started distributing pronoun badges. What's your pronoun?' adding the hashtags "inclusion", "equality" "diversity" and "unitedforinclusion". They then proceeded to hand out purple badges bearing pronouns such as 'he/they,' 'her/they and 'they/them' and - the corker - 'Just ask me.' How good to see public money spent on such worthwhile ways to safeguard the citizen in the street! This experiment is, thankfully, taking place in an all-male prison but hopefully it will spread to mixed jails so that if a woman does have the bad luck to be raped by a man called Regina where once he was. Reg, she'll know what *gender* her assailant is and address them accordingly. After all, as the judge told Maria MacLachlan - essentially telling her to lie under oath - it's only 'respectful' for women to respect the pronouns of their attackers. In October 2021 it was announced that female prisoners who called transgender prisoners by the 'wrong' pronoun could be punished with time added to their sentences.[5] After a prison rape by an alleged fellow female, a woman may well wish to see a doctor - but the doctor may not see a woman, but rather 'the anatomy and physiology of bodies with vaginas' as a September 2021 edition of the official medical journal The: Lancet put it. The old sawbones line 'First do no harm' (not strictly part of the Hippocratic Oath, but a pretty good rule to live by if you're in the business of life and death) might be better reframed as 'First do men in mini skirts feelings no harm.' Still, the muddled medics were in good company, as at the September 2021 the Labour Party's conference were busy assuring the electorate that not only women have cervixes. Now the only British party never to have a female leader, I fully expect the first be-frocked person to front the Peoples Party to have been born a man.

It's shocking but not surprising that more civil servants are from privileged backgrounds than they were in the 1960s - part of the Woke side-hustle against social mobility, which may explain a lot of the abject silliness currently taking place, such as the Northern Ireland civil service informing employees in the September of 2021 that there was no longer any need to use the word 'lesbian' as 'gay' would do (though I doubt that the T will not be erased from the ever-burgeoning LBGTQ alphabet soup) and that so-called natal women and men should be 'encouraged' to call themselves by the 'correct' terms of cis women and cis men.

But meet the new bossy-boots, same as the old bossy-boots; in June 2021 it appeared that Google had been harbouring a 'head of diversity strategy' named Kamau Bobb who had blogged in 2007 that Jews had an 'insatiable appetite for war and killing.' Though Google 'unequivocally condemned' the statement, they kept him in employment - after all, if diversity is the most important quality for a company to have, it makes sense to include anti-Semites, as there are so many of them. Happily, there are signs that the house of red cards that Woke built is even more fragile than the precarious mental state of the most vociferous Wokers would suggest.

A survey in February 2021 found that only one in eight black Britons believed toppling statues of dead men associated with slavery was worthwhile. In May 2021 the new chairwoman of the Equalities and Human Rights Commission, Baroness Falkner. said it was "entirely reasonable" for people to challenge the biological status of women who were born as men. In the same month the Communities secretary Robert Jenrick said that there must be amendments to building regulations to ensure separate toilets for the two sexes in new buildings. The thought of all those tantrum-having architects was a thing of beauty indeed. Also in May - a very merry month indeed for we of the sentient persuasion - the Culture Secretary Oliver Dowden more or less suggested a working-class cultural uprising when it came to cultural heritage bodies, by now largely involved in a crazed attempt to out-Woke each other:

> 'Museums and other bodies need to have genuine curatorial independence. But that independence cuts both ways. Heritage organisations should be free from government meddling, but the people who run them also need the courage to stand up against the political fads and noisy movements of the moment…as national institutions, heritage organisations should take into account the views of the entire nation: the people for whom they were set up, and whose taxes pay for them. That's why I want to make sure the boards of these bodies are genuinely diverse and not solely governed by people from metropolitan bubbles. I want a grandparent in Hartlepool or Harwich to feel as represented by their decisions as a millennial in Islington.'

But to me, as a person who openly lists their official hobbies as philanthropy and spite, one of the greatest pleasures of the Woke Wars is when the bed-wetting cry-bullies believe they've won - and then have their tragic little triumphs over-turned. This is what happened when in June 2021 the work of the artist Jess de Wahls was banned from the Royal Academy of Arts gift shop as she had written the black magic words 'a woman is an adult human female' adding the killer line 'I worry because this notion of 'wrong think' and wrong speak' feels eerily reminiscent of my East German childhood, and that's actually quite terrifying.' Within a week the RA had apologised and reinstated her work - four attractive if conventional embroidered flower patches. But the damage - or rather, the publicity campaign - had been done, with de Wahls HERETIC designs selling out time and time again from her own website: 'I will embroidery vaginas & other female only work & there is feck all you can do about it,' she informed Diddums Inc on Twitter. As with J.K Rowling, the sight of a woman holding her nerve was becoming a rare, exotic event; an honourable mention to that modern Galileo of gynaecology, the Scottish student Lisa Keogh, who was suspended and then reinstated by Dundee University for the (flat) earth-shattering statement 'women have vaginas' in this new Eden where there must be no Eves lest the Adams run shrieking with outraged envy. 'It was a modern day witch hunt,' Miss Keogh commented of the episode. Yes - it's called a Woke Trial.

The anti-Woke fun and gains continued. Ellen 'Be Kind To Each Other' DeGeneres - seemingly the Johnny Carson of Woke - was revealed as being more of an Imelda Marcos, with workers on her show revealing a culture of toxic tyranny, including 'racism and intimidation' backstage. A man who identified as a deer was shot by hunters in South Carolina. Shawn Mendes misgendered Sam Smith during a Jingle Ball introduction, bringing a festive tear to Them's eye. And even at the height of the Tory government's perceived mishandling of the pandemic, a survey by a Labour organisation warned that the lost Red Wall seats of the North would never be re-taken until the party of the workers ceased to 'be drawn into debates on divisive cultural and identity issues' - that is, until it wakes up from Woke.

After a year of global lunacy, signs that an epidemic of common sense was just around the corner broke through like an early spring after a long winter. In December 2020 Cambridge University, previous a bastion of Woke madness, updated their Statement on Freedom of Speech so that speakers may be barred only if they are likely to use 'unlawful speech' or cause other legal problems. The frankly gorgeous philosopher Dr Arif Ahmed spearheaded the campaign:

> 'A lot of people nowadays feel as if they're living in an atmosphere where there are witch hunts going on, a sort of academic version of Salem in the 17th century or the McCarthyite era. If a view is idiotic we should be quite free to say a view is idiotic. If a religious or political or other position is a tissue of bigotry and superstition, then we should be free to

say those things without fear that somebody would find it disrespectful.'

In the same month the Scottish parliament backed an amendment by the Labour MSP Joanna Lamont which meant that rape survivors would be allowed to choose the sex rather than the pretendy-gender of those examining them after an attack, as - insensitively - many women feel safer with female medics in such traumatic circumstances rather than with a man in a frock sticking his big beer-carrying hands up them. For once, the actual injuries of women took precedence over the hurt feelings of men. Mastercard turned its back on the masturbators of Pornhub, that Woke Bro horn of cornucopia which regularly showcases the rape of children - they'll just have to toss their lives away over deep-fake images of J.K. Rowling drowning in a swimming pool of filthy lucre instead. And just in time for Christmas, after a case lasting two years and untold amounts of public money, Kate Scottow,[6] arrested in December 2018 at her home in front of her then ten-year-old daughter and 20-month-old son, was cleared of committing a crime by calling a man 'a pig in a wig' on Twitter.

While judgments are the backbone of political progress, it's individuals who give it oomph and pizzazz. I often think that the most use anyone can ever be on earth - apart from giving away money - is to inspire others. No one past the age of twelve needs heroes, but this is my roll-call of the people who stand up for everything - curiosity, fearlessness, generosity - Woke isn't. Some of them make odd bedfellows - but what an honour to be in bed with them, snug and safe from the impotent fury of the Wokers.

Frances Barber, the lifelong Labour activist who said of her monstering by Corbynites 'I found that the people I was fighting with on Twitter hadn't come from places like I had. There was usually family money, often a public school education and Labour was more of a hobby for them, whereas it's always been a way life for me.' Jennifer Saunders, in a radio appeal for a women's charity, affirming actual biological sex more frequently than anyone since the Commodores did Three Times A Lady - every other word was woman. (It felt so rebellious - how weird is that!) Rupert Everett, with a moue of distaste, saying 'We're in such a weird new world, a kind of Stasi it feels like to me, and if you don't reflect exactly the right attitude, you risk everything just being destroyed for you by this judgmental, sanctimonious, intransigent, intractable, invisible cauldron of hags around in the virtual world.' The actor Janes Dreyfus blasting 'They WANT to hate. They YEARN to find people to demonise. They ADORE to denounce. They REVEL in making threats. They OBFUSCATE when challenged. They DENY simple truths. They ACT like feral teenagers. They HATE women.'

Graham Linehan pointing out that some trans-activists who have 'glommed on to the movement' are 'a mixture of grifters, fetishists, and misogynists...all it takes is a few bad people in positions of power to groom an organisation, and in this case a movement. This is a society-wide grooming.' John Lydon saying 'I never thought I'd live to see the day when the Right-wing would become the cool ones giving the middle finger to the Establishment and the Left-wing become the snivelling self-righteous ones going around shaming everyone.' The rapper Zuby 'identifying' as a woman to break the British women's deadlift record - and then identifying back to male. Grayson Perry shrugging 'The Left is more venal and has more antipathy to the opposition than the other way round - I would say the Right on average are friendlier and more open.'

The philanthropists Marcus Rashford and Stormzy, the activists Nimco Ali and Ayishat Akanbi. The beautiful and brilliant politician Kemi Badenoch - surely the third female leader of the Conservative Party, when Labour are still electing the latest stale pale male? Harry Miller, silver-fox super-cop turned TERF champion. Trevor Phillips and Tomiwa Owolade, generations apart but similarly excellent writers on the pride and persecutions of being black Britons. Patrick Hutchinson, the BLM marcher who carried an injured white counter-protestor to safety when their respective mobs clashed. J.K. Rowling, who started out so gentle and sweet but became toughened in the Twittersphere to the point where she now resembles a warrior queen from Game Of Thrones: Joanne of Wessex, Protector of Tomboys. The breathtakingly brave Keira Bell ('I look back with a lot of sadness - there was nothing wrong with my body') who took on the state-sponsored genital mutilation of children.

The most interesting of times, either a blessing or a curse, depending on whether one is of the tough or the tender tribe. 2020 was the year which promised perfect vision and then turned out to be the twelve months in which we were instructed to willingly blind ourselves; an ongoing project with the formidable pockets of resistance to it I've mentioned but no end in sight by the end of 2021. Entering the crazy world of identity politics is like being locked in a hall of mirrors with a borderline personality disorder coach party. 'Stop looking at me funny! Why are you ignoring me? Go away, I hate you! Come back, how dare you reject me!' But where there is destruction there will be pushback - and the violent virtue-signallers are going to get a whole lot more than they bargained for. As the great black social commentator Mo Kanneh Tweeted over a photo of John Cleese as the now-censured Basil Fawlty: 'This is all going to negatively impact on black people - we didn't ask for, or want, this cultural purge.' The Woke are like Daleks - what comes after all the EXTERMINATE business? They turn on each other. The end of Woke could conceivably end in a glorious bout of in-fighting to the death, as the ever-growing number of allegedly oppressed minorities (Furries? Plushies? Adult Babies?) splinter in all directions and engage in one last big all-you-can-beat hissy-fitting Woke War of All Against All. The Wars Of the Poses!

How will they sustain themselves, these creatures who create nothing and who see danger everywhere? They won't be breeding in sufficient numbers, that's for sure - a survey showed that 92% of left-wing activists in Berlin live with their parents, which added to ever-rising age at which generations lose their virginity does indicate that the Woke will burn up the best years of their lives in an impotent fury of porn and tantrums. The upcoming generation already shows signs of rebelling against the slimy straitjacket of Woke and any day now the overgrown toddlers who fill their nappies and spit their dummies over everything from J.K. Rowling's superior grasp on biological science to Jodie Comer's pulling power are going to wake up and find themselves 40 and no longer able to use youth as an excuse for being so parasitic, so intellectually lazy and so scared of any opinions which challenge their own.

Because we don't have to live in an atomised world where every thought is an 'ism' and every person an 'ist' where we're all furiously beeping our horns at each other as we kill time stuck in the cul-de-sac of identity politics. The human spirit (yes, that old thing) could rally at the eleventh hour and we might awake from our sleepwalking. And then we'll think 'It was all a horrible dream!' as we gaze around dazedly at each other, strangers and good companions, on a piece of rock hurtling through space, going somewhere, together.

## Notes

[1] https://en.wikipedia.org/wiki/Free_love

[2] https://www.thelondoneconomic.com/news/top-10-pointless-degrees-56750/

[3] https://www.thetimes.co.uk/article/universities-are-a-safe-haven-from-censorship-a-sanctuary-of-free-speech-and-tolerance-pgpvqb7rv

[4] https:// www.theguardian.com / education / 2018/oct/30/uk-universities-struggle-to-deal-with-toxic-trans-rights-row

[5] https://insidetime.org/women-face-punishment-for-using-wrong-pronouns/

[6] https://www.christian.org.uk/news/woman-cleared-of-wrongdoing-in-misgendering-case/

# INDEX

Greater Manchester Police, 59
Green Party, 181
Greenpeace, 181
Green, Susie, 119
Greer, Germaine, 21, 24
Grey, Christian, 66
Grice, Shana, 58
Guardian, 20, 24, 27, 28, 33, 34, 40, 133, 146, 163, 168, 172, 219, 231
Gutenberg, Johannes, 239

**H**

Hachette, 5
Hadid, Bella, 52
Haka, 17
Hamas and Islamic Jihad, 29
Handler, Chelsea, 185, 234
Harley, Steve, 125
Harman, Harriet, 43, 63, 113
Harradine, Karen, 147
Hawkins, John, 208
Haynes, Gavin, 13
Healey, Denis, 25
Healy, Matt, 96
Heathrow Airport, 181
Hebdo Charlie, 134
Henry Jackson Society, 236
Henry, Lenny, 225
Hensher, Philip, 29
Hewson, Eve, 196
Hill, Max, 63
Hindley, Myra, 112
Hines, Sally, 241
Hippocratic Oath, 242
Hirsch, Afua, 172
Hirsch, Joy, 173
Hitler, Adolf, 4, 20, 39, 68, 138, 165, 206, 229, 236
Hoey, Kate, 42
Hole, Cheryl, 94, 229
Holland, Jools, 134
Hollywood, 11, 39, 70, 84, 182, 189, 190, 191, 198, 209, 211, 233
Holmes, Sherlock, 3
Holocaust, 132, 144, 145, 224

House of Commons, 158
House of Lords, 181
Howard. Terrence, 232
Howe, Darcus, 133
Howe, Geoffrey, 25
Hughes, Ted, 226
HuffPost U.K, 33
Human Rights Commission, 45, 243
Hurley, Liz, 189
Hutchinson, Patrick, 246

**I**

International Pronoun Day, 83
In The Heat Of The Night, 3
Invictus Games, 209
Islam, 56, 85, 132, 133, 134, 135, 234
Izaakson, Jen, 106

**J**

Jackson, Glenda, 42, 158
Jackson, Michael, 142
Jama, Maya, 232
James E. L, 64, 66-67
James, Sid, 64
Jamil, Jameela, 232, 234
Jenner, Bruce, 100
Jenner, Caitlyn, 6, 100
Jenner, Kendall, 195
Jenrick, Robert, 243
Jingle Ball, 244
John, Sir Elton, 180, 233
Johansson, Scarlett, 198
Jones, Owen, 52, 222
Jordan, Michael, 232
Joyce, Eric, 70
Jung, Carl, 12

**K**

Ka'ai, Tania, 17
Kanneh, Mo, 247
Kassam, Raheem, 141
Kaufman, Gerald, 41
Kardashians, 24, 195
Kardashian, Kim, 233
Kemal, Ali, 17
Kendal, Frankie, 218